JOURNALISM
IN THE
DATA AGE

Jingrong Tong has produced an excellent and very timely book on digital journalism. It covers all of the main developments and areas of debate with outstanding clarity. It provides a full and well-rounded picture of the central issues facing journalists in the digital age and will be an essential textbook for students studying journalism.

Professor Colin Sparks
University of Westminster

Journalism in the Data Age offers a well documented, thoroughly researched and highly accessible account of the pervasive and disruptive changes to many aspects of journalism and journalists' s professional practice, products and relationships with audiences, triggered by the emergence of new digital communication technologies.

Professor Bob Franklin
Cardiff University

SAGE was founded in 1965 by Sara Miller McCune to support the dissemination of usable knowledge by publishing innovative and high-quality research and teaching content. Today, we publish over 900 journals, including those of more than 400 learned societies, more than 800 new books per year, and a growing range of library products including archives, data, case studies, reports, and video. SAGE remains majority-owned by our founder, and after Sara's lifetime will become owned by a charitable trust that secures our continued independence.

Los Angeles | London | New Delhi | Singapore | Washington DC | Melbourne

JOURNALISM IN THE DATA AGE

JINGRONG TONG

Los Angeles | London | New Delhi
Singapore | Washington DC | Melbourne

Los Angeles | London | New Delhi
Singapore | Washington DC | Melbourne

SAGE Publications Ltd
1 Oliver's Yard
55 City Road
London EC1Y 1SP

SAGE Publications Inc.
2455 Teller Road
Thousand Oaks, California 91320

SAGE Publications India Pvt Ltd
B 1/I 1 Mohan Cooperative Industrial Area
Mathura Road
New Delhi 110 044

SAGE Publications Asia-Pacific Pte Ltd
3 Church Street
#10-04 Samsung Hub
Singapore 049483

Editor: Michael Ainsley
Assistant editor: Cassandra Seibel
Production editor: Prachi Arora
Copyeditor: Rosemary Campbell
Proofreader: Sunrise Setting Limited
Marketing manager: Susheel GokarakondaX
Cover design: Lisa Harper-Wells
Typeset by: KnowledgeWorks Global Ltd.
Printed in the UK

Library of Congress Control Number: 2021944190

British Library Cataloguing in Publication data

A catalogue record for this book is available from the
British Library

ISBN 978-1-5264-9733-8
ISBN 978-1-5264-9732-1 (pbk)
eISBN 978-1-5297-3741-7

CONTENTS

LIST OF FIGURES AND TABLES

LIST OF BOXES

ABOUT THE AUTHOR

Jingrong Tong is Senior Lecturer in Digital News Cultures at the University of Sheffield. Her research focuses on the impact of digital technology on journalism, social media analysis and environmental communication.

ACKNOWLEDGEMENTS

Chapter 10 is developed from my article: 'Journalistic Legitimacy Revisited: Collapse or Revival in the Digital Age?', published by *Digital Journalism* in 2018 6(2), 256–273, doi: 10.1080/21670811.2017.1360785). I would like to thank Taylor & Francis for granting me the right to use the related content in this book. I am so grateful to all of the journalists who kindly shared with me their experiences, views and insights about journalism. The book is developed from my more than ten years of teaching journalism in UK universities. For their active participation in the discussions about the related topics, I thank my students on the *Digital Journalism for a Global Society* module at the University of Sheffield, the *Media/Journalism Issues* module and the *Data Journalism* module at Brunel University London, and the *Online Journalism* module at the University of Leicester. I would like to thank Michael Ainsley of SAGE for his support for this book project. Finally, special thanks go to my family for their love and support along the way.

This book is dedicated to my parents: Zhaoli Wang and
Changsen Tong, who taught me never to give up.

ONE
INTRODUCTION

What does journalism look like today? Journalism appears to be quite different now from what it was decades ago. Old-fashioned, shoe-leather journalism, which means journalists walk from place to place to collect and report news, may still be practised and appreciated. Yet, journalists need to – and are able to – do much more than that. With the assistance of digital technology, they may develop stories from large chunks of data, and, apart from text, their stories may contain graphs, maps and virtual reality (VR) animations. News stories can be instantaneously disseminated to many places in the world and be accessed by users with their smartphones and tablets. Journalists may be no longer employed by a legacy news organisation such as *The New York Times* but self-employed through starting and operating their own journalism businesses. Within newsrooms, algorithms are used to understand audiences and to write news reports automatically. A lot of people, who we used to call audiences, have started to produce and distribute content on the Internet. Such content is overloading the Internet, with some of it even being fake. Tech giants such as Google and Facebook (now Meta) have emerged, reaching positions of prominence, while a significant proportion of audiences and advertising revenue have moved to the platforms provided by these technological companies. These are only some examples of the recent developments in journalism, which are so relentless and profound that we are still endeavouring to understand them.

This book explores the development of journalism in the era of digital technology. It comes at a time when new forms of journalism have emerged and flourished in the digital environment. In this environment, social activities and lives are continuously and rapidly transformed into quantified digital data. To mark the importance of this digital transformation and datafication process to the communication environment, this book refers to the period during which these changes have taken place as 'the data age'. In this age, the practice of new forms of journalism, such as data journalism or computational journalism, requires journalists to obtain interdisciplinary knowledge. The emergence and practice of these new forms of journalism also significantly shape journalism and the relationship between journalists and audiences. These critical changes in journalism exert pressure on us to develop a systematic and profound understanding of what journalism now is and its status in society.

This book's focus on the influence of digital technologies on journalism, however, does not mean that it embraces the technological determinism thesis, which sees technology as determining the development of societies and human cultures (Kennedy, 1993; McLuhan, 1964). Instead, it will consider the joint influence of digital technologies and social factors, such as the market and politics, on journalism.

Journalism in the Data Age is formed in three parts. First, I discuss the transformation of the communication environment, as well as the resulting challenges and opportunities that are faced by quality journalism. Second, I address the evolutionary changes in journalism by examining four new, crucial forms of journalism: online journalism, data journalism, computational journalism and entrepreneurial journalism. Finally, I look at three aspects of the state and the status of journalism as a profession in society in the data age: journalist-audience relationships, journalistic autonomy and journalistic legitimacy.

In terms of how to use the book, readers can (but do not have to) follow the sequence of the chapters. You can also choose to focus on the chapters that most interest you. You can find 'key questions', 'key concepts' and 'exercises' in each chapter (except for the Introduction and Conclusion). Most chapters have 'boxes' containing detailed discussions of relevant cases, concepts or topics. These features can help you comprehend and think critically about the main topics that are discussed in the book. You are also encouraged to explore your own views and discuss the examples and cases of your choice. By so doing, you can broaden and deepen your knowledge and understanding of journalism in the data age.

TWO

THE COMMUNICATION ENVIRONMENT IN THE DATA AGE

KEY QUESTIONS

- What are digital technologies?
- Are digital technologies 'disruptive technologies'?
- What main features can you identify in the current communication environment?
- What does the application of digital technologies mean for journalism?

KEY CONCEPTS

digital technologies
the Information Technology Revolution (ITR)
digitisation
digitalisation
datafication
decentralisation of communication

connectivity
virtuality
time-space transformation
convergence
post-industrial/information/network society
disruptive information technologies

In the history of life on Earth, with dramatic changes happening in the natural environment, new species appeared, while old species were either wiped out – if they failed to migrate or evolve – or evolved to adapt to the new environment. Similarly, new forms of journalism have emerged upon the arrival of the data age. Journalists have started to adopt new skills and methods in response to the profound changes in the communication environment. To gain a thorough understanding of these new forms of journalism, we need to understand the communication environment.

This chapter serves this purpose. It will first discuss the concept of digital technologies – the technological foundation of the data age – and the Information Technology Revolution (ITR). It will then explore the five principal features of the current communication environment that are closely relevant to journalism and their implications for journalism. The last part of this chapter addresses a question that arises as to whether, and if so, to what extent, digital technologies are 'disruptive information technologies' for journalism.

Digital Technologies and the Information Technology Revolution (ITR)

Our current communication environment is awash with digital technologies. In this book, the term *digital technologies* refers to a wide range of 'technologies in microelectronics, computing (machines and software), telecommunications/broadcasting, and optoelectronics' (Castells, 1996: 29). They include not only the Internet, computers, smartphones and other portable electronic devices, but also information and communication technologies, like satellites, optical fibres, cables and chips. The number of digital technologies began to surge in the 1970s, and continues to grow.

Digital technologies have been rapidly integrated into, and have profoundly changed, people's everyday lives. Significant social change has occurred in the interactions between digital technologies and society. The global economy, for example, has been a primary driving force for, and has benefited from, the development and penetration of digital technologies. In the 1970s, accompanying the advent of the Internet, there was a crisis in the Fordist manufacturing economy and Western capitalism. At the time, capitalism urgently sought to restructure and to expand globally, looking for new markets, new sources of labour and new resources. The invention of the Internet suited this need well by facilitating the establishment of global commercial operations, such as global production and consumption systems. As well as in the economic sector, changes have happened in almost all aspects of human society. These changes are so profound that society has been greatly transformed.

Scholars have discussed whether, and if so, to what extent, these changes indicate the emergence of a new type of society. Some scholars (see, for example, Castells, 1996; Forester, 1986, 1990; Halal, 1993) argue that the avalanche of social change fuelled by digital technologies signals the coming of the Information Technology Revolution (ITR). Thus, a new type of society is being formed in the wake of the deep and rapid – but not yet universal – penetration of digital technologies. This society is referred to as the 'post-industrial society', the 'information society' or the 'network society' (see Box 2.1) (Bell, 1973, 1976, 1979; Castells, 1996). In this new type of society, production, consumption and communities take forms that are so different from those in an industrial society that our 'material culture' has been transformed. As a result, we have new ways of doing things, such as employment, producing, consuming, publishing, entertaining and communicating.

Other scholars (see, for example, Hodge & Coronado, 2005; Webster, 1997, 2006), however, are not convinced that we should see these changes as a revolution and that our present society can be entirely distinguished from previous forms of society. They, for example, have highlighted that, despite all the changes, old, established social forms, such as 'class structure', continue to exist in this 'new' system. Some scholars (see, for example, Brants, 1989) even see the idea of the information revolution as having been constructed by different actors, like industrial actors, actors involved in policymaking, the European community and the mass media. These different actors play their own parts in defining technological developments as the information revolution and making it a dominant discourse to pave the way for economic growth.

━━━━━ **BOX 2.1** ━━━━━

'Information society' and 'network society'

'Information society' and 'network society' are both used to refer to post-industrial society. The work of Manuel Castells, a renowned sociologist, has discussed these two concepts extensively. For Castells, the two ideas are interrelated – if not completely interchangeable. A network society is 'a society where the key social structures and activities are organized around electronically processed information networks'. An information society refers to a 'specific form of social organization in which information generation, processing, and transmission become the fundamental sources of productivity and power because of new technological conditions' (Castells, 1996: 21 and 695). Both types of society are a result of informationalism, which means that information is the pillar of the economy and underpins the fundamental functions of society.

Other scholars, however, hold views that differ from those of Castells on the concepts of information society and network society. Van Dijk (2006), for example, uses the two concepts to 'typify contemporary developed and modern societies marked by a high level of information exchange and use of information and communication technologies (ICTs)' (p. 19). His concept of network society focuses on the changes in these societies' organisational forms, infrastructures and structures. In defining network society, he stresses the co-existence and integration of social and media networks, as well as the social changes caused by them (van Dijk, 2006). However, Castells' emphasis is on electronically processed information networks and how such networks have changed social organisations and social structure.

Five Features of the Communication Environment in the Data Age

In the data age, the communication environment has five features that are important for journalism: (1) being digital: digitisation and digitalisation; (2) decentralisation of communication and connectivity; (3) time-space transformation; (4) virtuality; and (5) datafication. These features are the prerequisites for the evolutionary changes in journalism that will be discussed later in this book.

(1) Being digital: digitisation and digitalisation

Today, we are immersed in digital environments. Our immersive experiences result from the digitisation and digitalisation of communication and information. Digitisation refers to a technical process in which data, such as text, pictures, graphics, videos and sounds, is converted into a digital form. Digitalisation means the process of digital transformation – the changes in many aspects of society caused by digitisation and the application of information communication technologies – and as a result these aspects have a digital nature. The universal use of the binary digits: 0 and 1 (see Box 2.2) to code, store and distribute information enables the digitisation and digitalisation of society.

BOX 2.2

The binary number system

Silicon transistors, the fundamental component of the chips used in most kinds of electronic devices, like computers, only have two states: 'on' or 'off'. Computer scientists model them as 0 or 1, i.e., 0 represents 'off' and 1 represents 'on'. Information is represented and stored using these binary numbers. The binary number system was initially used for mathematical calculation purposes but has extended to almost everything that we are doing now.

Three features – compatibility, reproducibility and transmissibility – distinguish digital information from old forms of information, like that printed on paper. Digital information is detached from, and compatible across, platforms, companies and devices. It can be easily changed, reproduced, manipulated and distributed over enormous distances. It can be quickly transmitted in large amounts and at a high quality. For example, the content published on web pages can be modified and forwarded to Facebook easily by a single click on a mobile. The news content published by the BBC on its website can be consumed on different devices, such as tablets, mobile phones, PCs and even TV boxes like Roku or Fire Stick. These qualities of digital information make possible the functioning of digital society and its main characteristics, such as technological, corporate and media convergence (see Box 2.3), big data and social media platforms.

■ BOX 2.3 ■

Technological, corporate and media convergence

Technological convergence refers to a tendency in which different digital technologies come to perform the same tasks. In the past, different media and devices had separate and distinct functions. For example, we would use a camera to take pictures, a DVD player to view films, a fax machine to fax documents and a television to watch TV programmes. Today, some or all of these functions are integrated into a single device, such as a computer, laptop, mobile phone, tablet, and even a smartwatch. As users, we find that we can use one device to do different things, and the same content can be consumed by using different devices.

Corporate convergence is the convergence and concentration of media ownership, a trend towards operating media organisations across previously distinct industry boundaries following mergers and acquisitions. Corporate convergence greatly facilitates technological and media convergence. It is much easier for different businesses in the same conglomeration to collaborate and change in terms of resource allocation, compatibility, transaction costs, distribution, products and services, revenue models, and market and business strategies. Businesses in the same group follow a common standard, which allows different types of networks to connect, or a particular network to provide various communication services.

Facilitated by technological and corporate convergence, content produced by different types of news media looks similar, and it can move across various media platforms and be consumed using a wide variety of digital devices. These features are those of media convergence.

When it comes to journalism, a consequence of technological, corporate and media convergence is a striking resemblance in the content that is produced by the broadcasting or print media. Technological, corporate and media convergence also means that news content in its digital form can flow freely between different platforms and be created, changed and consumed on multiple devices. Convergence is underpinning the rise and development of online journalism (discussed in detail in Chapter 4).

■ EXERCISE 2.1 ■

Record how you consume media content every day for a week. Write down related information, such as which devices you use for this purpose, when, where and which types of media content you read, watch or listen to. Think about what your media consumption habits tell you about convergence and how convergence may influence journalism. Do some research to discover what facilitates media convergence. For example, it will be helpful to look for news about the mergers or acquisitions of media or telecommunication companies. Try to think about what these business activities mean for media convergence? It will also be useful to think about what similar functions different technologies, such as mobiles, tablets and computers, have. Would these similar functions help media convergence?

(2) Decentralisation of communication and connectivity

The Internet is an infinite web of numerous nodes that are interconnected through ties with no absolute centres. Nodes and ties can be different things in different contexts. For example, nodes can be routers, web servers, and the computers of organisations and individuals. Ties can be cables or wireless signals through which data can be transmitted quickly.

Although far from being universal, the broad application of the Internet turns the world into a well-connected global village. In theory, regardless of where they are based, individuals, organisations and regions are connected online beyond national boundaries, and they can send messages to one another freely and instantaneously.

The transition from Web 1.0 to Web 2.0 technologies makes the decentralisation of communication and the connectivity of the Internet possible. Web 1.0 and 2.0 tools represent two different ways of 'doing things' online. The former merely allows ordinary users to download and read data on the Internet. By contrast, the latter affords users the ability to upload and share data on the Internet. The shift from Web 1.0 to 2.0 empowers users by giving them new functions on the Internet, such as interactivity. With Web 2.0 tools, any users who have digital media literacy and the willingness to participate in public communication can produce and disseminate information and interact with one another (Solomon & Schrum, 2007). This ability of users breaks down the news media's monopoly on public communication and turns public communication from being largely vertical to being a combination of vertical and horizontal communication (see Box 2.4).

The arrival of Web 2.0 tools has also led to a digital culture of 'remix' and 'remixability', which refers to the phenomenon and ability of Internet users to continuously remix and diversely reproduce information and content (Manovich, 2005). Such information and content are transformed in the course of flowing across different online sites and platforms. This process of remediation involves the remixing, reusing and repurposing of information and content produced by Internet users (Deuze, 2006). Imagine you need to attend a job interview. You may search online, find some tips for job interviews and then compile a list of useful things to consider in preparation for your job interview.

Another example of 'remix' and 'remixablity' is computer programming. For programmers, they may not need to write code from scratch, as the public accessibility of open-source code online means they may be able to find relevant, useful code and easily use it in their own programs in a way that serves their needs. Although having appeared nearly two decades ago, this remixing culture on the Internet has become increasingly prominent. It has become a driving force behind – and has also benefited from – the rise of social media platforms such as Instagram and TikTok and the development of the open-source movement, which advances making products such as software, content and information publicly accessible for free and legally. While the availability of digital tools such as Faceswap (a free Deepfake app) and TikTok's Time Warp Scan Filter makes remixing easier, issues such as authenticity and copyrights emerge surrounding the remixing culture on the Internet. For example, suppose someone wants to produce a picture of themselves caught up in a tsunami. To achieve this, they may access some tsunami pictures on the Internet, combine them with their own photo using tools such as Photoshop, use Time Warp Scan Filter to add some effects and share the combined photo on their TikTok account. In this case, the remixing of the photos may have copyright implications with the authenticity of the combined photo being questionable. Moreover, if they use Faceswap to swap their own face with that of a celebrity in their photo and then share it on social media, there may be other issues such as privacy concerns.

BOX 2.4

Vertical and horizontal communication

Vertical communication refers to the old model of public communication where information flows or cascades from cultural elites, like the news media, to mass audiences who are deemed to be at a lower level in the communication hierarchy. Infrequently, information will be transmitted upwards from audiences to the news media. Horizontal communication means the transmission of information among individuals at the same level in the communication hierarchy. In an information society, public communication mixes vertical and horizontal communication, as both models of information flow co-exist.

A simple example of vertical communication is that you read a news story produced by, say, *The Guardian* through one of its news apps or on its printed newspaper, and your sharing of this news story to your friends on Twitter or WhatsApp is a type of horizontal communication.

Despite the decentralisation of communication, control still exists in online communication (see the discussions in Chapter 9). For example, countries such as China and North Korea practise Internet censorship through various means, ranging from online regulations and bans to the adoption of firewalls. In other countries, like the United States (US) and the United Kingdom (UK), although there is no explicit censorship, regulations limit online communication amidst concerns over issues such as privacy, national security and hate crime.

Control also exists at the organisational level. Organisations like the BBC may have moderators for their website, and information may be checked and moderated by moderators before appearing on their website. Corporate social media platforms, such as Facebook, Twitter and Instagram, have their own policies on filtering, removing and publishing content. In 2019, for example, Twitter announced the banning of any political advertising globally. They even ban certain users from using their service. In 2021, for example, in the wake of the accusations about Donald Trump's incitement of the attack on the US Capitol, Facebook, Twitter and other social media companies banned Donald Trump from their platforms. Social media firms use algorithms to detect harmful content and to automate batch removal. They also hire human content moderators to review and clean content that appears on their platforms. By 2018, some 7,500 content moderators had worked for Facebook (Wong & Solon, 2018). Therefore, the Internet is not entirely free, with control remaining.

Scholarly views vary on the social value of the decentralisation of communication. The decentralised communication structure and the great connectivity of the Internet are seen to provide ample opportunities for the public to participate in everyday politics and political events, such as the Arab Spring movements, the Queer movements, the #metoo movements and the Black Lives Matter protests. While weakening the cultural authority of journalists, this decentralised structure, manifested in news and current affairs blogs, and other types of online communication, such as the whistleblowing platform WikiLeaks and social media platforms, contributes to holding power accountable. The influence of such platforms has been demonstrated in successful examples, including the Drudge Report's revelation of the Clinton-Lewinsky scandal in the US in 1998 (see Box 2.5), the case of Sun Zhigang in China in 2003 (see Box 2.6), and the revelations made by WikiLeaks about Iraq and Afghanistan war logs and military operations in 2010 (see Box 2.7). Some studies (see, for example, Azenha, 2006; Castells, 2001; Goggin, 2011) also celebrate the Internet's potential for creating and delivering innovations. The rise of YouTube, for example, has presented new possibilities for users to express themselves and develop an identity.

BOX 2.5

The Drudge Report and the Clinton-Lewinsky scandal

In 1998, the then US President Bill Clinton's alleged sexual relationship with Monica Lewinsky, a former White House intern, was first revealed by the Drudge Report, a news blog, rather than by the mainstream news media. This scandal led to the impeachment of Clinton, who was, however, acquitted later (Shin, 2018). This case shows the power of news blogs, which are deemed to have fewer organisational restrictions.

BOX 2.6

The case of Sun Zhigang

Sun Zhigang was a migrant worker in Guangzhou, China. In 2003, he was detained because he failed to present his residential ID to the law enforcers who stopped him while walking on the street. He later died in custody, which was exposed by the *Southern Metropolitan Daily* as the result of physical abuse by the police. This event attracted such massive attention on the Internet that the Custody and Repatriation system was abolished. This case shows the power of the Internet and online public participation in China in the early 21st century (Yu, 2006).

━━━━━━━━ **BOX 2.7** ━━━━━━━━

WikiLeaks: Iraq and Afghanistan war logs

In 2010, WikiLeaks disclosed massive batches of classified US military files relating to the wars in Iraq and Afghanistan to news outlets, such as *The Guardian*, *The New York Times* and *Der Spiegel*. The leaks exposed US troops' killing of civilians and torturing of prisoners (Davies & Leigh, 2010). Although controversial, WikiLeaks' leaks have drawn the world's attention to the problems surrounding the US military operations.

Yet despite showing promise, online public participation is also considered to be transient, short-sighted and influenced by social and political contexts (see, for example, Tang & Yang, 2011). Scholars are also concerned about the credibility of digital information published by 'men in the street' (Mihailidis & Viotty, 2017; Tandoc, Lim, & Ling, 2018). Especially in the past five years, worries have deepened over fake news (see Box 9.5 in Chapter 9), or misinformation, which is circulated on, and facilitated by, the Internet in general and social media platforms in particular. In the era of information overload, which is worsened by the use of artificial intelligence (AI) algorithms to generate fake news, it is difficult to discern genuine from fake information. Despite being unproven, fake news and misinformation are even reportedly thought to have influenced important political events such as the presidential elections in the US and the EU referendum in the UK. Hate discourses that are constructed and promoted online are extremely worrying in a politically turbulent and volatile time. These have resulted in new problems for the practices, autonomy and legitimacy of journalism (discussed throughout the book, for example, in Chapters 6, 9 and 10).

(3) Time-space transformation

Closely associated with the decentralisation of communication and connectivity is the transformation of the time and space relationship. The application of digital technologies, along with the invention of other technologies in areas like logistics and aviation, has significantly shortened the time needed to complete activities and processes (Harvey, 1990). As a result, social relationships and systems, such as production, consumption and employment, have been lifted from locales, and they are able to span space indefinitely without geographical limitations (Giddens, 1990). Time-space transformation has deterritorialised news production and consumption, as well as other aspects of journalism, such as journalists' employment.

Time-space transformation reorganises almost all aspects of our lives. From a production and consumption perspective, Harvey (1990) argues that the compression of time and space suggests the rise of flexible accumulation (production and consumption). It differs from the previously industrial Fordist production and consumption (see Box 8.1 in Chapter 8) in three ways. First, the extensive use of outsourcing and automated

machinery, which can be easily changed to suit different needs, makes flexible production possible. This change signals the importance of catering to the fast-changing needs
and tastes of global consumers when producing products. Second, the well-developed
global logistical and delivery system offers the basis for extending the production system worldwide and accelerating the global consumption of goods. Under the Amazon
Prime system, for example, consumers receive goods on the same day or the day after the
placing of their order. Third, the shortened circle between production and consumption
diminishes the time required between capital investment and a profit turnover, which
stimulates the circulation of capital in markets. A side effect of these changes prompted
by post-industrial flexible accumulation, however, is the so-called post-modern aesthet-
ics, featuring individuality, personalisation and fast-changing fashions. These changes
signal the reduction in the half-life of products and the aesthetic shift towards instanta-
neousness or ephemerality (see Box 2.8). They also have profound implications for the
media consumption habits of audiences (discussed in detail in Chapter 8). The prevalence of ephemerality means that audiences' attention span for news may be short and
transient. Journalists and the news media may thus need to continuously offer audiences
something new and exciting, and something that can quickly replace 'old' (forms of)
content, in order to retain their attention.

BOX 2.8

Ephemerality

Ephemerality is a term that is used to describe the short-lived or transient nature of an
object. This means that the period between the birth and death of the object is short,
instantaneous or even transitory (Hassard, 2002). Such objects are often disposable and
can be quickly replaced. Disposable coffee cups, face masks and plastic packaging and
the speedy obsolescence of mobile phones are everyday examples of ephemerality. Its
implications for journalism are that the time it takes for a piece of news or a new form
of news reporting to become 'old' is dramatically reduced and journalists may find
themselves in demand to relentlessly produce something new and appealing in order to
keep audiences' attention. You can find more discussions in studies such as David Harvey's
The Condition of Postmodernity and Alvin Toffler's *Future Shock*.

Time-space transformation also creates flexibility in employment. The technological affordances of digital technologies facilitate the possibility of global operations and
stimulate the appearance of a flexible workforce. When it comes to the news industry,
the changes in employment are demonstrated in a news organisation's workforce going
global and the emergence of entrepreneurial journalism (see the discussion about entrepreneurial journalism in Chapter 7).

Take the job market, for example. Despite severe job losses in the news industry,
new jobs – often de-territorial and networked – have emerged, such as those remotely

based jobs providing sub-contracted or outsourced media content to employing news organisations and supporting some parts of their news production process. In 2008, Roy Greenslade of *The Guardian* called for a shift from in-house subediting to complete outsourcing (Greenslade, 2008). In 2009, Telegraph Media Group outsourced its subediting to Pagemasters, a company based in Australia, which only charged £45 for a page (Brook, 2009). Ed Roussel, the then digital editor, also revealed that apart from subediting, other works such as video production and distribution, web publishing and software development had also been delegated to other companies that might be based in Bulgaria or India so that the media group could save costs and remain profitable (Brook, 2009). In 2010, the *London Evening Standard* followed suit, outsourcing some of its subediting work to the Press Association (Brook, 2010). Ten years later, newspapers' fervour for outsourcing was still unabated. As of 2021, in the US, quite a number of newspapers have outsourced their printing (News & Tech Staff Report, 2021). In these examples, with job losses accelerating in the UK or the US, more jobs were created somewhere else globally. These new types of job suit entrepreneurial journalists, who can take over desk-based jobs such as subediting regardless of where they are based, although they may not be able to take up outsourced jobs of printing.

These changes also indicate there is a tendency towards the individualisation of work and flexible work. In the context of journalism, the increasing job precarity of journalists is associated with this trend of individualisation. Given that employees' skills and education are continuously redefined and become crucial in their performance evaluation at work, even valuable workers may become vulnerable, for reasons of health, age, gender discrimination, or lack of capacity to adapt to a given task or position.

(4) Virtuality

The fourth important aspect of the communication environment is virtuality. 'Virtual' does not mean 'unreal'. Instead, it means something that is intangible and cannot be physically touched, but that can be felt and experienced in an environment (Shields, 2003). In the context of digital technologies, 'virtual reality' refers to the immersion experience of users in a technologically mediated environment, such as video games, online forums and films. Virtuality makes it possible to experience things which we cannot experience in the offline world. A simple example is that of taking a virtual tour of the Moon, as offered by NASA, which can give the virtual experience of visiting the moon without actually going there.

The virtuality of the communication environment creates possibilities for journalists to develop new types of content and innovative ways to deliver news content. The application of virtual reality (VR) technologies, for example, facilitates the emergence of immersive journalism. Immersive journalism uses VR technologies and creates VR content which allows users to immerse themselves and to have a first-person experience. Over recent years, with the extensive use of multimedia materials, such as audio, videos, photographs and data visualisations in news reporting, the storytelling aspect of news articles has changed, and users can experience immersion without wearing VR goggles. Chapter 4 will discuss immersive journalism as part of the development of online journalism.

(5) Datafication

Our society is profoundly 'datafied'. Datafication means an omnipresent process that is continuously transforming our social lives and actions into quantified data (Mayer-Schönberger & Cukier, 2013). In this context, data means information or content that appears in – or can be converted to – the digital format of zeros and ones. The digitisation of our activities and lives leads to the constant, rapid proliferation of digital data. Most of our everyday activities, ranging from tapping fingers on mobiles to scanning the barcodes on our groceries, are creating data. When we drive on highways, the speed cameras automatically read the number plate of our car and save the data into the database of Highways England in the UK, or its equivalents in other countries. When doctors prescribe antibiotics for patients, their prescriptions become figures and numbers in governments' medical databases. Such data is enormous in quantity, comes from different sources and increases continuously. It also forms valuable resources that are beneficial to human societies. Through mining and analysing data, one can gain knowledge of and insights into human behaviour and society. Not only governments but also businesses, academics, journalists and other social actors want to harness the benefits of data.

The datafication of our societies is closely related to the rise of data journalism and computational journalism (discussed in Chapters 5 and 6). This is partly because data offers enormous reporting resources for journalism, and partly because of the role played by journalism in facilitating data access and exposing stories hidden in data. Government bodies are major holders of public records data, which refers to data produced from information in the public domain. Many governments in the world have started to open part of this data to the public. In 2009, in the US, President Barack Obama issued his Memorandum on Transparency and Open Government in order to take government transparency to an unprecedented level. His initiative greatly propelled the development of the open data movement. The UK and other democratic countries followed suit. Open data is a by-product of Freedom of Information, which was approved in a United Nations General Assembly Resolution in 1946 (Afful-Dadzie & Afful-Dadzie, 2017). In countries that have Freedom of Information laws or similar regulations, such as the UK and the US, governments' open data initiatives facilitate liberating data held by governments for the public and journalists to use. However, over recent years, the development of open data has been stagnating. One principal reason for this is the increasing public and political concerns over user privacy and national security. Citizens also may not be able to benefit from data due to barriers such as a lack of data literacy (see more discussions about open data and Freedom of Information in Chapter 5). As for data held in the private sector, tech giants, such as Google, Facebook and Amazon, hold even more significant amounts of data. Data is such a valuable asset that such organisations may be unwilling to share it for free Journalists can therefore play a much needed role in pushing for the release of data and using data to inform the public. Data-related journalistic practices and their implications for journalism and society will be discussed thoroughly in Chapters 5 and 6.

Are Digital Technologies 'Disruptive Technologies'?

Along with the emergence of the post-industrial society (see Box 2.1), the proliferation of digital technologies has shaken up the news industry, substantially transforming not only journalistic practices and products but also media markets. Questions thus arise about whether, and if so, to what extent, digital technologies are disruptive or sustaining for journalism and the news industry. The answer to this question is both yes and no.

The developments in the communication environment provide opportunities for journalism to reinvigorate itself and to engage with audiences. In the digital and virtual environment, for example, journalists may find it easier to collect information and contact news sources. The emergence and increasing popularity of data journalism (Chapter 5) and automated journalism (Chapter 6) generate new ways of holding power to account, telling stories and interacting with the audience. Big news media organisations have started to hire people globally. Thanks to the prevalence of digital technologies, entrepreneurial journalists have cheap or free platforms on which to run independent journalism projects and manage their journalism brand (discussed in Chapter 7). Using the latest technologies can help meet the aesthetic and functional preferences of the audience, whose members are increasingly digital natives. Collecting and analysing the data about the consumption behaviour of audiences provide a quantified understanding of those audiences. Such knowledge helps the news media engage with their target audiences (discussed in Chapter 8).

Yet despite these opportunities, digital technologies also bring disruption to journalism in four ways, which will be discussed in the remainder of this section.

(1) Disrupted media markets

The first disrupted area for journalism concerns media markets. The concept of 'disruptive technologies' was first introduced and developed in the domain of business. Bower and Christensen argued that the advent and adoption of new technologies might change established market orders and remove leading players from their top positions (Bower & Christensen, 1995). How businesses perceive and respond to the arrival of new technologies is crucial. In the 1990s, there was a tendency towards undervaluing the power of the Internet among news industry leaders and journalists (Gilbert & Bower, 2002). Newspapers missed out on opportunities to benefit from the Internet:

> Many industry leaders were slow to respond, until they realised the technology's potential threat. Then they responded aggressively and rigidly – so much so that most newspaper publishers missed the opportunity to capitalise on

> Internet-enabled markets.... Initially, many newspaper managers undervalued the Internet. ... But then editors and business managers became nervous. ... Coming to see the Internet as a serious threat, newspaper publishers began investing heavily in defensive measures. ... Unfortunately, in their rush to defend the print franchise, many newspaper executives missed the independent opportunity.
> (Gilbert & Bower, 2002: 97–98)

Gilbert and Bower's comments provide a valuable perspective through which to understand the market failures of news organisations in the earlier years. What they discussed, however, happened before the worsening of the financial crisis in journalism in the 2010s. In the second decade of the 21st century, the news industry has been desperate to embrace the opportunities brought about by the Internet, trying all kinds of new business model experiments in a vain (so far) attempt to take advantage of digital technologies (discussed in Chapter 3).

(2) Disruptions to news production processes and newsrooms

In addition to media markets, the disruptions caused by digital technologies to journalism have also resulted in news production processes and newsrooms becoming increasingly digitalised and converged. In the wake of the convergence of networks, content and devices, global newsrooms started their digital transformation from the early 21st century (see Box 2.9). The digital transformation of newsrooms resulted from the adoption of digital tools and content management systems, which makes the digitalisation of news collection, production and dissemination possible. It leads to the convergence of different forms of journalism – such as print, broadcast and audio journalism – into online (and multimedia) journalism (see the related discussion in Chapter 4). As a result, print, broadcast and audio journalism now bear a close resemblance to one another on the Internet.

The need for journalists to update their journalistic skills and methods has accompanied media convergence. On top of basic journalism skills, journalists need to learn new skills, like video and audio making, multimedia competence, data processing, online/social media storytelling, and even digital marketing. New skills to learn may also include (but are not limited to) how to make vertical videos for Instagram, techniques to make 360° videos for Google Cardboard and other simple VR apps, the knowledge to engage young people on social media and to increase impact, and the skills to analyse large-scale data. Digital technologies can be disruptive for this reason: journalists need to update their skills continuously, otherwise they face the risk of being laid off. This threat may lead to skill-based precarity for journalists; they may feel insecure about their jobs because of the constant need to update their skills quickly in order to adapt to the fast-changing media environment (Chapter 10 has more related discussions).

BOX 2.9

Digital transformation and the convergence of newsrooms

Establishing server-based, tapeless or paperless newsrooms was usually the first step in the digitisation and media convergence of newsrooms. From the end of the 1990s (around 1997), for example, the BBC, adopting automated tapeless production and equipping PC workstations with editing facilities, started transforming its newsroom into a digital newsroom. The digital production system, or content management system, digitalised and reorganised the production system around a central server, replacing the 'old' analogue tapes with hard disks to store the data (Saltzis, 2006). The BBC newsroom became a news centre (Cottle & Ashton, 1999). The data gathered by reporters through the use of digital technologies, such as tapeless cameras, was in digital form, which made inputting that data into, and disseminating it within the system, effortless. The data was stored in a central hive and could be used by multiple users at the same time. Every personal computer at each workstation had digital editing facilities, and, therefore, was compatible with the system (Fletcher, Kirby, & Cunningham, 2006). The introduction of digital technologies into newsrooms, however, took place at an uneven pace. Sky News, for example, was hesitant to purchase an expensive digital newsroom system, while its competitors, such as BBC News and ITV, had already done so (Saltzis, 2006).

The digitalisation and media convergence of UK and US newsrooms are exemplified in the BBC, *The Daily Telegraph* (both in the UK), and The *Tampa Tribune* (in the US). Convergence culture is not exclusive to the Anglo-American context. It is a global trend and is evident in newsrooms worldwide. News organisations elsewhere, such as Austria, Germany, Spain, Norway, South Korea, China, India and Egypt, have also experienced this wave (see related studies such as Menke et al., 2018; Na, 2011; García Avilés, Meier, Kaltenbrunner, Carvajal, & Kraus, 2009; García Avilés, León, Sanders, & Harrison, 2006; Erdal, 2009; Tong & Lo, 2017; Zhang, 2009, 2012; Aneez, Chattapadhyay, Parthasarathi, & Nielsen, 2016; Abdulla, 2013).

Although not a universal occurrence, media convergence and the digitalisation of newsrooms often led to changes in the office layout of newsrooms, as well as in their organisational structure (Thurman & Lupton, 2008). Members of staff supporting multimedia production were moved to work together under the same roof. Such changes facilitated the co-operation of staff members in different areas. *The Daily Telegraph*, for instance, moved to its news hub in 2006, paving the way for its integration of the news editing and page design phases (Reece, 2006). In 2007, the title tried to achieve editorial integration by bringing staff from *The Daily Telegraph*, *The Sunday Telegraph* and the website into one division. *The Guardian*, *The Mirror* and other British newspapers experienced similar transformations. They invested substantially to support their websites. Likewise, in the US, news organisations tried to bring staff from TV, the Web and newspapers to work together. The Tampa Group, for example, completed the integration between a website (TBO.com), a paper (Tampa Media Group) and a TV channel (WFLA) by moving them together.

Globally, digital transformation and newsroom convergence started from the late 1990s and continue to develop in the 21st century. Some newsrooms have achieved this more recently. The newsroom of NRK in Norway, for example, completed its physical integration in 2013 (Larrondo, Domingo, et al., 2016).

(3) Disruptions caused by tech giants

One major source of such disruption is the role played by tech giants in information collection, production and dissemination in the data age. Among others, Google, Facebook, Twitter, Instagram and YouTube have become the main platforms on which ordinary people communicate for all kinds of purposes. Social media and other tech giants are a double-edged sword. They are a threat to the traditional media in three ways. The first is the migration of audiences and the profits of the legacy news media to new players, like Facebook and Google, causing further deterioration in the financial situation facing journalism (see Chapter 3). The second refers to the pressing need for the legacy news media to engage with their audiences and advertisers. News content merely becomes part of the information that is available to readers on the Internet in general and in particular on social media. The content produced by the news media and journalists may have to compete with a mass of digital information and content for the audience's attention, advertisers' investments and social and political influence (see Chapter 8). The third is the rampant proliferation of fake news and misinformation on the Internet, particularly on the platforms of these technological companies, that may also disrupt the autonomy and legitimacy of journalism (see related discussions in Chapters 9 and 10).

Despite posing threats to journalism, social media also offer new ways of distributing news and of managing the relationship with the audience for the news media (see Chapter 8). In addition, social media companies, and other tech giants – such as Google – have begun to provide journalists with free, useful tools and even development grants (see Chapter 5). The advent of the new tools and technologies offered by tech companies, such as Google Flourish and 360° cameras, facilitates the production of digital, multimedia and immersive content so that journalists can cater to the tastes of audiences, an increasing number of whom are digital natives.

(4) Being global as a disruption

Last but not least, disruption is related to the global nature of journalism in the data age. Traditionally, journalism was local. However, today, globalisation is evident in journalism in at least three aspects – audiences, journalism practices and organisational operations. Along with the international spread of the websites and the apps of news outlets, the audience, journalism practices and the operations of the news media have all become global. The global nature of journalism practices and the media business has downsides.

For the news media, their competitors now include local, national and global news outlets, as well as news aggregators like Google, and even social media platforms. Likewise, journalists may find themselves competing with international counterparts for the same jobs, which deepens their job precarity. These all show the disruptive influence of digital technologies.

These opportunities and disruptions, as well as the resulting changes, will be explored in detail in this book. The discussions about them will prepare you to understand the influence of digital technologies over journalism. They will also prompt you to think about what journalism is today, what status it has in society, and what it needs in order to serve its role in democracy.

EXERCISE 2.2

Imagine if you are a journalist, or are looking to build a career in journalism, what challenges and opportunities will digital technologies create for you? What skills would you need to learn? Would you need to learn new skills and techniques all the time? Would you find practising journalism easier? Would you produce journalism of better quality? Would you feel digital technologies could help you to find a job or start your own journalism projects? Would you find difficulty in securing a job? If so, what reasons might there be for this? If you want to practise independent journalism, where might the funding come from? Would digital technologies help you raise money? Alternatively, imagine you are an audience member, do you pay for journalism? How do you perceive journalists and their work? Do you see them as doing a good job by bringing you quality news? Do you trust the news that is published by the news media? Do you see journalists as different from those ordinary users who create content on the Internet? Collecting all your thoughts together, can you find some arguments and counterarguments for the statement: digital technologies are disruptive technologies?

Summary of the Chapter

This chapter sets the context for the discussions about the changes in journalism in the book. It addresses the concepts of digital technologies and the Information Technology Revolution in its first part. Then, it explores the changes in the communication environment in the data age, before discussing whether, and if so, to what extent, digital technologies are disruptive to journalism. The new forms of journalism that have emerged in response to these changes have been integrated into newsrooms. The following chapters in this book will unpack what these new forms of journalism are and what they mean for journalism.

■ END OF CHAPTER EXERCISE ■

You have read about the digital communication environment being different from that of the pre-Internet age. However, digital technologies are so pervasive that you may feel they are part of your life. You may not understand what the pre-digital communication environment looked like, especially if you have not experienced the 'old' media era. You may not see the differences in the communication environment between the pre-Internet age and the current digital and data age. Try to think of situations in which these digital technologies, such as the Internet, mobiles and tablets, did not exist. What do you think personal and public communication would be like? How would you talk to your family and friends if they live far away from you? How would you do your shopping? How would you access the news every day? Compare what you would do today, and in these situations, and make a list of the differences. If you have started to think about how these changes are associated with the way news is produced, distributed and consumed, then make another list outlining the main features of the news that you read every day. Then compare the two lists and see which changes in the communication environment may have led to particular features of the news that you consume today.

■ FURTHER READING ■

Castells, Manuel (2013). *Communication Power.* Oxford: Oxford University Press (Chapter 2). This book offers an account of the transformation of power in the Internet age through an analysis of political events and social movements. Chapter 2 in Castells' book discusses in detail the changes in the communication environment under the influence of digital communication technologies. However, given that this book was published in 2013, the discussions do not address more recent phenomena of communication, such as fake news.

Lindgren, Simon (2017). *Digital Media & Society.* London: Sage (Chapter 1). Lindgren provides an introduction to several key concepts and topics that are related to digital media and society. Chapter 1 introduces you to the concept of digital society, which encompasses discussions of the idea of being 'digital' and the main features of the digital media ecology.

THREE

THE CRISES OF QUALITY JOURNALISM

━━━━━━━━ **KEY QUESTIONS** ━━━━━━━━

- What has caused the financial crisis of journalism?
- What is the traditional business model of news media? To what extent is it still viable today?
- What new business models have emerged? To what extent are they successful?
- Is quality journalism in crisis? If so, what is the crisis? How bad is it? What are the causes of the crisis?
- How have digital technologies and the market influenced the financial crisis in journalism and the crisis of quality journalism?

━━━━━━━━ **KEY CONCEPTS** ━━━━━━━━

business models

paywalls

quality journalism

content farms

investigative journalism

audience migration (to the Internet)

audience metrics

Journalism is in crisis. As we explored in the previous chapter, digital technologies play a pivotal role in transforming the communication environment in which journalism is practised, distributed and consumed. This chapter will continue to discuss how the changes in the communication environment have led to the double crises of journalism: the financial crisis of journalism, and the crisis of quality journalism. It explores the news media's traditional and new business models and analyses how technological innovations and market transformation have both interacted and jointly influenced journalism. With the arrival of digital technologies, audiences and advertising have substantially migrated to the Internet. The shifting news consumption habits of audiences, along with the rise of new players, like Google and Facebook, have delivered a heavy blow to the news media's revenues. Quality journalism is under threat as a consequence of news organisations' priority of combating financial difficulties (over the quality of journalism). Using audience metrics and analytics, news organisations are able to understand their target audience better than ever. The urgent need to succeed – or survive – in the media markets puts pressure on news organisations to cater to the needs and interests of audiences, which, however, may not be beneficial to public interest journalism (see detailed discussions in Chapter 8). As a result of reduced costs and resources and news organisations' reluctance to offend potential advertisers, tabloid journalism may prevail over quality journalism, especially investigative journalism, as the latter requires more resources to produce and is more likely to annoy those in power than the former (discussed later in this chapter). The discussion in this chapter will direct you to think critically about the driving needs behind the emergence of new forms of journalism (discussed in Chapters 4–7). It prompts you to start thinking about the reformed journalism–audience relationship (discussed in Chapter 8) and why it is important. It also urges you to recognise the news industry's imperative to deal with the emerging problems surrounding journalistic autonomy and legitimacy (discussed in Chapters 9 and 10).

The Financial Crisis of Journalism

Traditionally, the printed news media sold single copies of papers, subscriptions and advertising space in order to remain financially sustainable. Commercial broadcasters similarly sold advertising space on the basis of their ability to attract audiences to their content. Media content and the access to audiences are two products sold in the 'dual product' markets of the news media (Picard, 1989: 17). Advertising and circulation/subscription revenues are thus their lifeblood. However, over the past two decades, newspapers (and to a lesser extent, commercial broadcasters) have experienced a sharp decline in revenues. The traditional business model seems no longer to be a viable one. The losses in advertising revenues were the product of several contextual changes, including economic recessions, fierce market competition, the changing reading habits of audiences – especially those of younger generations – and the popularity of digital technologies (Franklin, 2014). In the revenue-driven news industry, the financial plight of news organisations has had a severe impact on journalism.

In Anglo-American countries, revenue losses started to haunt the news industry from 2003. Since around 2008, when advertisement revenues moved in significant quantities to the Internet, financial sustainability has become a primary concern for news organisations (Curran, 2010; Franklin, 2014). In the United States (US), in 2013, if measured by revenues, the news industry shrank by 40 per cent from its 2003 size (The Pew Research Center's Project for Excellence in Journalism, 2013). In 2017, daily (print and digital) newspaper circulation continued to decline, dropping 11 per cent and 10 per cent, respectively, from 2016 (Pew Research Center, 2018). The situation is not much brighter in the United Kingdom (UK). Since the start of the 2000s, the UK press has suffered considerable declines in circulation, advertising revenues and the numbers of audiences. For example, the Telegraph Media Group saw a 50 per cent fall in its annual profits in 2018 (Sweney, 2018b). Figure 3.1 shows a dramatic decrease in UK newspaper circulation between 2007 and 2019. In 2019, the circulation of most UK national newspapers dropped to less than 40 per cent of that in 2007. In 2020, some UK national newspapers such as *The Times*, *The Telegraph* and *The Sun* refused to publish their circulation figures, while others reported further declining circulations (The BBC, 2020).

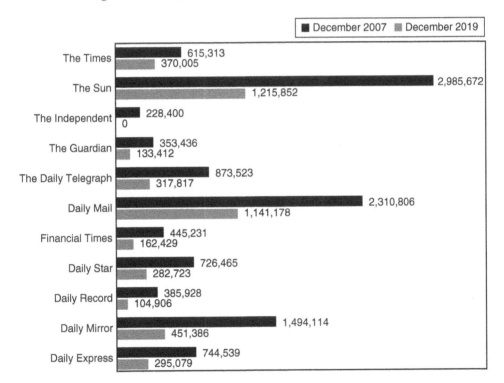

Figure 3.1   The changes in UK newspaper circulation between 2007 and 2019

Source: Data was compiled from https://www.theguardian.com/media/table/2009/jan/09/abc-december-national-newspapers and https://pressgazette.co.uk/national-newspaper-abcs-full-figures-december-2019-observer/ (accessed on 16 March 2020).

Note: The Independent ceased as a print edition and became digital only in 2016. The newspapers' Sunday counterparts have not been included in the data.

European countries, such as Finland, France, Germany and Italy, have also reported similar stories about the news industry in crisis (Brüggemann et al., 2016). In Spain, from 2007 to 2010, the circulation revenues of the press dropped 14.2 per cent, following a sharp decline in the sales of newspaper copies (Casero-Ripollés & Izquierdo-Castillo, 2013). Against the backdrop of austerity, severe advertising and circulation revenue losses hit the Greek news industry (Touri, Kostarella, & Theodosiadou, 2017).

The news media in Asian countries, such as China, encountered similar problems nearly a decade later than their Western counterparts. After 2009, for example, the newspaper circulation and advertising revenues in Australia shrank continually and significantly (Carson, 2015). At around the start of the 2010s, newspaper circulations rose in some Asian countries, such as China and India, as well as in South American countries such as Brazil, in stark contrast to the withering newspaper markets in developed economies (Brock, 2013). Later on, the situation in these countries, however, has started to change. The Chinese news media began to see revenue losses from 2013, after more than ten years of profit. Their financial crisis became particularly severe from 2016 (Tong, 2017a; Wang & Sparks, 2018). Likewise, the Brazilian news media have encountered enormous financial pressures, resulting in dramatic changes in the cultures of both newsrooms and journalism, as shown in the case of *Valor Econômico* (Undurraga, 2017).

In India, in the 2010s, the news media were still thriving, due to particular social, political and commercial factors, as well as the relationship between journalism and politics (Chadha & Koliska, 2016; Devi, 2019; Kalyani, 2017; Prasad, 2019; Udupa & Chakravarrty, 2012). News media owners and even journalists and editors often have a close relationship with powerful politicians or political parties in exchange for political and commercial benefits. Recent years have witnessed the concentration of political power coinciding with that of corporate media ownership (Maheshwari & Sparks, 2018). Nevertheless, the news media's growth has slowed down under the influence of the Internet and the changed reading habits of readers in India (Aneez, Neyazi, Kalogeropoulos, & Nielsen, 2019; Rodrigues, 2017).

In the Arab world, the increase in the circulation and advertising revenues for traditional news media has slowed (Guaaybess, 2019). For similar reasons, such as the migration of audiences and advertising to online platforms, signs of declining revenues have appeared from around 2011 (Shawli, 2021). In Saudi Arabia, for example, the income from the sales of print media fell from $407.6m in 2005 to $271.2m in 2015 (Oxford Business Group, No year). In seven Middle East and North Africa (MENA) countries including Qatar, the UAE, Tunisia, Jordan, Egypt, Lebanon and the KSA, newspaper readership significantly declined between 2013 and 2019, and in some countries, such as Qatar, the drop was more than 50 per cent (Dennis, Martin, Lance, & Hassan, 2019). In recent years, likewise, the Egyptian print media have suffered from shrinking circulation and advertising revenues, losing audiences to the Internet (Allam, 2018). In the first quarter of 2020, for example, Omnicom Group, an American media company, reportedly suffered a slump in its advertising revenues in the Middle East and Africa (ARAB NEWS, 2020).

Despite some exceptions, such as India, and variations in timing and place, in terms of changes in the financial situations of the news industry, the overall trend is therefore that financial turmoil is either enveloping the news media or lurking in their future. In their attempt to mitigate the financial crisis of journalism, most news media have given their top priority to urgently looking for viable business models and new ways to engage their audiences. As a result, it is natural for news organisations to go online, to be digital, and to experiment with novel funding models so that they can make the most of the opportunities that are offered by digital technologies.

Going Online and the Business Model Experimentation of the News Media

Going online and being digital are vital strategies that most of the news media have adopted in order to cope with the financial turmoil they are experiencing. Online experiments by news media organisations started as early as the 1970s, such as *The New York Times'* Information Bank, an online, interactive retrieval system (database), which was initiated in 1969 (Bourne & Hahn, 2003). However, news outlets did not start moving online and becoming digital until the 1990s or the early 2000s. In 1994, only around 30 newspapers in the US had gone online – in terms of launching their websites – though many already had online versions on paid-for databases like AOL and CompuServe. *The New York Times* launched its website (www.nytimes.com) in 1996. In the UK, *The Daily Telegraph* had the first British newspaper website (www.telegraph.co.uk) in 1994, while the BBC created its news website (www.bbc.co.uk) and its online branch in 1997. Other news media followed suit. By 1999, the number of newspapers going online had risen to 4,925 worldwide (Brown, 1999). One prominent feature of online news media is 'being digital', i.e., journalistic content is published and delivered in digital form (Chapter 2 discusses 'being digital' in detail).

In the meantime, news outlets have started to explore the viability of alternative business models. Today, no news organisation relies on just one business model. Instead, they draw on a hybrid of business models and revenue streams for profits. Legacy news media set up paywalls to deal with the threat that is posed by free content and news aggregators 'snatching' away journalistic content, audiences and advertising, with no or little costs. Although the situation has improved, with Google, for example, saying they will now pay selected publishers for high-quality news (Cellan-Jones, 2020) and agreeing to pay News Corporation for its journalism in 2021 (Hern, 2021), the threat posed by news aggregators taking news and advertising away from the news media still remains. In cases where laws and regulations are involved, some tech giants respond strongly. In 2021, for example, Facebook blocked users in Australia from viewing or sharing news content about a law proposed by Australian authorities to request tech giants to pay news media for news content appearing or content linked to on its platform (The BBC, 2021).

Since the mid-1990s, different types of paywalls have been introduced. Their development has experienced four stages – starting from the experimental phase (1994–2000), through the failed trial phase (2001–2007) and Murdoch's paywall crusade phase (2008–2010) to the popularising of the paywall phase (2011–2014) (Arrese, 2016). The four stages symbolise the ongoing transition from free content to paywalls, and the legacy media's struggles to find funding models that are adaptable to, and viable in, the digital environment. In the process, big legacy news outlets, such as those from Murdoch's media empire and *The New York Times*, have played a crucial role in experimenting with paywalls (Arrese, 2016).

Once hailed as a lifeline, the business model of paywalls has proven to be not universally viable. Not generating enormous revenues for news outlets, paywalls may put off readers who may not be keen to pay for content. Quite a lot of news organisations have erected paywalls but have quickly removed them. News outlets such as the *San Francisco Chronicle* in the US, *The Sun* in the UK and the *Southern Metropolitan Daily (nanfang dushibao)* in China are in this group.

As of 2021, news organisations such as *The Times* and the *Financial Times* in the UK, *The New York Times* in the US, and *Mainichi Shimbun* and *Asahi Shimbun* in Japan still operate paywalls for their online content. Roughly, two types of paywalls exist. The first type is those hard paywalls that offer no free content, such as the *United Daily* in Taiwan, and *The Times* and the *Financial Times*[1] in the UK. The second refers to those soft, or metered, paywalls that provide users with some free content; in particular, they give users certain free content over a specific period of time. However, if users want to read more, they will need a subscription. *The New York Times* in the US, and *The Daily Telegraph* and *The Independent* in the UK belong to the second type (for more discussions see Yang, 2012; Mayhew, 2019a; Musariri, 2018; Newman, Fletcher, et al., 2018).

Scholars (see, for example, Chyi, 2012; Chyi & Lee, 2013) argue that it does not matter how news organisations charge for content, what matters is that users may not be willing to pay for content. Despite scholars' pessimism about paywalls, however, some news organisations, like *The New York Times*, have reported their success. In 2020, for example, *The New York Times* had 7 million subscribers, whose subscriptions boosted the paper's digital revenue (Lee, 2020).

Other business models include inviting readers to make 'micropayments' – i.e., readers pay a small fee for articles they read; offering free online content but selling newspaper apps, as exemplified by *The Guardian*; bundling subscriptions for content published on multimedia platforms; and carrying advertising on mobile devices. News organisations also use crowd-funding, encouraging individuals to make donations to support journalism. Occasionally, they even organise events and training sessions to raise money.

These alternative funding models have created both opportunities and new problems. The upside of adopting paywalls, subscriptions or donations is the chance to ally with readers in order to fund quality journalism. A good example of this is Mediapart in France, which relies on its subscribers to support its independent investigative journalism (see a discussion on Mediapart in Benson, 2019). However, erecting paywalls may lead to the commodification, or 'monetisation', of journalism (Pickard, 2011; Sjøvaag, 2016). Paid content is seen as representing high-quality content. Paywalls are considered to contribute to a democratic deficit, as they may eventually include highly educated (and well-off) elites but will exclude those who cannot afford paywalls from quality news. Such exclusion would leave financially disadvantaged and marginal groups underserved by the news media. *The Guardian*'s strategy (see Box 3.1) might offer a third way of coping with this problem. While making its online content free to access, the newspaper charges for its apps, such as *The Guardian Daily*, and encourages readers to donate to support its quality journalism. In so doing, the paper can increase the accessibility of quality content for readers, while it can still seek to make a profit to ensure its financial sustainability.

BOX 3.1

The business models of *The Guardian*

As of 2021, *The Guardian* did not have a paywall for its online content. However, it required a digital subscription for its *Live* (Premium) app and *Daily* app. The digital revenues earned by the owner of *The Guardian* and *The Observer* increased to £108.6m in 2017 (Waterson, 2018a). *The Guardian* has also introduced the business model of encouraging readers to donate to support the paper financially (Viner, 2018). Since 2016, *The Guardian* has started to seek crowd-funding from its readers, asking them to contribute to maintaining the financial sustainability of the newspaper (Bond, 2017). In 2017, its income from readers' support even exceeded its advertising revenue (Mayhew, 2017). In 2018, it said in an editorial that 'more than a million people worldwide have contributed to *The Guardian* in the last three years, with 500,000 paying to support the publication on an ongoing basis' (Waterson, 2018b). Despite being promising and inspiring, *The Guardian* still cannot claim that it is financially sustainable. In 2020, the paper published its 2019/2020 statutory financial results for the year to 29 March 2020. The results show that its primary financial goal was achieved in 2020, with revenues of £223.5 million, slightly down from £224.5 million in 2019. To ensure long-term sustainability and growth, the paper announced strategic changes and a decision to reduce costs, including staff redundancy (GNM press office, 2020).

In their article about the pros and cons of digital paywalls, Victor Pickard and Alex Williams, two media scholars, discussed related copyright and antitrust concerns surrounding paywalls (Pickard & Williams, 2014). It is uncertain whether extending the consent given by authors for print publications to become online publications is legally acceptable. There have also been concerns expressed over potential, secret deals struck among news media competitors over prices which may impair fair competition among the news media.

As for non-profit journalism (see examples in Box 3.2 and Box 3.3) and journalists practising entrepreneurial journalism (see a detailed discussion about entrepreneurial journalism in Chapter 7), crowd-funding has become one of their primary funding models, in which journalists receive 'micropayments' from ordinary people to finance their reporting. Through facilitating the rise of non-profit news media, independent news media and entrepreneurial journalism, crowd-funding potentially alleviates some of the problems caused by layoffs. It has the potential to help journalists make their journalistic dreams come true and thus fulfil their career ambitions. This is important, in particular in the context of journalism in crisis. However, crowd-funding is not perfect, as new problems, such as those concerning financial sustainability, stress and independence, have arisen (discussed in more detail in Chapter 7). An analysis of three crowd-funded news organisations in Germany, Hungary and Russia, for example, reveals that crowd-funding has burdened journalists through financial instability and increasing their work-load, which has therefore driven down their occupational happiness (Zaripova, 2017).

BOX 3.2

weReport and Taiwan FactCheck Center

Taiwan-based weReport (wereport.org), is an excellent example of crowd-funded non-profit journalism. It is an innovative business model where ordinary people sponsor journalists to report. Relying on micropayments made by ordinary users, i.e., readers, journalists can report on topics which may not be covered otherwise. With crowd-funding, weReport aimed to support journalists to conduct investigative journalism. weReport was launched in 2011 but stopped accepting donations and applications in 2020. The decision was made in response to a decrease in the amounts of donations and the number of applications after nine years of operation (Lo, 2020). In 2020, the same group of founders launched another independent, non-profit, donation-based news outlet: the Taiwan FactCheck Center (tfc-taiwan.org.tw), which was aimed at resolving the problems caused by fake news and misinformation.

BOX 3.3

ProPublica

ProPublica is another excellent example of non-profit journalism that has adopted multiple funding models. The US-based ProPublica, 'an independent, non-profit newsroom', is famous for its (often data-driven) investigative journalism. It received its founding funding from the Sandler Foundation. Apart from this, it has also been supported by other foundations, e.g., the Knight Foundation, and donations from readers. Between 2008 and 2020, ProPublica won the Pulitzer Prize six times and received other awards for its excellent journalism (www.propublica.org).

Another type of funding has emerged in recent years. Internet giants, such as Face-book and Google, have launched their own projects to support local journalism (Ingram, 2018). In the UK, in January 2019, for example, the Community News Project was launched collaboratively by the National Council for the Training of Journalists (NCTJ), Facebook and news publishers, such as JPIMedia, Reach, and the Midland News Asso-ciation (Wrenn & Cox-Brooker, 2018). Apart from providing training and developing a partnership with news organisations, the Google News Initiative offers the Digital News Innovation Fund to support journalism. The implications of the involvement and finan-cial support of these tech companies as patrons for journalism, however, remain unclear. Although serving as an alternative (financial) resource, their sponsorship gives rise to a key issue of whether, and if so, to what extent, would their involvement impair the independence of journalism. Tech giants like Facebook and Google play an increasingly important role in our economic, political and social lives. They monopolise and gate-keep digital commerce and communications in the data age. Their power thus needs to be put under close public scrutiny. This recent emergence of collaboration between journalism and big Internet companies raises vital questions about the possible restraints (direct or through self-censorship) this could place on journalists seeking to scrutinise their operations. This problem, however, is not exclusive to this particular collaboration between tech giants and journalism. It also exists in any crowd-funding journalism projects involving audiences' financial support. With audiences and other social actors becoming funders, how will journalistic autonomy be influenced? You can find related discussions later in this chapter and in this book, for example in Chapters 7, 8, 9 and 11.

EXERCISE 3.1

Select several news outlets and explore whether they have erected paywalls in one way or another. Ask yourself and fellow students if you/they would like to pay for the content behind the paywalls and what are your/their reasons for their decisions. In particular, if the answer is 'no', give some thought to your views on the reasons why you/they would not want to pay, and the implications that this has for journalism. Think about the questions that this raises, such as: if even journalism students do not want to pay for journalism, who will? How can journalism survive if we all have the free content mentality? In your opinion, what feasible funding models are available to the news media?

Why Has Advertising Migrated to the Internet?

Advertising has migrated to the Internet for three reasons. First, the news media are no longer the primary platforms on which advertisers can find their target audiences. With the rise of Internet-based news outlets, media markets have been significantly transformed. Multiple media players can be found in the media market. They may be big legacy media, such as the BBC, *The Guardian*, or *The Independent*. These players can be online media outlets, such as *The Huffington Post* (www.huffpost.com), or news aggregators, such as Google News and Yahoo! News. Also joining them in the market are independent non-profit newsrooms such as ProPublica, and hyperlocal sites/community sites that contain online news or content services about a town, village or even a single postcode, or other small, geographically defined communities. We can see that some journalism start-ups (discussed in Chapter 7) have also grown into big players in the markets. *The Huffington Post*, for example, was founded as a website in 2005, and it quickly became the second-most-used online news brand in the US (Newman, et al., 2017). It receives its financial support from advertising revenues and investors. The Internet group AOL bought it for US$315 million in 2011. At the time of writing in 2021, it is owned by BuzzFeed.

The news media compete with so many players for audiences' attention that they may not win the attention competition. With little or no investment in journalism, news aggregators, such as Google News and Yahoo! News, can offer users a wide variety of free news products (Berte & Bens, 2008). In addition, user-generated content (UGC) provides users with free content that does not have to abide by the principles of journalism and is entertaining, apolitical and trivial. With their content being sharable and instantly delivered, social media platforms, such as Facebook and Twitter, have become leading platforms for exchanging news and information. While entertainment providers such as Amazon Prime, Netflix, YouTube and Apple Music bring them relatively free or cheap entertainment content, audiences may not have the time or appetite for news on serious political and social topics.

In 2019, based on a YouGov survey of more than 75,000 online news consumers in 38 countries, the Reuters Institute for the Study of Journalism published a report outlining the latest developments in news audiences. The survey shows that news was merely one of the forms of online media content that users could purchase. When asked to choose only one media subscription among those for online video, music and news for the next year, only 7 per cent of participants under 45 years old said they would select online news (Newman, Fletcher, Kalogeropoulos, & Nielsen, 2019). Another 2019 study found that young audiences and readers have stopped trying to read the news published by the mainstream news media (Flamingo and the Reuters Institute for the Study of Journalism, 2019).

The second, and related, reason for advertising moving to the Internet is the changed news consumption habits of audiences, which are becoming increasingly fragmented and disoriented (for more discussion about this see Chapter 8). No longer sitting in front of televisions or holding a print copy of newspapers or magazines, audiences may read news in a way that suits their life and work schedule, which means their reading time may be 'small' and fragmented. For example, instead of sitting down to read carefully, they may quickly go through news on mobiles while they are waiting for a bus or sitting on a train. That audiences can choose what they want to consume and decide when to consume it results in a trend towards audience fragmentation. Audience fragmentation is a consequence of the formation of segmented audience clusters made up of like-minded people who like to be connected and share information (see also the discussion about the 'echo-chamber' effect in Box 8.6 in Chapter 8). Audience fragmentation has emerged along with the disappearance of the mass audience and the rise of narrow-casted audiences, whose consumption is significantly individualised, privatised and fragmented. Apart from fragmentation, audiences are also increasingly disoriented in the data age. Audiences' attention may be easily lost and they can be distracted in the wake of excessive online information and hyperlinks. The fragmentation and disorientation of news audiences, as well as the disappearance of the mass audience, suggest the difficulties faced by the news media in catching and maintaining audiences' attention. When it comes to advertising revenues, such difficulties mean that news media are less capable of providing advertisers with a critical mass of readers in the way they used to be able to do, and, at the same time, they cannot give advertisers particular subsets of the target audience as precisely as tech giants like Google and Facebook.

The third reason relates to the profound penetration and pervasive presence of the Internet giants such as Google in the evolved value chain in the online advertising market, which has new types of advertising pertinent to the online environment and in which the link between users' content consumption and publishers gaining advertising value from such consumption has been broken. Advertisers' focus on clicks means that clicking on news content somewhere else other than on the news media's websites does not necessarily bring any value to news media.

As a dominant player, for example, Google gains revenue at each stage of the online advertising value chain (Geradin & Katsifis, 2020). Search advertising – advertising appearing among search results on search pages – for example, has emerged and grown rapidly since its appearance in 2000. In the US, Google receives around $40 billion annually from advertisers (The Justice Department of the United States, 2020). In 2019, Google's search revenue reached $34.3 billion in the US (Kang, McCabe & Wakabayashi, 2020).

While the conventional news media struggle to retain the attention of audiences, search engines and social media platforms, like Google and Facebook, can offer advertisers 'targeted' advertising, based on analysis of the data collected in relation to the behaviours of Internet users. With their ability to track and measure audiences' involvement and the effectiveness of the advertisements, these Internet giants outperform the traditional news media in obtaining advertising revenues and thus have dominated digital advertising markets. In 2019, for example, Google and Facebook accounted for more than half of all US digital advertising spending (Wakabayashi & Hsu, 2021).

Under the influence of these three factors, the news media are no longer the primary – let alone the only – platform for advertising. They have lost the target audiences of advertisers to the Internet. The news media's early strategy of going online originated from their fear of the Internet. In 2010, at the Bloomberg Business Week Media Summit, Jon Klein, the then president of CNN US, even said that he feared Facebook more than Fox News with regard to competition. He said that 'the competition I'm really afraid of are social networking sites' as 'that's an alternative that threatens to pull people away from us' (*The Independent*, 2010). The substantial exodus of audiences and advertising to the Internet, and the role played by tech giants like Google and Facebook in this process have proved that there was a foundation for his worries.

Online advertising is often seen as disrupting press advertising. The surge in the numbers of alternative online advertising channels, and the migration of classified advertisements to the Internet, have posed enormous challenges to advertising on the traditional news media (Berte & Bens, 2008). That said, along with the new advertising formats that are emerging, in theory, the traditional news media can also benefit from online advertising markets. Interactive online advertising, for example, is one type of innovative advertising adopted by traditional news media to adapt to online advertising marketing. It has the potential to engage users by encouraging interactivity with them. Its audience engagement and interactivity can also be measured by metrics.

However, as was also discussed in the previous chapter, the news media have not adequately grasped the opportunities that are offered by online advertising markets, due to their slow response to disruption and 'routine rigidity' (Gilbert & Bower, 2002; Gilbert,

2005). The past success and established routines of the news industry have led to an 'inertia', which prevents them from fully embracing the new opportunities provided by digital markets (Boczkowski, 2005; Gilbert, 2005). To overcome such 'inertia' requires the industry to re-invent itself and to implement organisational reforms (Christensen, Skok, & Allworth, 2012). News organisations will have a long-term struggle to survive in the changed communication environment, as exemplified in the case of *Aftonbladet*, a major newspaper in Sweden (Åkesson, Sørensen, & Eriksson, 2018). After 20 years struggling to shift from a conventional print-based newspaper to a digital media company by embracing digital media and markets, the newspaper is still considerably based on print publication and has developed ambidextrous strategies to engage and integrate both new and old technologies and markets. Apart from news organisations' struggles to embrace digital markets, the adoption of new types of digital advertising has posed new challenges to journalism, particularly journalistic authority and legitimacy (this point will be discussed further in Chapter 10). Take native advertising (see Box 10.2 in Chapter 10). Native advertising is a type of advertising that in its appearance is identical to the editorial content of the news outlet. Its rise is allegedly bringing some hope to cash-strapped newsrooms, but raises mounting concerns over the related ethical issues, such as blurring the boundaries between journalism and advertising.

EXERCISE 3.2

Take a look at the website of a news aggregator, such as Google News. Think about how the content is 'produced' and distributed to audiences. Does Google News produce its news stories? Who initially makes and publishes the news stories? You can compare the news visible on your Google News page with that of your friends. Do you receive the same kind of news? Very likely, you will find Google News presents different content to different people. Think about the reasons for the differences and how this happens. Think about the consequences for quality journalism and journalism generally.

Job Cuts and the Closures of Newsrooms

In response to their financial losses, news organisations have cut jobs and even closed down news outlets. Academics (see, for example, Curran, 2010; Franklin, 2012, 2014) have portrayed rather miserable, or even apocalyptic, scenarios for the current situation and the future of Anglo-American journalism. Words, such as 'haemorrhaging' and 'bleeding', are used to describe the scope of job cuts and newsroom closures.

In the Anglo-American world, job losses were noticeable from 2008. In that year, in the US, around 25 per cent of jobs in newspapers in 2001 vanished (The Pew Research Center, 2009). The situation has not improved since then. Between 2008 and 2017, the number of US newsroom jobs (including those in newspapers, TV and radio) declined by 23 per cent. The situation was worse for newspaper employment, which dropped by 45 per cent, from 71,000 in 2008 to 39,000 employees in 2017 (Grieco, 2018). Local and regional newspapers have suffered particularly severely. In 2008, the New York *Daily News* announced a 50 per cent cut to its editorial employees. Likewise, in the UK, local and regional newspapers, such as those in the Trinity Mirror Group (now Reach plc) and those in Northcliffe Media, shrank their editorial teams by more than a thousand jobs between 2008 and 2009 (Curran, 2010).

There is a striking resonance in other parts of the world. In China, for example, the closure of news outlets and job losses hit the news industry hard from around 2016, as a result of the joint influences of the market, politics and digital technologies (see the case of China in Chapter 9). The news media in Australia has also witnessed widespread job losses and redundancies. In particular, its local journalism has suffered badly from job losses.

Digital teams and online journalism are not much better off. In 2018, Rogers Media in Canada, announced that it was to cut about 75 full-time jobs from the digital content and publishing team and thus downsize it to about 150 members (The Canadian Press, 2018). In January 2019, BuzzFeed, HuffPost and Gannett announced about 1,000 job cuts (Darcy & Kludt, 2019). A month later, the number increased to about 2,000 jobs lost among online news providers, including BuzzFeed (Bell, 2019).

The closure of news outlets, especially at local levels, is another response by news-groups to their financial losses. In the UK, Trinity Mirror closed seven local newspapers in 2014 and another four in 2017 (Johnston, 2014; Stuart-Turner, 2017). In January 2019, Harlow, an Essex town of 80,000 people, lost its last print newspaper, the *Harlow Star* (Waterson, 2019a). In the US, about 2,000 newspapers were either closed or merged between 2003 and 2018 (Morris, 2018).

The impact on quality journalism of job losses and newspaper closures of this scope should not be underestimated, as it is closely related to the quality of journalism. The remainder of the chapter will discuss the consequences of the financial crisis in journalism on its quality.

The Decline of Quality Reporting

As we discussed, above, in the media sector, one noticeable change that has been brought about by digital technologies is the transformation of the media market. The power of the market is tricky. Market power can liberate the media from the interference of the state. Mature and developed markets help to increase the professional status of occupations. With sufficient financial support, the news media are able to commit to substantial investments in journalism and long-term journalistic investigations.

However, the market can also turn into a constraining force. News media organisations' pursuit of financial profit may sacrifice quality journalism, a lifeline for democracy. Journalism is a costly practice that needs enormous amounts of investment. The failure in media markets is thought to be one of the main reasons for the abandoning of quality journalism – journalism that has ethical practices, serves the public interest and democracy, informs citizens properly and holds power to account. Take investigative journalism for example (see Box 3.4). Investigative journalism is one type of quality journalism. In addition to commercial considerations, news organisations can have concerns about investigations that may potentially damage their relationships with powerful institutions or individuals, and this may lead to the removal of institutional support for investigative journalism. In addition, the closures of local or regional news outlets impair the ability of the news media to report on local issues. As a consequence, there has been a lack of diversity in news content, and the legacy media have increasingly lost contact with local communities.

■■■■■■ BOX 3.4 ■■■■■■

The disappearance of investigative journalism

Investigative journalism is a particular form of journalism that involves significant amounts of investigation, intending to hold power to account. Investigative reporting is central to the watchdog role of the media in the public sphere. It contributes to democracy by nurturing an informed citizenry. However, investigative journalism 'pits the press against power' and disrupts the usual patterns of the 'indexing' of the views that are expressed by mainstream government sources. These practices may upset the sometimes cosy world of daily reporting, as rightly pointed out decades ago by Glasser and Ettema in their classic work 'Investigative Journalism and the Moral Order', which is still applicable to today's journalism (Glasser & Ettema, 1989). Take investigative journalism in the UK, for example. After the 'golden era' of the 1970s, the decline in British investigative journalism became prominent in the 1990s and early 2000s (see further discussions in de Burgh, 2008). Its decline weakened the public scrutiny power of journalism and thus further impaired the legitimacy of journalism. One explanation is that investigative journalism, which takes a great deal of time, is expensive, and the related 'potential legal risks/costs' are high (Aldridge, 1998: 118). News organisations may also fear the effect on their relationships with the powerful. They may not be able to afford to damage such relationships, especially in circumstances in which they are suffering from severe financial losses.

However, more recently, crowd-funding and the prevalence of data have facilitated a revival of investigative journalism (see detailed discussions in Chapters 5 and 7). Over the past decade, investigative journalism has been resurrected under the influence of a variety of factors, ranging from the emergence of data journalism to alternative funding opportunities (Leigh, 2019). The publication of influential data-based investigative reports such as those on the UK MPs' Expenses Scandal (in 2009), the NSA Surveillance Exposures (in 2013) and the Panama and Paradise Papers (from 2016) conveys a positive sign of the revival of investigative journalism to the world (see discussions about these cases in Chapter 5).

The increasing concentration of media ownership in the hands of a few people is also believed to threaten the diversity and quality of journalism. Media owners' desire to maximise profits has led to the rise of tabloid journalism, or even of paparazzi journalism, a type of tabloid journalism with a focus on sensationalism. In addition to this, critics (see, for example, Hallin & Mancini, 2004) worry that high media concentration will lead to commercial censorship and the instrumentalisation of journalism, meaning the use of journalism as an instrument by media owners in pursuit of their own political aims and capital.

In the data era, the political power and influence of tech giants have grown dramatically with their wide reach of online populations and extensive political lobbying. In 2020 Google and Facebook had much more reach with respect to the UK adult digital population than all the UK news media sites added together (Ofcom, 2021). Tech players are also endeavouring to cast political influence. In the US context, for example, a data-driven investigation published by *The New Statesman* revealed an overall huge year-on-year increase in political lobbying spending by big tech companies such as Facebook, Google, Amazon, Microsoft and Apple trying to influence the US federal government. In 2020, the 15 tech companies analysed by the paper accounted for almost a quarter of the total political lobbying spending made by nearly 700 communications and electronics companies, which is the fourth highest-spending sector in US federal lobbying (Swindells, 2021). With the growing influence and power of big tech companies, the extent to which news media owners can use journalism as an instrument to their political benefit has become precarious, with potential implication for quality journalism.

A threat to the quality of journalism may also come from news organisations' need not only to reduce costs, but to fill editorial space. To fulfil this need, they may begin to use cheap – or even free – content. Some news organisations have even opted to use 'aggregation, content farms and Huffinization' – a new method of news production and dissemination (Bakker, 2012) (see Box 3.5). As a result of this, (quality) content is no longer king.

■■■■■ BOX 3.5 ■■■■■

'Aggregation, content farms and Huffinization' (Bakker, 2011, 2012)

The concepts of 'content farms' and 'Huffinization' have emerged in academic discussions since 2011. They refer to a phenomenon whereby (usually free) online content is cheaply produced by freelancers and amateurs, like bloggers or social media users, in order to boost the traffic of the websites of the news organisations, as best exemplified in The Huffington Post (Bakker, 2011, 2012). On a content farm, algorithms, or the combination of humans and algorithms, aggregate free content from the Internet, which is an example of remixing, as discussed in Chapter 2. The emergence of 'content farms' is news organisations' strategic response to the harsh competition in media markets and the lack of viable funding models in practice. Heavily adopting news aggregation and content produced by ordinary Internet users or volunteers, news media can effectively produce content at no, or low, cost (Bakker, 2011). Several issues arise around the emergence of 'content farms' – such as a reduction in the quality of journalism, the treatment of journalists, copyright, verification and accuracy, and algorithms' biases. These two concepts – 'content farms' and 'Huffinization' – contrast with other scholarly arguments about the importance of niche journalism. Niche journalism targets niche audience markets, cherishes creative values and provides quality journalistic content (see, for example, Cook & Sirkkunen, 2013; Picard, 2006). As you will find, for example, in Chapter 7 on entrepreneurial journalism, to be successful it is crucial for entrepreneurial journalism start-ups to identify, target and engage niche markets.

━━━━━━━━ **EXERCISE 3.3** ━━━━━━━━

Try to find two examples of content produced on 'content farms' and think about how this content was produced. The examples need not necessarily be published in the English language. Also, think about why the host websites would like to provide audiences with content of this type and what are the consequences for quality journalism? Would quality newspapers, like *The Guardian* and *The New York Times*, do this? What does the news media's use of free, or cheap, content, produced by amateurs mean for journalists and journalism? Does it mean fewer jobs for professional journalists? Can the host websites ensure the credibility of such content? What role is played by algorithms in the emergence of 'content farms'? If the content has errors, who should shoulder the responsibility? Should news be original?

The desire of news organisations to boost audience engagement may also pose a threat to quality journalism. The need to compete for the attention of users may compromise public interest considerations. One key influencing factor is newsrooms enthusiastically using metrics, such as website visiting rates, and web-page viewing or click rates, as an essential measurement for the success of a report. This measurement will potentially encourage journalists to write something sensational in order to catch the eye of Internet users, rather than something important that citizens need to know, as exemplified in the cases of mainland Chinese and Taiwanese journalism (Tong & Lo, 2017). In Tong and Lo's study, the urge to survive the crisis in media markets was the main driving force behind the tabloidisation of two newspapers – one was based in mainland China and the other Taiwan. That audience metrics were used to judge the success of a news story commodified audiences and pressured journalists to produce sensational stories that would become viral on the Internet. Due to this metrics obsession, as shown in Tong and Lo's study, the question of how news organisations can engage with audiences but still serve the public interest becomes a pressing challenge.

With the prevalence of the free-content mentality, only those readers who care about, and can afford, quality news will pay for it. In the meantime, tabloid newspapers, such as *The Sun* and the *Daily Mail*, which do not currently have paywalls for their online content, cater to the needs of audiences who have a taste for infotainment content and embrace their free news treats. In the longer term, a potential consequence is that media markets become further stratified. Quality papers will heavily depend on their long-term, small, but stable, often elite and well-off readers for revenues. With no paywalls, tabloid papers rely on big audiences (in the case of the *Mail*, worldwide) to generate advertising revenues and offer free content to their readers. In between these two tiers may rise a third camp of news providers composed of entrepreneurial journalism projects (see related discussions in Chapter 7). For example, there have emerged journalism start-ups like overtone.ai, using AI technologies to curate and provide quality news.

The quality of journalism is, thus, under threat in the wake of the financial crisis that is being faced by the news media. Quality journalism, however, is necessary for a healthy democracy. The deterioration of quality journalism has profound implications for the relationship between journalism and the state, as well as the level of autonomy that journalism can have (see the discussions in Chapter 9).

Accompanying these problems are also the concerns around the legitimacy of journalism (see the discussions in Chapter 10). Legitimacy justifies the acts of social groups and organisations and makes them acceptable to other members of society. Journalistic legitimacy is the source of justification for the cultural authority of journalism in collecting, producing and disseminating information, and in defining reality. The cultural authority of journalism, in turn, consolidates its legitimacy. Journalists need to endeavour to maintain journalistic legitimacy, as it is a dynamic process rather than a fixed one.

Journalism needs a sustainable future. There is, thus, an urgent need to reinvigorate journalism and regain and solidify journalistic legitimacy. The emergence of new forms of journalism has brought about opportunities in the data age. However, to what extent will these opportunities contribute to the easing of the crises in journalism? The following chapters will explore these issues and questions.

Summary of the Chapter

This chapter discusses two crises facing journalism: the financial crisis, and the crisis of quality journalism. It explores the economic plight of the legacy news media and their efforts to seek innovative forms of journalism and viable funding models. Before addressing the crisis in quality journalism, it discusses the reasons why advertising and audiences have migrated to the Internet and, in particular, the role played by tech giants, like Google and Facebook, in speeding up this tendency. The chapter raises questions as to whether, how and to what extent new forms of journalism can help to mitigate the crises in journalism, which will be discussed in the following chapters.

END OF CHAPTER EXERCISE

Think about this interesting paradox. The proliferation of free online content takes away the resources for journalism and the justification for making quality news. It may not be worth the effort to produce and publish quality content, as doing so is costly and may bring low financial rewards. Meanwhile, however, quality content is needed more than ever in a time of information overload when users may receive content of varying quality, and even fake news and misinformation. If the audience realises the importance of quality content and is willing to pay for it, the news industry may be able to survive the financial hardship that it is facing and may even thrive again. So, think about the two sides of the situation. Do you agree that publishing quality content can help to alleviate the lingering financial crisis faced by the news media at a time when fake news has become rampant? If so, to what extent?

━━━━━━━━ **FURTHER READING** ━━━━━━━━

Curran, James (2010). The future of journalism. *Journalism Studies, 11*(4), 1–13.
Franklin, Bob (2014). The future of journalism: in an age of digital media and economic uncertainty. *Digital Journalism, 2*(3), 254–272.
These two articles accurately outline the financial predicaments faced by journalism and the bleak future ahead for journalism, as well as the problems with which journalism needs to deal as an occupation.

Bakker, Piet (2012). Aggregation, content farms and Huffinization: the rise of low pay and no pay journalism. *Journalism Practice, 6*(5–6): 627–637. Bakker's article, published in 2012, was developed from a conference paper he gave in 2011. It discusses an important phenomenon which helps us to understand the significant influence of the shifting digital environment on the quality of journalism.

Note

1   As of 2021, the *Financial Times* offers schools, students aged 16–19 and teachers free online subscriptions, see https://ft.com/content/7ab6a9ec-1e4e-11e8-aaca-4574d7dabfb6 (accessed 20 December 2019).

FOUR

ONLINE JOURNALISM

===== **KEY QUESTIONS** =====

- What is online journalism? What are its main features?
- How have the ways to deliver news changed in the digital environment?
- What features does digital storytelling have?
- How has the rise of online journalism transformed journalism skills and job markets?
- Is online journalism better journalism?
- How has the prevalence of online journalism changed journalism cultures?

===== **KEY CONCEPTS** =====
---

online journalism
multimedia
deterritorialisation
interactivity
hyperlink
immediacy

transparency
hypertextuality
immersion
digital storytelling
5Ws and 1H

Online journalism is journalism that is published and delivered on the Internet. You may ask, shouldn't journalism be online? You ask because you may take for granted that online is the normal way of publishing and consuming news. Today online journalism is so pervasive that it has become 'normal' and even lays the foundation for most other new forms of journalism that are digital. Yet, this is only part of the story. Journalism is not always online. Online journalism is only one form of journalism, though predominant, and there have been ongoing, gradual developments in journalism moving from offline to online. Given online journalism's importance in itself and to other forms of journalism, gaining a thorough knowledge of its features and developments is crucial for our understanding of journalism in the data age.

The chapter will first examine the rise and development of online journalism, its key features, and the related changes in storytelling. It will then explore the emerging need for new skills in order to gather, cover and disseminate news before discussing how this need is transforming job markets. The last part of the chapter discusses the resulting changes in the cultures, quality and sustainability of online journalism.

The Rise and Development of Online Journalism

Online journalism means that newspapers and broadcasters, whose products used to be distinguishable from one another, now offer content in the digital format – though for most news outlets, their news content is also delivered in the traditional print, broadcast or radio format. Often multimedia and digital, online news content may contain text, audio, videos, images, interactive features, timelines, charts, graphs and maps. The practice of online journalism thus blurs the traditional distinctions between print and broadcast journalism.

Online journalism emerged in conjunction with the strategy by news outlets to produce online versions in the mid-1990s, as we explored in Chapter 3. Online news has established itself as an essential form of journalism in fewer than two decades, being rapidly integrated into traditional journalism in tandem with the digital transformation of newsrooms and the changing news consumption habits of audiences. The publishing and delivery of journalism first moved from offline – print, radio and broadcast – to the Internet, and later to portable devices, such as mobile phones and tablets.

Early years

From the late 1990s to the 2000s, news outlets cautiously tried out different technical features of the Internet for distributing their content in an attempt to adapt to the digital environment. Their endeavours mark the start of the transformation of journalism in its forms, concepts and relationship with its audiences.

Legacy news media going online gave rise to online journalism. Although going online partly originated from news media's fear of the Internet (discussed in the previous chapter), they also wanted to make the most of it. *The New York Times*, for example, explained the strategy behind the launching of its website (www.nytimes.com) in 1996: 'The electronic newspaper … is part of a strategy to extend the readership of The Times and to create opportunities for the company in the electronic media industry' and 'our site is designed to take full advantage of the evolving capabilities offered by the Internet' (Lewis, 1996). With their websites launched, the news media began to publish their content on the Internet, and online journalism began.

In the early years, multimedia elements in online journalism content were fewer in number and less diverse than they are today. For example, apart from text, the web pages of *The New York Times* published between 1996 and 1999 mostly contained pictures and hyperlinked textual headlines with limited interactive functions, such as 'Search the Site'. In the early 21st century, more innovative and diverse forms of online news content appeared. It was during the wars, conflicts and natural disasters of the time that online journalism showed that it had great potential to inform and engage audiences. In the aftermath of the 9/11 attack in the United States in 2001, for instance, the news media noticed a massive increase in the traffic on their websites (Bradshaw & Rohumaa, 2011). Online journalism's potential for audience engagement spurred the news media to look for new ways to deliver online news.

Later, news outlets introduced new digital elements, such as interactive graphs, timelines and live blogs, in order to tell stories creatively and engagingly. For example, the web page of *The New York Times* published on 30 March 2003, contained interactive graphs about 'Actions in Iraq' and slide shows of pictures of soldiers and the families of victims. When it comes to covering emergency events, such as conflicts, crises or natural disasters, the use of timelines and live blogs in news allows journalists to update audiences regularly with the latest information as events unfold. These new forms of news content originated from the live sports coverage that was initiated by Guardian.co.uk in 1999 (Thurman & Walters, 2013). Live blogs, usually including timelines, geo-information and small pieces of the latest information about particular events, are well suited to the needs of news organisations to tackle the challenges of immediacy and audience engagement, as well as the flexible, fast news consumption of their audiences. During crisis events, such as earthquakes or tsunamis, the news media frequently publish updates through live blogging, including content contributions made by citizens on the scene. Timelines and live blogs, for example, were extensively used in the news coverage of the 7/7 London bombings of 2005 and the Haitian earthquake of 2010. The continuous updating of information turns news reporting into something ongoing, interactive and happening in real time.

Accompanying the rise of online journalism is the emergence of a global trend in which user-generated content (UGC) is incorporated into news output, for three reasons. First, journalists are not always at the scene of events. Equipped with digital devices, such as cameras and mobile phones, ordinary people may take pictures and videos of the events which journalists can use in their news stories. Early examples of incorporating UGC into news include using the footage taken by passers-by or passengers in the coverage of the 9/11 attacks in the United States (US) in 2001 and the 7/7 London bombings in the United Kingdom (UK) in 2005. In this sense, UGC helps to enhance the coverage of events like natural disasters, conflicts and war zones that may be inaccessible to journalists (Cooper, 2017).

Second, the integration of UGC into traditional reporting, easily adaptable to the forms of timelines or live blogs, also results from the attempt of the news media to engage audiences. Maintaining the connection with local communities is especially crucial for local and regional newsrooms, so it is important to publish content that comes from social media or that is sent in by local community members in order to establish and demonstrate such a connection.

Third, the adoption of UGC by traditional journalism is driven by the economic motivations of news organisations to reduce costs while improving revenue (Vujnovic, Singer, et al., 2010). As we discussed in the previous chapter, some news organisations tend to use increasing amounts of UGC and other free, or cheap, content that has been contributed by amateur writers, in pursuit of profit (Bakker, 2011). Adopting UGC is thus also their strategy for coping with their need to fill the infinite online space, but to decrease the workforce and downsize newsrooms to save costs.

For these reasons, newsrooms worldwide have moved to include UGC as part of the news stories produced by journalists. UGC also appears on its own in the dedicated coverage of news outlets such as the BBC's 'Have Your Say'.

▬▬▬▬▬ EXERCISE 4.1 ▬▬▬▬▬

Choose a news outlet – either print, radio, broadcast or online only – and examine the content on its website. Try to identify whether it uses UGC in its news content. If so, where and how does it use UGC? You may want to look for the use of UGC on live blogs and in the news coverage about emergency events, such as crimes, political crises and natural disasters. Think about whether, and how, such uses will influence the work and role of journalists. For example, can ordinary users replace journalists in creating and publishing news content? Can journalists still have control over the content of the news stories published by them?

Recent developments

Multimedia content

Since the 2010s, producing and publishing multimedia content has become a routine element of online journalism and is practised globally. Apart from the universal use of conventional elements, such as pictures, audio and videos, the news media have shown a firm intention to experiment with using innovative tools, such as data visualisations, drones (see Box 4.1) and Virtual Reality (VR) gadgets (see Box 4.2), for storytelling.

======= **BOX 4.1** =======

Using drones in journalism

Despite related ethical concerns like privacy, drone technologies – or so-called uncrewed aerial vehicles – are considered to bring in new angles to stories and offer new opportunities for news gathering, particularly in crisis or disaster reporting, or in collecting data in the face of controls on the media. Recent prominent cases using films taken by drones in online news articles include those on the 'Sunda Strait tsunami' by *The Guardian* (Farrer, 2018), on the 'Hong Kong 2019 protests' by the BBC (The BBC, 2019c) and on mass burials of COVID victims in Jakarta by Reuters (Reuters, 2020).

======= **BOX 4.2** =======

Using VR for journalism

Along with the advent of immersive technologies, such as VR cameras and goggles, news outlets, such as the BBC, *The New York Times*, The Guardian and VRT (Belgium), have also started to produce 360° video news, giving audiences an immersive and 'first-person' experience (Van Damme, All, De Marez, & Van Leuven, 2019). Overall, there are three types of VR news stories. The first type consists of events such as crises and disasters that can evoke empathy and compassion in the audience. Amongst others, prominent examples include 'The Displaced' and 'Miles of Ice Collapsing into the Sea', commissioned by *The New York Times*, 'Limbo' by *The Guardian*, and 'We Wait' and 'Inside the Horrors of Human Trafficking in Mexico' by the BBC.

The second consists of VR films that help to tell complicated stories. When covering topics of great complexity, journalists often need to introduce a lot of detail into news stories in their efforts to engage their audiences, who may have limited background knowledge. VR films can assist in mitigating this. A typical example of this is *The New York Times*' 'Fight for Falluja', which helped audiences to understand the Arab world and the battles between Iraqi forces and ISIS.

The third type, also attractive to VR story producers, consists of topics that require the 'first-person' experience of audiences in order to understand them. *The New York Times*' 'Seeking Pluto's Frigid Heart' and 'Walking New York', as well as several of *The Guardian's* VR experience programmes, including 'Songbird', 'Celestial Motion', 'Crime Scene' and 'Solitary Confinement' exemplify this type of VR news story.

However, given that VR stories target a niche market, the future of using VR as a mainstream form of news reporting is precarious, and the news media are reflecting on their efforts to utilise VR as a new way of news reporting. In 2019, for example, the BBC decided to abandon its VR strategy (The BBC, 2019b) and to dismantle its VR team, formed only two years before.

There are three different ways to use multimedia content in news stories. In most daily online news articles, such as 'International Criminal Court May Investigate UK "War Crimes Cover-Up"' by the BBC, the use of multimedia content is supplementary, and the text is still the main storytelling element.

However, multimedia content can be the primary, dominant storytelling element, creating an immersive and interactive environment for audiences. The news stories: 'Concrete and Coral: Tracking Expansion in the South China Sea', 'Rohingya Camps' (http://fingfx. thomsonreuters.com/gfx/rngs/MYANMAR-ROHINGYA/010062VK4VN/index.html) and 'Shock Tactics: Inside the Taser' by Reuters, 'The Pessimist's Guide to 2028' by Bloomberg News, and 'The Uninhabitable Village' by *The New York Times*, are good examples of this.

Text and multimedia content may play equally important roles in telling the story, as shown in 'Antarctic Dispatches' by *The New York Times*. In this story, while multimedia elements, such as interactive graphs, maps, pictures and VR films of the Antarctic, generate a high level of interactivity and immersion, the detailed and beautiful text tells audiences the story of the situation.

To summarise, in the present day, multimedia content in online news articles ranges from text, pictures, videos, audio, graphs, animations to games, data visualisations, interactive gadgets, datasets and even virtual reality (VR) films. The growing prevalence of multimedia content makes online news articles increasingly interactive, hyperlinked and immersive (these features will be discussed later in the chapter).

EXERCISE 4.2

The discussion in this section includes some examples in which multimedia content is used as a supplementary or as the dominant element, or as an element that is equally important to the text. Now it is over to you. Find three news articles, respectively incorporating the three ways of using multimedia content in news stories. Compare and discuss the extent to which multimedia content contributes to the storytelling in the news articles of your choice. Also, try to think about the implications for journalism skills of the heavy use of multimedia content in news articles. Does it mean journalists have to learn multimedia skills to be employable? Which skills do you want to learn to prepare for your future career? Video production skills? Podcast production skills?

News delivery

Today, online news is delivered – and audiences access and consume the news – across platforms, through the homepages of the websites of the news media, their applications (apps) on portable devices, and social media platforms. News delivery has become increasingly SMS- (short message service), MMS- (multimedia messaging service) and app-based. From the early 21st century, news organisations started to employ SMS or MMS technologies to deliver the news – in particular, breaking news – to audiences, not only in Western societies, such as the UK and Germany, but also in the Global South, such as China and Africa (Westlund, 2013). In China, for example, the *Yunnan Daily* Press

Group started to use SMS, WAP (Wireless Application Protocol) and MMS news services in 2002 (Liu & Bruns, 2007). Mobile phone-based news delivery has become alternative revenue sources for the Xinhua News Agency (Zhang, 2012). In Africa, for example, the *Daily Monitor* began experimenting with SMS news from 2007 and had 30,000 SMS subscribers in 2011 (Bürén, 2011).

In the wake of the proliferation of mobile apps, news outlets began to introduce news apps and to deliver news content to portable devices, such as smartphones, tablets, and even smartwatches. Multimedia content that is delivered through these apps can be any, or a combination of, the following: short headlines, the full text of news articles, videos, audio, photos, graphs and live streaming. The news media have also started social media pages to try to engage audiences. Especially for regional, local and hyper local newsrooms – such as the titles owned by *Reach* (previously *Trinity Mirror*) (in the UK), *The Boston Globe* (in the US), *Kaleva, Etelä-Suomen Sanomat* (ESS) and *Turun Sanomat* (all three in Finland) – a social media presence becomes extremely important for audience engagement and for connecting with local communities. The situation elsewhere is almost the same. The *Apple Daily* in Hong Kong, *The Korea Herald* in Seoul, the *China Daily* in Beijing and the *Asahi Shimbun* in Tokyo, for example, all launched news apps and social media pages in recent years.

Two driving forces behind this switch from Internet browsers to mobile devices are (1) the technological affordances of new devices to get connected, and (2) the audience becoming growingly task-driven and lacking time to sit in front of the computer for a task. The decision by legacy media to use apps is a response to changes in the way audiences access news. Consuming the news on mobile phones suits the modern time-poor lifestyles of audiences well. Not only can people access and navigate news articles quickly and easily whenever and wherever they wish, but they can also personalise the content they want to receive. Studies (see, for example, Newman, Fletcher, et al., 2017; Rosenstiel & Mitchell, 2012; The Nielsen Company, 2014) have found that audiences across the globe now spend more time consuming digital content on their smartphones than on larger screen devices, such as computers.

The news media are continually experimenting with digital technologies to test the best way to engage audiences and deliver their content. In the process, old apps may be replaced by new ones. *The Guardian's* free Eyewitness app for iPad, for instance, was introduced as a standalone app in 2010. However, in 2014, it was discontinued and integrated into *The Guardian's* new apps for tablets.

Launching apps was also expected to provide a new source of revenue. However, there is no definitive conclusion to be drawn about whether online distribution and in particular app-based, news delivery can produce financial sustainability. There has been some good news about getting income from digital subscriptions. *The New York Times*, for example, reported an increase in its 2018 digital revenue, with online subscriptions growing by 18 per cent, and it saw a further jump in its digital revenue and subscriptions in 2020 (Peiser, 2019a; Lee, 2020). Likewise, *The Guardian* witnessed a revenue increase of 3 per cent in the 2018–19 financial year, with more than half of the income originating from the Internet (Waterson, 2019b). It is, nevertheless, still uncertain how profitable and sustainable the sales of apps and digital subscriptions may be. The mentality that online content should be free puts users off paying for content. For users who are satisfied already with free news content received from news aggregators such as Google News, from the news media without paywalls such as the *Daily Mirror* or the *Daily Mail*, or even social media platforms, it is unlikely they will pay for news. The success of digital subscriptions therefore is down to the degree of users' appreciation of, and need for, quality news and the affordability of subscriptions. Ironically, in the context of global political and economic uncertainties, the phenomenon of fake news may be able to help news media to gain more subscriptions through justifying the importance of high-quality, verified news and information.

News delivery through mobile devices and social media platforms has given rise to the practice of mobile journalism (often shortened to Mojo) and social media journalism. Mojo means a form of journalism in which journalists use portable devices, such as smartphones and tablets, to create, edit and deliver multimedia content for websites or social media platforms. The practice of Mojo has been rapidly adopted by newsrooms around the globe, as shown in the examples of WJZY in the US, *Der Spiegel* in Germany, the *Léman Bleu* in Switzerland, the BBC in the UK, Al Jazeera, and the *Hindustan Times* in India. The BBC's story 'Sharing with Strangers' is a typical Mojo TV story, which Dougal Shaw, Senior Video Innovation journalist of BBC News, shot using an iPhone.

Social media journalism, closely related to Mojo, refers to journalism happening on social media platforms, or to journalists using social media platforms to publish and distribute news. Journalists turn to social media platforms for news sources, despite the difficulty in establishing the credibility of social media content. In addition, news organisations increasingly use social media platforms, such as Twitter, Instagram, Facebook and WeChat (a counterpart of WhatsApp in China), to distribute news. A new generation of users, who interact with news organisations on social media, has been nurtured.

Meanwhile, social media companies also actively seek collaboration with news organisations by providing tools for journalists. In 2016, Facebook launched Facebook Live, a live video stream tool, which allows users to send their videos to their contacts on Facebook. The news media, such as BBC News and ITV News, have incorporated the tool on their Facebook page and deliver videos via Facebook Live. Media outlets from around the world, such as the *taff* TV show in Germany, ITV News in the UK, the Eastern Broadcasting Company in Taiwan, the Teletrece Media/News Company in Chile, and the Firstpost News & Media website in India, have had success with using Facebook Live. Twitter's Periscope offers similar functions, such as live streaming and newscasts. Google's AMP (Accelerated Mobile Pages) stories (www.ampproject.org/stories/) is another example of this. Tools, such as Snapchat, which are provided by social media platforms, potentially offer a new way of news gathering and engaging the audience. However, these tools' usefulness is yet to be proved. There is uncertainty over how widespread the demand by journalists is to use these tools to collect information, how many have the skills to do so and if audiences wish to use them to consume news. Questions over the stability and sustainability of social media tools and user stickiness are other issues. Using these tools might well succeed in boosting the news media's connections with younger audiences such as Generation Z, referring to those people who were born from the late

1990s to the 2010s. However, young users tend to shift from one social media platform to another, while users of other age groups may not be keen to use them as their main news channels. In addition, an extensive use of these tools increases the news media's reliance on particular social media platforms. The specific user groups associated with these tools, and also managing and maintaining user groups nurtured by using these tools, are beyond the control of news organisations. In 2021, for example, after less than six years' operation, Twitter discontinued Periscope as a service, largely due to waning usage. This means users of the news media's services which were created using this tool may be lost. It is uncertain whether, and if so to what extent, the users of Periscope can be retained and shifted onto other platforms by the news media which used it to engage audiences.

Six features of online journalism today

Today, online journalism has six features: deterritorialisation, interactivity, immediacy, transparency hyperlinks, and immersion. While enriching the news consumption experiences of audiences, however, these new features also raise new problems. These six features are explored below in more detail.

Deterritorialisation In theory, deterritorialisation exists. Online publication means a potentially global audience, regardless of where they are based geographically. In 2018, 15 per cent of the digital-only news subscribers of *The New York Times* were from countries other than the US (Wang, 2018). In 2019, only 18 per cent of the circulation of the UK-based *Economist* was from the UK (*The Economist*, 2019). *The Financial Times* and *The New York Times* have a Chinese language version of their websites. *The Guardian* has launched *Guardian Australia* and *Guardian US* to target an online and global audience. In 2019, the BBC reported that it had a global audience of 426 million per week (The BBC, 2019a). In 2021, the *China Daily*, the English-language newspaper of China, had more than 330 million readers across the world, up from 200 million in 2020 (*China Daily*, No year). In 47 of the more than 100 countries where it operates, RT (Russia Today) enjoyed 100 million weekly viewers in 2018 (Ipsos, 2018). These are among many examples that demonstrate the global expansion of the news media.

However, in reality, global reach and access may be limited by many contextual factors. Key among these contextual factors are language barriers, the digital divide, national policies and local audiences' interests. It is for these reasons that a global audience may not exist.

- **The language barrier** is a significant obstacle to news media's global reach. English-language news media, for example, will not reach audiences with no, or a low, English proficiency. Likewise, news media in other languages are unlikely to be consumed by users who do not know these languages.
- **The digital divide**, a term originally referring to disparities in access to and use of the Internet associated with users' demographic and socio-economic attributes, continues and has even deepened – in terms of infrastructures, audiences' online literacy and skills, as well as their usage of the Internet, affordability of the Internet

and subscriptions to the news media and their other social markers, such as age. The deepening digital divide will limit the extent of the global reach of the news media, as not everyone can afford or is willing or able to access the content of global media. The paywalls of the news media also deter those audiences who may be avid to consume their products, but unable to afford the subscriptions.

- **National Internet policies**, such as Internet censorship in China, Iran and North Korea, also play a crucial part in restricting the news media from reaching global audiences.
- Another vital factor is that **local readers and viewers** may not be interested in the content published by international news outlets. It is difficult for the news media, in particular newspapers that have a more national or international orientation than television does, to have global appeal. Especially in the current time when narrowcasting, which means news content targeting a specific group of people, instead of broadcasting prevails, the individual needs and particular local tastes of audiences may further the fragmentation of the audience, which makes achieving global reach more difficult.

Interactivity refers to the tools created to allow users to interact with the website or app of the news media. The 'Gender Pay Gap' interactive gadget that is used by the UK's Reach plc (formerly Trinity Mirror) is a good example. Using this gadget, users can type in their postcode and find out about the gender gap in the average salary for the place in which they live, and the potential salary they might earn if they were of the opposite gender. During the coronavirus crisis that started in 2020, a BBC gadget, used to discover 'How many cases are there in your area?', has a similar function, through which audiences can find out how many confirmed cases there are in the area in which they live.

Immediacy (also see Box 10.1 in Chapter 10) is a result of the instantaneity of the publication and transmission of online information. Immediacy first means the immediate breaking of news on the Internet: the time between the occurrence of the events and the circulation and distribution of the information about them is extremely short. This feature also means the instantaneous production and dissemination of news. Although showing online journalism's ability to report the world quickly, immediacy poses a challenge to journalists' commitment to accuracy, as under the pressure of short deadlines, journalists may not have enough time to fact-check the content.

Transparency and hyperlinks Transparency, which means making the news production process and related information and sources such as data, data sources and people involved transparent, is a feature of online journalism that is closely associated with the use of hyperlinks and hypertextuality (see Box 4.4). Achieving transparency through linking to the web pages containing the original or background information is believed to help repair public trust in journalism. It, however, also brings new problems to journalism. For example, that journalists lack control over the reliability of the websites to which their stories link may impair the accuracy of the journalism they deliver (see more discussions in Box 4.3).

━━━━━━━━ **BOX 4.3** ━━━━━━━━━━━━━━━━━━━━━━━━━━━━━━━━

Transparency and journalistic legitimacy and authority

Transparency is a double-edged sword for journalism. On the one hand, journalism has adopted 'transparency' as a new norm in order to enhance its credibility and legitimacy. The use of hyperlinks (see Box 4.4) and the publication of methodological notes, and even datasets for data stories (discussed in Chapter 5), are among the attempts to augment the transparency of journalistic reporting. On the other hand, however, the practice of being transparent potentially undermines journalistic authority by revealing the 'backstage' performances of journalists and disclosing and demystifying the previously hidden detailed information about how journalists cover events. In addition, when journalists link their articles to online resources, their journalistic credibility and legitimacy may also be damaged, as the reliability of these online resources is beyond their control. What is more, using digital technologies in journalism has brought about new problems in relation to transparency, such as algorithmic transparency (discussed in Chapter 6). Algorithmic transparency concerns the problems surrounding the transparency of algorithms. Being a black box, how algorithms work remains a mystery to journalists, and this fact will impair the credibility of journalistic work that involves a heavy use of algorithms. Algorithms may have subtly influenced journalistic work without raising the awareness of journalists, and through journalists' work, such influences may act insidiously in the public's minds with regard to the events reported by journalists.

━━━━━━━━ **BOX 4.4** ━━━━━━━━━━━━━━━━━━━━━━━━━━━━━━━━

Hypertexuality, hypertext and non-linear reading

Hypertextuality refers to the ability to link online content, such as web pages and sites with each other, while hyperlinks are the links which are usually clickable and embedded in news stories, and which can bring Internet users to the online content they link to. Hypertext, or text in a non-linear digital format, is text containing hyperlinks. Non-linear reading, which often happens in the digital environment, refers to a type of reading that does not follow the traditional habit of reading from the beginning to the end of a text but jumps from one text to another by following hyperlinks.

Immersion refers to engaging audiences by offering them virtual and immersive environments and experiences through the use of immersive technologies, such as 360° video and VR headsets. In technology-simulated enclosing environments, users get experiences from sensory feelings gained through immersing themselves in and interacting with signs. Such immersion experiences are said to help the news media retain audiences' attention and encourage their news consumption.

━━━━━━━━━━ **EXERCISE 4.3** ━━━━━━━━━━

Choose a news outlet and examine the features of its online content. Can you identify all, or most, of these six features? Discuss their implications for journalism. For example, think about whether deterritorialisation means the news outlet has a global audience. How does interactivity influence journalists' control over stories and the journalism–audience relationship? Does immersion blur the boundaries between journalism and entertainment?

Storytelling

In the data age, storytelling has become digital, multimedia, hyperlinked and immersive. The affordances of digital technologies, such as tablets, also enable the revival of long-form journalism, which offers distinctive, multimedia stories of high quality. The use of any, or a combination of some, of these multimedia elements – including sounds and visuals – in the content of news stories can have different effects, like triggering direct and emotional feelings, creating realism, providing contexts and increasing interactivity. Sounds can give your audience realistic feelings but also leave space for imagination. Videos and pictures vividly encompass and reconstruct what happened on the scene. Data visuals can lucidly visualise the patterns in data, while animation (re)constructs the happenings in the past, present or future in a fun way (Kolodzy, 2012). Podcasting (see Box 4.5), for example, represents a new way of immersive storytelling that gives audiences 'a first-person experience' through narratives (Mehendale, 2019).

Interactive gadgets and quizzes increase interactivity. The use of infographics leads to 'scrollytelling' – this is a new form of storytelling in, usually, long-form news stories that utilise multimedia, interactive content, in particular, infographics, to tell multifaceted stories (Seyser & Zeiller, 2018). Timelines and maps provide detailed temporal and geographical information, which offers context and enhances the sense of realism and holism. Storytelling with informative data visualisations allows audiences to explore and find information from the visuals.

━━━━━━━━━━ **BOX 4.5** ━━━━━━━━━━

Podcasting

Podcasting has become popular in the late 2010s. In 2019, the Pulitzer Prize Board even created a new category to recognise the rising importance of audio reporting, which is seen as representing the rebirth of audio journalism (Pulitzer, 2019). International, national and local news outlets have started launching their own podcast programmes, such as The Washington Post's podcasts, The New York Times' podcasts, the UK local news outlets' Google-funded Laudable project, and the donation-based (US) New Hampshire Public Radio's podcasts, such as Bear Brook (www.bearbrookpodcast.com). A broad spectrum of topics, ranging from current affairs, crime, health and science, to education, can be found in these programmes. The ubiquity of portable electronic devices, like phones and tablets, the availability of platforms like Spotify, the busy lifestyles of people, and the flexibility and immersion offered by podcasts that are easy to use, are among the reasons that podcasts have become popular.

An excellent example is the interactive investigative report: 'Hell and High Water' (Satija, Collier, Shaw, & Larson, 2016), jointly published by *The Texas Tribune*, *Reveal* and ProPublica, in 2016. In this story, a significant amount of multimedia elements, in particular maps and interactive gadgets, are used to tell the story. 'A New Age of Walls' series (Granados, Murphy & Schaul, 2016) and 'The Waypoint' by *The Washington Post* and 'The Injustice System' series commissioned by *The Guardian* in 2017, are also representative. Their extensive use of interactives and new technologies, such as VR, creates immersive, interactive storytelling.

These new ways of storytelling transform the conventional meaning of the 5Ws and 1H – What (happened), Who (did it or were involved), Where, Why, When and How (it happened) – tenets of journalism and give them new meanings:

who = a profile, a picture story, a video, a podcast

what = link to documents, official reports, write an FAQ (frequently asked questions), pictures, ask readers to send in views and pictures about what happened, link to special blogs, start a blog about a specific issue/event

where = maps, graphics, data on regions and countries

when = dates, background, context, a calendar, a timeline of significant dates and events

how = analysis, Flash interactive or animation, live Q&A for readers to engage with expert/issue. (Bradshaw & Rohumaa, 2013: 35)

These renewed understandings of the journalism basics suggest that online news articles have become extended, non-linear, contextual and fluid, reflecting the hypertextuality (see Box 4.4) of the Internet.

Also associated with the popularity of Mojo and social media journalism is the rise of vertical storytelling. Ole Reißmann, the Managing Editor at *Der Spiegel* at the time, for example, gave his opinion that horizontal storytelling is out of date with the advent and popularity of vertical stories (Reißmann, 2019). Vertical storytelling refers to a type of visual storytelling that suits users' reading habits using social media platforms and mobile devices. Its main features include interactivity, the adoption of narrow, long (rather than wide), close-up shots, using big-screen photos or portrait-mode videos, and presenting the elements of stories in a vertical structure. The story 'Algae Bio-curtains: Architects' Radical Solution to Capture Carbon' published by the BBC is a good example of this. The story was filmed horizontally by using a smartphone but edited vertically to be suitable to be shared on Facebook, IGTV (an Instagram's app with which users can watch long-form, vertical video published by Instagram creators) and Instagram (Shaw, 2019).

From Instagram and Snapchat stories to IGTV and Google's AMP Stories, news outlets are experimenting with vertical storytelling and these social media tools in an attempt to tailor their content to these platforms. Their efforts can be found in BBC Minute, Vice Reports, CNN, Financial Times on Instagram, The *Telegraph's* Visual Stories using Google's AMP Stories template and the BBC's AMP Stories for news. Content published on these apps has clear features of vertical storytelling, comprising close-up shots or videos, being portrait-mode and interactive and suiting smartphone screens.

▬▬▬ EXERCISE 4.4 ▬▬▬

Think about the differences between vertical and horizontal storytelling and why news organisations would go for vertical storytelling. Choose a news organisation and look up a news story that has been published on the website of the news organisation and a social media platform, respectively, by the news organisation. Compare the two versions of the same story and try to find the different features of storytelling on the two platforms. For example, can you spot the differences between vertical and horizontal storytelling? What are the features of vertical storytelling, as shown in the news article of your choice? If you use mobiles or tablets to read the two versions of the news story, what do you discover about your reading experiences?

New Skills, Practices and Jobs

Online journalists are expected to master multimedia skills to report across media platforms, including print, broadcast and social media. This need results from the convergence of content and devices (see Box 2.3 in Chapter 2 for a discussion about convergence). Accompanying media and technology convergence are the rise of cross-platform journalism, the convergence of roles in newsrooms and the corresponding changes in the practices of journalists. In digital newsrooms, news articles may be delivered across platforms and can be easily changed to suit the needs of different platforms. Fewer people are needed to run the system, but any single person may need to do more work and undertake multiple tasks.

The knowledge of multimedia skills and the availability of digital devices also make it possible for individual journalists to practise journalism on their own. That a single journalist can do the jobs that used to be done by a team of people gives rise to both backpack journalism – a type of journalism practised by a single journalist who takes on multiple tasks and roles, ranging from reporting (reporter), shooting (photographer and videographer), editing and producing (editor and producer) to selling and promoting news stories (advertiser and marketing person) – and entrepreneurial journalism, which means journalism start-ups (see detailed discussions about entrepreneurial journalism in Chapter 7).

The changes in journalism practices suggest that updating reporting skills becomes imperative. A print journalist will need to learn to shoot and edit pictures, audio and video recordings, while a radio or broadcast journalist will need to learn to write for publication, rather than, for example, a script. To be successful in job markets, they will need to learn more than that. A study of BBC News staff using social media content and UGC, for example, found that the incorporation of UGC into news work meant that BBC journalists felt it was necessary to learn new skills in order to collect and check online content (Johnston, 2016). The practice of Mojo and social media journalism has also changed the expectations of the skills that journalists should master and has flagged the importance of using mobiles and social media for journalism. New skills to learn also include multimedia production skills, like podcasting skills and techniques for using mobiles for journalism, Search Engine Optimisation (SEO) skills, audience engagement skills, basic HTML coding and programming skills, Internet search skills, and data processing and visualisation skills.

News organisations have begun to recruit reporters with up-to-date skills who are adaptable to the fast-changing digital environment. The BBC, for example, reportedly asked its experienced camera crew members to learn to shoot with iPhones so as to grasp the skills of Mojo (Scott, 2018). A study, analysing the content of more than 735 job postings published by 17 US media companies in 2008 and 2009, found that there was an increase in the organisations' desires for Web/multimedia skills, as well as the skills to deliver social media and mobile content (Wenger & Owens, 2012). The study was repeated several years later, analysing 1,800 job ads, posted in 2010 or 2015, by ten top US news companies. It revealed an increase in the demand for skills in social media and audience engagement (Wenger, Owens & Cain, 2018).

Universities have also updated their journalism curricula by trying to keep up with the latest developments in media convergence and online journalism. Take Mojo for example. In the wake of its introduction, social media reporting has gradually been embedded into the journalism curriculum (Bor, 2014). However, journalism education needs to do more to help journalists grasp the opportunities and meet the challenges of the new 'mobility paradigm' that Mojo has brought (Bui and Moran, 2019).

Although multiple skills are welcome and are valued by news organisations, multi-skilled journalists may not be universally present in reality for two reasons. First, it takes time to upgrade the skills of the overall workforce. Second, whether multi-skilled journalists can do a better job than journalists who specialise in one type of medium is doubtful. A print journalist may not be able to produce a beautiful radio or broadcast news story, while a broadcast journalist may not be able to write an excellent article.

Furthermore, there has been some hesitancy and resistance to the organisational requirements of being multi-skilled. An early prominent example of this is the BBC's bi-media experiment in the 1990s when reporters were required to receive training and take on multimedia jobs. Tremendous resistance from frontline journalists made this experiment unsuccessful (Hemmingway, 2008). This experiment has mostly been abandoned today, given that not every journalist is good at reporting for both radio and television. More recently, in the Dutch newspaper *de Volkskrant*, reporters no longer carried out multimedia tasks, and print and online newsrooms had even been separated. The newsroom showed evidence of 'de-convergence' under the influence of cultural resistance on the part of reporters, along with the lack of a valid business model (Tameling & Broersma, 2013).

With the rise of online journalism and media convergence, 'old' jobs are phased out, and new (digital and multiplatform) jobs are created. In the UK, in 2013, for example, the *Financial Times* hired ten journalists for digital roles, but laid off 35 journalists from other roles as part of its effort to reshape the paper to suit the digital age (Halliday, 2013). In 2018, *The Telegraph* announced the recruitment of 39 journalists to contribute to improving its digital journalism (Ponsford, 2017). In its restructuring process, in 2019, Reach plc (previously Trinity Mirror) cut some 20 national newspaper editorial jobs. However, a year later, it created five digital journalist jobs to serve its local and regional news websites (Mayhew, 2019b; Tobitt, 2020). New job titles have also emerged in response to the rise of Mojo, for example mobile journalists are employed, dedicated to reporting using mobile devices.

Key Debates About Online Journalism

The features of online journalism we have been exploring have triggered debates among scholars regarding (1) whether the new techniques and skills of online journalism can bring success to journalists and enable them to produce better journalism (see the discussions in, for example, Spyridou, Matsiola, Veglis, Kalliris, & Dimoulas, 2013; Spyridou & Veglis, 2016), and (2) whether, and to what extent, online journalism has changed journalism cultures, such as journalists' professional identity and values. Journalism scholars have offered different answers to these questions.

Does online journalism produce better journalism?

In the early years of the development of online journalism, a group of scholars (see, for example, Quinn, 2005) gave affirmative answers to this question, for three reasons. First of all, by benefiting from the accessibility of the Internet, journalists have new, alternative ways to gather news (Bradshaw & Rohumaa, 2011; Herbert, 2000). RSS feeds, a collection of non-RSS sources and social media sources have replaced the traditional data-gathering methods like scheduled daily reporting, tip-offs, phone-ins and press releases (Dick, 2012). That gathering news online is international and no longer bounded by territory can broaden news sources for journalists. This is true in particular in reporting emergencies and disastrous events happening on foreign soil.

Second, online news articles can include, and be linked to, extensive background and contextual information, which enriches news stories. The space of one piece of news article is limited. By following links included in a news article, however, audiences are able to access more content that is thought to be relevant but not included in the article. Such content can be other news stories on related topics, background information, data sources and other websites, such as government websites or other news media's websites. The use of hyperlinks in online reporting is thus seen to increase transparency, credibility and diversity (Jarvis, 2006; De Maeyer, 2012).

Third, the new features and the storytelling capabilities of online news articles help journalists to engage with and understand audiences better than before, therefore improving the relationship between audiences and journalists. Traditionally (in pre-Internet times), journalists kept their distance from those who read, watched or listened to their work. However, market pressures now make it crucial for purveyors of news to understand their audiences. Audience metrics give news organisations an understanding of online traffic and how much time the audience spends on one article or video. Apart from the element of interactivity that enhances audience engagement, tracking audience data also helps to establish an interactive relationship between journalists and their audience (see a detailed discussion about news audiences in Chapter 8). These three arguments therefore suggest that the shift to online journalism helps to deliver better journalism.

However, scholars have started taking a more critical view of these changes, in considering new problems correspondingly emerging in relation to labour conditions, fact-checking and verification, ethics and diversity in news. In terms of labour conditions, overall, working conditions in the newsroom are considered to be adverse. Studies (see, for example, Reinardy, 2011; Paulussen, 2012; Ekdale, Tully, Harmsen, & Singer, 2015) have found that journalists face greater work pressure, have low job security and are on the verge of and at risk of burnout due to a dramatic increase in tasks alongside a reduction in resources in digital newsrooms that have universally adopted online journalism. A study with journalists in the US newsrooms of television stations serving large media markets reveals that multimedia reporting can damage journalists' job satisfaction (Perez & Cremedas, 2014). Such unfavourable labour conditions cannot improve the quality of news and journalism.

Both online news gathering and hyperlinks generate new problems relating to fact-checking and working with trustworthy sources. The recent prevalence of misinformation and fake news (see Box 9.5 in Chapter 9) makes the verification role of journalists particularly important. An online experiment shows that fact-checking UGC can increase audiences' perception of the level of trustworthiness of a news article (Grosser, Hase, & Wintterlin, 2019). Nevertheless, it is hard – if not impossible – to check the credibility of the materials collected online or those to which there are links, in news articles. Partially for this reason, no ideal use of hyperlinks was found. For example, a study examining the use of hyperlinks in the newspaper websites' online coverage revealed that external hyperlinks were seldom used and thus the content to which the hyperlinks link was mostly limited to online newspapers' own resources (Dimitrova, Connolly-Ahern, Williams, Kaid & Reid, 2003).

Ethical issues are another key part of more critical explorations of online journalism. Take drone journalism. Although facilitating news gathering and media freedom, the practice of drone journalism also poses challenges to quality journalism, such as the low quality of drone footage, and triggers concerns over issues like privacy and air traffic safety (see related discussions in Adams, 2018; Lauk, Uskali, Kuutti, & Hirvinen, 2016).

Another example is Mojo. Practising Mojo may impinge on the quality of news as a result of journalists' over-reliance on public relations professionals for ideas and story tips, due to the lack of time and the pressure of deadlines (Blankenship, 2016; Kumar & Haneef, 2018). Although the fact that a single journalist can practise Mojo on their own empowers journalists with the possibility of completing multiple tasks, this affordance may also burden them by putting too much on one person's shoulders. A study examining the experiences of journalists at the *Hindustan Times* in India, reveals that practising Mojo both 'en-skills' and 'de-skills' journalists. Although they gained more multimedia skills, journalists did not have enough time to properly make Mojo stories (Kumar & Haneef, 2018). Additionally, the prevalence of mobile journalism is considered to facilitate the rise of lifestyle journalism and to change journalists' perceptions of their role (Perreault & Stanfield, 2019).

Another part of the criticism is related to that fact that journalism being online may not increase diversity in news content in terms of topics and news sources. In the context of Argentina, content homogeneity appeared in both print and online newspapers in 2005 (Boczkowski & de Santos, 2007). More recent studies have recognised similar patterns in other contexts, such as in the UK and Spain (see the related discussions in Fenton, 2010 and Odriozola-Chéné & Llorca-Abad, 2014). Other factors have been found to be more influential in shaping the diversity in news. For newspapers in Belgium, news content diversity was influenced more by the ownership and the nature of newspapers, and whether they were broadsheet or tabloid, than by their being in print or online (Beckers et al., 2017). Likewise, the organisational, political and professional contexts played a decisive role in influencing content diversity in online news media in the US, the UK, Germany, Switzerland, France and Italy (Humprecht & Esser, 2018).

Scholars' criticism also originates from the much-needed balance between skills and critical thinking. In the digital and converged world, having new skills but not understanding how to bring critical thinking to bear means journalists still cannot produce quality journalism. Critical thinking is an ability to think independently and critically and not see events from one fixed angle or mindset or automatically believe what we are told. This ability is crucial for fact verification and reporting ethically and for understanding and appropriately representing occurrences in the current environment, where there is a lot of political division and conflict and a great deal of mis- and dis-information. In an attempt to engage audiences by making and including substantial multimedia content, the news media may bring audiences more entertainment or politically polarising content, but less content relating to socio-political issues or less politically balanced content, the coverage of which is beneficial to democracy. This makes journalists' critical thinking ability particularly important.

How has online journalism changed the cultures of journalism?

The second question asks about the impact of online journalism on the cultures of journalism. On the one hand, changes in journalistic cultures have been identified.

The concept of news has changed. The distinctions between news producers and audiences have become obscure, along with the shifts in the journalist–audience relationship (discussed in detail in Chapter 8). Established notions of the professional roles and practices of journalism, for example, have been disturbed by the emergence of audiences as active users. New understandings of what journalism is have emerged, such as understanding journalism as 'connective journalism' or 'networked journalism' (Gade & Lowrey, 2011) – these two terms mean that journalism is practised through a collaboration among journalists, other professionals and/or citizens. Web analytics increasingly sway the practices, roles and professional values and norms of the journalists, as exemplified in a study examining the influence of audience metrics in different Australian newsrooms; although in this study such influence is dependent on the positions that journalists hold in the editorial hierarchy (Hanusch, 2017).

Meanwhile, the traditional culture of legacy newsrooms continues to influence news work and may even be in tension with newsrooms' digital culture that is emerging along with their digitalisation. A study with Norwegian journalism students who have worked in newsrooms as interns, for example, found such conflicts between traditional and digital culture, which had created friction in terms of their professional knowledge creation (Steensen, 2018).

Continuities thus exist in regard to journalism cultures, and the persistence of existing journalistic routines and values may hold back changes in journalism cultures. For example, traditional journalistic narratives have been found posing an obstacle to using immersion in journalism (Domínguez, 2017). In the context of Greece, online media, still clinging to traditional news production, have not fully employed the technological affordances of convergence (Doudaki & Spyridou, 2015; Spyridou et al., 2013). News agencies continue to dominate the content of Dutch news (Boumans, Trilling, Vliegenthart & Boomgaarden, 2018).

When it comes to UGC, overall, UGC has not much changed journalistic values and practices, as journalists are reluctant to incorporate UGC into their coverage, and they mainly see UGC as one type of amateur material. For example, Chinese journalists have been found to consider users to be amateurs and their content as having to be verified by professional journalists, in an attempt to defend their professional boundaries (Tong, 2015a, 2015b). Likewise, in the context of the UK, it was found that BBC journalists saw UGC as a type of ordinary audience material and few changes in journalistic practice were observed (Wahl-Jorgensen, Williams & Wardle, 2010).

Journalists still play a decisive role in collecting and curating content that is obtained from the Internet. A study of the use of UGC by British and Chinese newspapers, for example, suggests that the existing selection criteria and news value systems of journalism still determined how journalists used UGC in the coverage of disasters (Tong, 2017b). An observational study of how the BBC dealt with UGC at its UGC hub reveals the involvement of traditional gatekeeping barriers in the process to ensure the maintenance of core BBC news values (Harrison, 2010).

Summary of the Chapter

This chapter discusses the development and main traits of online journalism, which is the basis of the other new forms of journalism that will be addressed in the following chapters. The practice of online journalism, with six distinctive characteristics, gives rise to new ways of storytelling, in which interactivity, immersion and multimedia content are prominent. A shift from horizontal to vertical storytelling, along with the rise of app-based news delivery, transforms the news consumption experiences of audiences. Accompanying these changes is the necessity to update reporting skills to suit shifting job markets. In the final part of the chapter, two questions are raised and discussed concerning the key debates in the literature about the quality and cultures of journalism.

END OF CHAPTER EXERCISE

It is now time to reflect on what is vital for journalists if they want to produce quality journalism: skills, critical thinking, or something else. Look up news stories online that you feel might reflect good practice. Choose two – one short-form and the other long-form. Now try to unravel what makes you think they are quality news stories. Is it because of the skills used in making the stories? Is it because of the way the stories are told? Is it because they make you think about something important? Do you have any comments on the quality of the two news stories? Would you like to share them on social media? Then try to look for the responses of the audiences towards the two news stories on the Internet. For example, most news media allow audiences to leave comments or to forward news articles to social media sites. You can have a look at comments left by readers and at the figures showing how many times the stories have been forwarded to other online sites. You can even look for users' comments on social media sites. After you have had a good look at other audiences' responses, try to pull your thoughts together and give your answer to the questions regarding what counts as quality journalism today, whether quality journalism can be popular, and what is important when practising quality journalism.

FURTHER READING

De Maeyer, Juliette (2012). The journalistic hyperlink. *Journalism Practice*, 6(5–6), 692–701. This article explores 'hypertextuality', a vital concept in relation to the Internet and online journalism. It discusses discourses surrounding this concept that are constructed by textbooks, journalists and news outlets and how these discourses reinforce or conflict with existing journalistic values and identities.

Domínguez, Eva (2017). Going beyond the classic news narrative convention: the background to and challenges of immersion in journalism. *Frontiers in Digital Humanities*, 17 May, doi: https://doi.org/10.3389/fdigh.2017.00010. This article discusses the potential and challenges of using immersion as a reporting technique in news storytelling. It unpacks the phenomenon of immersion for journalism, and it critically evaluates the barriers and paths to immersive journalism.

FIVE
DATA JOURNALISM

━━━━━━━━━ **KEY QUESTIONS** ━━━━━━━━━

- What is data journalism?
- What is open data?
- What is big data?
- What is public records data?
- How has data journalism become integrated into newsrooms?
- What relationship is there between data and journalism?
- How do data journalists produce data-based news stories?
- Does the practice of data journalism change the concept of journalism?
- Is data journalism more objective than traditional journalism?

━━━━━━━━━ **KEY CONCEPTS** ━━━━━━━━━

data journalism	databases
data	'data state of mind'
open data	FOI (Freedom of Information) requests
public records data	'design subjectivity'
data visualisation	computer-assisted reporting

Since 2008, data journalism – a form of journalism telling stories in and with data – has started to flourish. It can be found in both daily short-form and long-form investigative news stories. Data journalism is thought of as significantly contributing to public discussions about issues that are in the public interest, such as public spending, political scandals, natural disasters and public health crises. Its increasing integration into newsrooms takes online journalism to a new level.

After briefly discussing the concept and history of data journalism, this chapter will explore its recent developments and current practices against the social backdrop of the open data movement and the phenomenon of big data. The chapter will then scrutinise the new skills that are required to practise data journalism and the implications that they have for the occupation of journalism. Key debates surrounding the emergence of data journalism will be introduced. Recent examples from around the world will be discussed in this chapter.

What is Data Journalism?

Defining data journalism

There is no single universal definition of data journalism. For some scholars (see, for example, Anderson, 2012; Hamilton & Turner, 2009; Young, Hermida, & Fulda, 2018), data journalism is mostly interchangeable with computer-assisted journalism, which originated from precision journalism, a concept advanced by Philip Meyer in 1973, and computational journalism. However, in alignment with other scholars (see, for example, Coddington, 2015; Stavelin, 2013), this book employs a definition that distinguishes the three types of journalism from one another (see the summary in Table 5.1). The principles of journalism, such as news value judgements, remain dominant in computer-assisted reporting (CAR) practices, guiding the use of computer algorithms and tools (Coddington, 2015). CAR is a professional process that is confined to journalists and involves no, or little, audience participation.

As for data journalism, it is a form of journalism that tells stories in and with data with the assistance of computer tools and algorithms (Tong & Zuo, 2021). It involves more participation by users – in particular, where crowd-sourcing (see Box 5.7) is used – in the reporting process, than computer-assisted reporting. But it focuses more on storytelling than computational reporting. The professional journalistic principles continue to be essential for data journalists and telling stories is still their primary aim in reporting.

When it comes to computational journalism, this puts more reliance on automation than computer-assisted reporting does. Apart from telling stories, one of its foci is on producing a solid product, platform or computational model for journalists to use instead of merely generating a story (Coddington, 2015; Diakopoulos, 2010; Stavelin, 2013). DocumentCloud (www.documentcloud.org), launched by former journalists from ProPublica and *The New York Times*, is a good example of computational journalism (see more discussions about computational journalism in Chapter 6).

Table 5.1 Comparing computer-assisted reporting (CAR), data journalism and computational journalism (drawing on studies such as Coddington, 2015; Diakopoulos, 2010; Stavelin, 2013; Tong, 2020)

Type of journalism	Main features
Computer-assisted reporting (CAR)	• Driven by human journalists' investigation with the assistance of computer tools and algorithms • Little audience participation • Aiming to tell stories • Using data as a supplement to telling stories with traditional journalistic techniques such as interviews and cross-checking • The size of data may not be big • Using social science methods to collect and analyse the data
Data journalism	• Still human journalistic investigation-oriented • More audience participation than CAR • Still aiming to tell stories • Data playing a primary role in telling stories • More computer tools and algorithms used to collect and handle data • May also use traditional journalistic techniques such as interviews and cross-checking • The size of data may be big • Using social science and computational methods to collect and analyse data
Computational journalism	• Producing and providing computational tools for journalists to use • Can also tell stories • Much more involvement of, and substantial role played by, the use of computer tools and algorithms in the whole process and more technical-expertise-centred • Very much focused on collaboration • Often large datasets and statistical modelling might be involved

Data and tools data journalists use for reporting

Data that data journalists deal with refers to information that is in digital format, or that can be digitised. Such information can be either structured (such as spreadsheets), or unstructured (pdfs or even hard copies). Structured digital information is what data journalists would like to use for analysis. Where possible, unstructured data should be converted to structured data before data analysis, although this requires data journalists to use special skills or tools.

Journalists adopt computer tools and algorithms to collect, store, clean and analyse data and to present their findings in such a way that it helps to tell stories. At the time of writing (in 2021), typical examples of computer tools and algorithms include, but are not limited to, OpenRefine, Python, R, Excel, Google Flourish and Google Sheets, and the Pearson Correlation Test. Interdisciplinary techniques, such as programming, data mining, analysis, and visualisation skills, are adopted in conjunction with traditional journalistic methods. Data reporting often involves the heavy use of figures, numbers and data visualisations, like tables, charts, graphs, maps and interactive gadgets, in storytelling. Influential examples of data journalism are seen in the MPs' expenses investigation by *The Telegraph* (*The Telegraph*, No year) and *The Guardian* (Rogers, 2009) in 2009 (the United Kingdom), the Panama Papers (global) (see Box 5.1), the 'Color of Debt' in 2015 (the United States), and the Tianjin Explosion in 2015 (China) (see Box 5.2). In most of these examples, journalists used large-scale data and, with the assistance of computer tools, told investigative stories, aiming to hold power accountable. In related data stories, data visuals such as graphs and maps are extensively used to facilitate storytelling. In more recent years, however, minimising the presentation of data analysis and highlighting human stories in data news articles have become more noticeable, as exemplified by the knife crime (Beyond the Blade) stories (see, for example, Barr, 2017; Younge, 2017), which were commissioned by *The Guardian* in 2017.

▬▬▬▬ BOX 5.1 ▬▬▬▬

The Panama Papers

The Panama Papers refers to a series of investigative reports that were published by global news media to expose offshore financial scandals. Two German journalists, Bastian Obermayer and Frederik Obermaier, received 11.5 million leaked documents about the offshore finance industry from an anonymous whistleblower, pseudonymised as 'John Doe'. The two journalists, with the assistance of the International Consortium of Investigative Journalists (ICIJ), collaborated with journalists from around the world in processing and analysing the documents. In 2016, their reports exposed offshore scandals involving those in power, such as important political and royal figures. For example, Jóhanna Sigurðardóttir, the then Icelandic Prime Minister, stepped down over the revelations. The analysis of the data encountered a considerable number of challenges in terms of encryption and data digging, mining and analysis skills. (See a detailed account of how they undertook the investigation, how they collaborated, and the challenges that they met in Obermaier and Obermayer, 2017.)

▬▬▬▬ BOX 5.2 ▬▬▬▬

The Tianjin Explosion

In 2015, a series of explosions of hazardous goods stored in a warehouse that was close to residential areas in Tianjin killed 173 people (*The Guardian*, 2015), injured over 700 others and caused extensive damage to buildings and the environment. Censorship was obviously in place after the explosions. News reports employing data reporting techniques can be seen in the coverage by a number of news outlets, such as the Southern Metropolitan Daily (*The Southern Metropolitan Daily*, 2015), and Tencent (*Tencent News*, 2015). These news articles managed to reveal the proximity of the warehouse to residential areas, which should have been avoided and therefore indicated that there were problems in government management and regulations. They are among early examples of data-based news articles in China.

Looking for stories, data journalists collect, clean, prepare, examine and analyse datasets that are often massive in size. A data journalism project is typically composed of five stages: data collection, cleaning, storage, analysis and presenting stories. Each of these stages involves the adoption of the appropriate tools and interdisciplinary skills (see a detailed discussion in Tong & Zuo, 2021). Common tools which are needed for each stage are summarised in Table 5.2.

Although data journalists use techniques and tools that are different to those of traditional journalists, practitioners (see, for example, Barr, Chalabi, & Evershed, 2019; Ottewell, 2018; Rogers, Schwabish, & Bowers, 2017; Tobitt, 2018) view data journalism as part of – rather than 'siloed' from – mainstream journalism and regard data journalism as simply another aspect of journalism. This is because, just like traditional journalism, data journalism is still about telling stories. To this end, data journalists need to employ data processing skills in tandem with using traditional journalistic skills, such as interview techniques. Interviewing helps to clarify and verify data, as well as to tell stories with the data (Tong, 2020).

Though conducted and published in the pre-digital and pre-Internet time, the Pulitzer-winning data-based *Color of Money* investigation in 1988 (Dedman, 1988) is an early, excellent example of data journalism, which used almost all the key elements and techniques of today's data reporting. Drawing on the findings from data analysis and interviews, this series of data-driven investigative reports told stories of racism against blacks in relation to home loans in Atlanta, the United States. The investigations drew on data collected from different sources and in various forms, mainly comprising lending data on computer tapes, obtained through Freedom of Information Act (FOIA) requests from the federal government, demographic data from the 1980 US Census updated with 1987 information from the Atlanta Regional Commissions, and relevant federal reports. On top of this data analysis, the journalist also carried out extensive interviews with the people involved. You can find similar features and techniques used in today's data-driven investigative journalism such as the 2015 'Color of Debt' (Kiel & Waldman, 2015), which was published by ProPublica, in which reporters revealed racial bias by lenders or debt collectors against black communities in three US metropolitan areas – St. Louis, Chicago and Newark.

Table 5.2 Common tasks and tools at each data reporting stage

Data reporting stage	Common tasks and tools
Data collection	• Downloading existing data(sets) from government websites • Obtaining data through Freedom of Information (FOI) requests • Collecting data by using traditional journalistic techniques such as interviews and cross-checking • Collecting data by using social science methods such as surveys • Collecting data by using data feed apps or algorithms, such as XML feeds (including RSS feeds) and Google Sheets • Collecting data by using social media APIs • Webscraping: using tools such as Google Sheets, Scraper, Octoparse, Beautiful Soup, HTML, programming languages such as Python, R, Java and JavaScript to collect data.
Data cleaning	• Data cleaning is a process of improving the quality of data such as correcting errors and incorrectly formatted data in a dataset so that the data can be read and analysed by the computer • Cleaning data by using Excel, OpenRefine, Google Sheets, programming languages such as Python, R, Java and JavaScript. • Using tools to extract data from pdfs such as Tabula and structured data such as CSV or Excel files although such tools may not be sufficient to tackle all sorts of PDFs
Data storage and management	• Using tools (for simple, small-scale data files) such as Excel and Access to store and manage data • Obtaining knowledge of data repositories including databases (for large-scale datasets) and using related tools such as MySQL, Microsoft SQL Server, PostgreSQL, Elasticsearch, and Oracle to store and manage data
Data analysis	• Using tools for different analysis purposes such as Excel, OpenRefine, SPSS, NVivo, MySQL, Elasticsearch plus Kibana, Gephi, QGIS, programming languages and statistical packages such as Python, R, Spark, Java and JavaScript • Obtaining statistical knowledge and techniques, such as linear regression analysis and using them to analyse data • Using social science methods such as (corpus) linguistic analysis and thematic analysis to analyse data
Data visualisation	• Visualising data and findings by using tools such as Excel, SPSS, NVivo, Elasticsearch plus Kibana, Gephi, Adobe Illustrator, Tableau Public, WebGL, Inkscape, D3.js, Chart.js, Google Flourish, programming languages and statistical packages such as Python, R and Java

━━━━━━━━━ **EXERCISE 5.1** ━━━━━━━━━

Find and read two classic data-driven investigative reports: the 1988 *Color of Money* investigation, commissioned by *The Atlanta Journal* and *The Atlanta Constitution*, and the 2015 *'Color of Debt'* (both in the United States). Try to identify similarities and differences between the two investigations and their stories in terms of the collection, processing and use of data, tools, methodologies and emphases.

In terms of practices, one big difference between data journalism and traditional journalism is the need for data journalists to master different computer tool kits and skills in order to collect and process data and to tell stories. They must get a handle on the skills of data collection, cleansing, analysis, visualisation and presentation. They will still need to tell stories with the patterns that they identify in the data, and such data is often large-scale in quantity and comes from different sources.

The essential skills for data journalists are thus comprised both of traditional journalism basics and of the interdisciplinary skills in areas such as data science, computer science and statistics. Such skill requirements are often spelt out in job descriptions. For example, in 2017, an ideal candidate for the role of data editor at ProPublica was expected to have received 'training in mathematics' and to have achieved 'proficiency in R or in using Python for data analysis' (ProPublica, 2017). Likewise, in 2018, a job ad in *The Guardian* for a data journalist required the candidate to have 'statistical and analytical experience', 'skills with desktop spreadsheet and database software, such as MS Excel, SQL, and MS Access', and 'knowledge of basic statistics and statistical software packages (SPSS, R, Stata, etc.)'. In 2019, the *Financial Times* was looking for a data journalist to join its New York team. The paper stated: 'In addition to clear written English, numeracy and the ability to think statistically are vital, along with expertise in handling data in spreadsheets and statistics software such as R or a scripting language such as Python'. Such requirements reveal that the expected skills and knowledge of a data journalist or editor are far beyond those usually required in the traditional journalism domain. They are supposed to integrate skills from the disciplines of statistics, data analytics and computing into the conventional craft of journalism.

━━━━━━━━━ **EXERCISE 5.2** ━━━━━━━━━

Select a data news story and identify the skills that might be involved in producing the article. Look for related information, such as methodology, to understand how the reporter(s) undertook the news report. It would also be helpful to understand where the data used in the story came from, which techniques and tools were employed, and how data was used to tell the story. Finally, you can make a list of the key skills and tools that you would need to learn and another list of the key databases with which you would need to familiarise yourself if you want to be a data journalist.

A Brief History of Data Journalism

Data has always been at the heart of journalism. Reporting on disasters, for example, requires a good understanding of the level of severity of disasters through interpreting numbers about the affected areas and people. Environmental journalists will need to read and understand the numbers that suggest ecological changes. Numbers of crime occurrences have been central to the work of crime reporters. Likewise, numbers are the pillars of both financial and sports reporting – for example, *The Wall Street Journal* was once famously referred to as 'a data product' by Simon Rogers (Rogers, 2014).

Although they may not be produced by journalists, examples bearing the features of today's data journalism appeared as early as the 18th and 19th centuries. One excellent example is the cholera map that was made by John Snow in 1854 (Rogers, 2013b). Snow was a Victorian doctor, rather than a reporter. His work in analysing and visualising cholera deaths told a story in a way that everyone could understand. Although not intended to be a journalistic piece, the work of John Snow resembles that of data journalists in two ways. First, his story is based on his statistical analysis of data collected about the disease and the public water pumps from which people drew their drinking water. Second, the map he made vividly visualises the connection between cholera deaths and the water pumps in London's Soho. His work is considered to have set a model of practice for data journalists (Rogers, 2013b). The same is true of the work of Florence Nightingale, who in 1856 reported mortality in the British Army during the Crimean War (Kopf, 1916; Rogers, 2010). As a leading figure of modern nursing, she collected data, analysed it and visualised her findings, vividly presenting the severity of the issues.

During epidemics in the 19th century, the news media also tried to use visualisations to present how these situations were developing. In 1849, for example, when cholera broke out in New York City, the *New York Tribune* (then the New-York Daily Tribune) made a line chart visualising the deaths in the city (Klein, 2016). This practice was quite rare in 1849 – a time when newspapers were still typeset manually, the Internet did not exist and no one had access to computing technologies or used the data-processing skills and concepts that we can find in today's data journalism practices.

The prototype of modern data journalism started in newsrooms such as *The Guardian*, *The Times*, the *Financial Times*, *The New York Times* and *The Economist* decades ago. Graham Douglas, the Head of the Graphics Department at *The Economist* at the time of writing (in 2019), for instance, discussed how *The Economist* made charts in the 1980s, with tools such as pencils, rulers, protractors, stencils and scalpels (Douglas, 2018).

In particular, two developments in modern journalism in the United States (US) paved the way for the emergence of data journalism. One is the rise of computer-assisted reporting, which is often considered to deliver more accurate news articles than traditional journalism can. The other is the adoption of social science methods in journalism or collaborations between academics and journalists. Two successful early examples of these are the 1967 Phil Meyer investigation into the Detroit Riots (The Detroit Urban League, 1967) and the 1968 examination of biases in the Dade County criminal justice system, which was commissioned by the *Miami Herald* (Cox, 2000; DeFleur, 2013). In the case of the Detroit Riots in 1967, Meyer collaborated with local newsrooms, collecting and analysing data from the people in the riot area in order to understand why the riots happened, and the contextual factors that influenced their occurrence and development. His seminal book, *Precision Journalism*, published in 1973, advocates using social research methods to collect and analyse data in journalistic reporting (1991). In the case of the Dade County criminal justice system in 1968, computer programs were written to analyse data in the public records, which were manually entered into a computer. The analysis showed the existence of biases in the Dade County criminal justice system (DeFleur, 2013).

The use of computer tools and collaboration between academics and journalists have become common in data journalism today, as shown in the investigation into the emergence of new forms of populism in Europe, which was commissioned by *The Guardian* in 2019 (Lewis, Barr, Clarke, Voce, Levett, & Gutiérrez, 2019; Lewis, Clarke, & Barr, 2019). Like the Detroit and Dade stories, *The Guardian*'s investigation involved a close collaboration between journalists and academics, the use of social science methods such as linguistic analysis and discourse analysis, as well as a combination of data analysis and interviews. This investigation was part of *The Guardian*'s new populism project, which began in 2018 (*The Guardian*, No year–a). In this investigation, a team of data journalists, beat journalists, interactive, visual and design specialists, investigative journalists and academics delivered data-based stories and commentaries, greatly extending the paper's coverage of the new populism and taking it to a new level.

Since Meyer published his work in 1967, data journalism has developed significantly. Three institutional factors have propelled its development. The first is the adoption and acceptance of data-processing skills and computer-assisted reporting in journalistic work (especially since the 1990s). The second refers to the news industry's recognition of computer-assisted reports, as shown in Bill Dedman's *Color of Money* (1988), discussed above, winning a Pulitzer prize.

The third is the more recent establishment of organisations or groups, such as the National Institute for Computer-Assisted Reporting (NICAR) (see Box 5.3), the Global Investigative Journalism Network (GIJN) (a network of non-profit investigative journalism organisations that produce news stories and provide training and resources for journalists), Hacks/Hackers (a community of journalists and technologists collaborating to explore new ways of storytelling), the Centre for Investigative Reporting (a non-profit investigative news organisation that provides training for journalists), Journocoders (a community of journalists and members of other occupations working in the media to share technical skills for use in reporting), The Bureau of Investigative Journalism (TBIJ) (a non-profit news organisation that produces investigative stories), the European Journalism Centre (EJC) (a non-profit organisation that provides training and resources such as grants) and DataJournalism.com (a website created by the EJC and supported by the Google News Initiative, providing resources for data journalists). These organisations support the development of data journalism by providing communities, resources and training, which cash-strapped newsrooms may not be able to offer to journalists who are interested in data journalism.

Journalism schools, such as the one at the University of Missouri in the US, also play an important role in facilitating the development of data journalism. In the 2010s, data journalism noticeably entered the university curricula in other countries. In the UK, for example, universities such as Goldsmiths University of London, Cardiff University, Brunel University London and the University of Sheffield launched data journalism courses or modules. Despite these positive developments in journalism education, most data journalism courses or modules are still confined to the US and Europe. These modules and courses also lack academic input as there has been a shortage of academics who are able to teach interdisciplinary data or computational journalism courses (Heravi, 2019). Overall, globally, journalism education in the higher education sector needs to keep up with developments in data journalism.

BOX 5.3

NICAR

The NICAR is short for the National Institute for Computer-Assisted Reporting of Investigative Reporters & Editors (IRE). The NICAR provides many resources for data journalists, ranging from databases to information about tools and skills and regarding jobs. It organises conferences and training events. The annual NICAR conferences, for example, are among the key conferences for data journalists. Its mailing list truly 'serves as a forum on the techniques of investigative reporting and ideas for investigative stories' (IRE, No year). Questions about technical problems and data access are asked on a daily basis, and list members generously offer answers to assist others.

Internet giants, like Google, and open-source communities, such as D3.js communities, have provided free and easy-to-use tools, which are an excellent aid for cash-strapped newsrooms and for journalists who lack specific coding skills in adopting data skills for their work. Free tools, such as Google Fusion Tables, Flourish, Google Sheets, OpenRefine and Tabula, significantly enhance the capability of journalists to collect, clean, analyse and visualise data at low, or no, cost. Take Google, for instance. The web service of Google Fusion Tables, launched in 2009, offered a useful tool for processing, managing and visualising data. *The Guardian's* 2011 riot reports, for example, used Fusion Tables to map riot incidents. Although Fusion Tables was retired in December 2019, Google published a list of alternatives to replace it. One alternative is Google Flourish, which is easy to use. With the templates on Flourish, journalists who do not have coding skills can map findings quickly. Google Dataset Search makes it easier to find and discover datasets. In addition, open-source tools and programming languages, such as OpenRefine (a tool useful for handling data), Tabula (a tool for extracting data from pdfs), D3.js (a JavaScript library for manipulating and visualising data), Gephi (a tool for analysing and visualising networks) and Python (a programming language), as well as their online mutual-help communities, have become an essential part of the development of data journalism globally.

The Development of Data Journalism Today

The background: big data, open data and the Freedom of Information (FOI) Acts

The development of data journalism today has benefited from two things in its context: (1) the rise of the phenomena of big data and open data, and (2) the passage and implementation of the Freedom of Information (FOI) Acts. As we discussed in Chapter 2, our everyday activities – clicking buttons on a web page, tapping on mobiles and swiping plastic (credit or debit) cards to make a payment – are producing enormous, even abundant, amounts of data every single second. Such data is astonishingly large in quantity and comes from different sources, with its continually increasing quantity producing what is called big data (see Jin, Wah, Cheng, & Wang, 2015 for a detailed definition of big data). The rapid proliferation of big data offers excellent reporting resources for data journalists, although they need to master particular skills to make the most of these resources.

Additionally, the ideal of open data has propelled data journalism forward. The open data movement promotes the idea that data should be made freely available to everyone, so that users can use, change and republish the data as they wish, without restrictions from copyright, patents or other mechanisms of control. In 2009, government initiatives, such as https://open.canada.ca/en/open-data (the US) and data.gov.uk, were launched, aiming to open up part of the public records data that is held by governments and authorities. This has considerably advanced the open data movement (see Box 5.4 for more information about open government initiatives in the world).

BOX 5.4

Open government initiatives and data portals in the world

On 21 January 2009, President Barack Obama signed the Memorandum on Transparency and Open Government, which marked a milestone for the open data movement. In the memorandum, he wrote: 'My Administration is committed to creating an unprecedented level of openness in government. We will work together to ensure the public trust and establish a system of transparency, public participation, and collaboration.' Following his move towards greater openness, the US government opened up thousands of datasets on its data portal: data.gov.

Other governments followed suit. In 2009, for example, the UK's data.gov.uk was launched to open up non-personal UK government data. Canada launched its open data portal, data.gc.ca in 2011, and its second and improved version in 2013. In 2012, Brazil launched the final version of its Open Data Portal: dados.gov.br. In Europe, Germany launched its open data portal, govdata.de, in 2013 and joined the Open Government Partnership (OGP) in 2016. From 2013, Sweden started and developed its national open data portal, oppnadata.se (discover more about open data in the European area in Iglesias, 2013). Apart from their own open data websites, European governments publish their open data on the European data portal.

In Asia, the Philippines has launched several open government initiatives, such as the Full Disclosure Policy Portal (FDPP), the OpenStat of PSA (the Philippine Statistics Authority), the data portals of Open Data Philippines, and the Freedom of Information (FOI) programme. The Japanese government adopted the Open Government Data Strategy in 2012 and launched data.go.jp in 2014 in order to host the government's open data.

Some authoritarian countries have also started to set up their own online platforms on which they publish their data. In China, for example, the Chinese government's Public Information Online was launched in 2009, although most of its content is made up of the government's policies and official documents. The National Bureau of Statistics of China hosts data such as national statistics, surveys and censuses on its website (http://stats.gov.cn/english/). In 2011, Singapore started its government data portal: data.gov.sg, hosting datasets from 70 public agencies. Since 2014, Russia has had its own open data portal, data.gov.ru.

Other organisations, such as the Open Data Institute (ODI), Open Government Partnership, Open Knowledge Foundation, and other open data campaigns, work with data holders to help them open up their data. The Global Open Data Index and the Open Data Barometer evaluate the state of open data in different societies, as well as how governments are publishing and using open data. International organisations, such as the World Bank (World Bank Open Data) and the United Nations (UNdata), also provide their own data portals.

In theory, opening up public records data can increase the transparency of our society and ensure that citizens are well-informed, so that they can better understand the work of governments and policymaking and can make informed decisions and suggestions about government policies. In reality, not all public records data is open data, and it is also uncertain how, and to what extent, the public are using open data. Even the development of open data is stagnating. In 2018, for example, the *Open Data Maturity in Europe Report* revealed that the level of open data maturity – a term referring to the extent to which and how well organisations publish and consume open data – across the EU had fallen from 73 per cent in 2017 to only 65 per cent (European Data Portal, 2018).

EXERCISE 5.3

Explore up to three government data portals of your choice and think about what factors might influence the democratic potential and development of open data. You can reflect on the difficulties and challenges you may encounter in looking for data, how easily you can find and understand the datasets that are available on the chosen data portals, and how effectively they can enable you to develop news stories. In the next step, think of a reporting topic. Try to find a dataset from any of these government data portals that may give you a story. Think about how you can use it to tell a story about the reporting topic.

The passage and implementation of the FOI Acts in some countries was also a driving factor for data journalism in those countries. In the UK, the FOI Act was passed in 2000 and entered properly into force in January 2005. Under the Act, public authorities must publish certain information about their activities, and members of the public have the right to request information from public sources. Such information includes recorded data, such as 'printed documents, computer files, letters, emails, photographs, and sound or video recordings'. Likewise, in the US, under the Freedom of Information Act (FOIA), journalists have the legal right to access and request information from the government and public authorities. However, not all countries protect journalists' rights to access data and information at the constitutional level.

━━━━━━ **EXERCISE 5.4** ━━━━━━

Try to find two examples of FOI requests – ideally, one successful and one unsuccessful – on the Internet. Compare them and think about why one was successful, but the other failed. Think about what these would tell us about the transparency level of governments and their relationship with the news media.

The mutually beneficial relationship between data and journalism

The discussion in the previous section shows that we live in a big and open data environment, which provides fertile soil for data journalism. The relationship between data and journalism is mutually beneficial (see the detailed discussion in Stoneman, 2015). Data needs journalism for three reasons. First, not all public records data is made publicly available. Second, open data does not necessarily lead to genuine openness and may not reach a mass audience. Most open data remains unexamined, and to understand open data appropriately, users need to have a certain level of data literacy. Third, big data, part of which is open data, offers excellent opportunities for understanding human society, and it needs to be analysed so as to reveal its meanings.

Journalism also needs data to recover from its decade-long financial deficits and to fulfil its democratic role. As discussed in Chapter 3, the survival of journalism, particularly investigative journalism, has been threatened by severe editorial budget cuts and fierce competition. Data journalists celebrate the opportunities offered by open data, as seen in a debate between Michael Bauer (the Open Knowledge Foundation) and Aron Pilhofer (Associate Managing Editor of *The New York Times*) in 2014 (Blanquerna – Universitat Ramon Llull, 2014). Additionally, data journalism offers a potential business model in which data and data services might be profitable. ProPublica, for example, runs Data Store, in which some datasets are free, but others charge fees for using them. From its launch in 2014 to 2016, the Data Store brought in $200,000 (Bilton, 2016).

The current state of data journalism

In 2008, the successful publication of data stories by leading news outlets, such as *The Guardian* in the UK and *The New York Times* in the US, marked the start of the flourishing of data journalism today. A 2017 study by Google News Lab about data journalism in the US and Europe reveals that 42 per cent of journalist participants regularly used data in their work to tell stories, and 51 per cent of news organisations had at least one data journalist (Rogers et al., 2017). Most frequently seen in investigative journalism, the use of data has started to play an important role in daily news reporting, as demonstrated during the COVID-19 pandemic in 2020. News organisations, such as *The New York Times* (Cook, 2019), have also started doing in-house training, thus enhancing the ability of journalists to use data for reporting.

There are three reasons for news media welcoming data journalism in the past decade. First, data-based news articles have the potential to hit the front pages and/or become exclusives or scoops. This potential can be seen in data stories – such as the populism revelations by *The Guardian* in 2019 (Lewis, Barr et al., 2019), the level of NHS staff taking sick leave due to stress in *The Observer* (Kirk, 2015) in 2015, the 'Doping Scandal' in *The Sunday Times* in 2015 (all in the UK), and 'Denied Justice' in the *Star Tribune* in Minneapolis (in the US) in 2018 and 2019. Second, the publication of data-based news articles and data may help news organisations and journalism win back the trust of readers. Third, as discussed earlier, datasets that are collected, created and curated by journalists may serve as an alternative revenue stream.

Big legacy news organisations such as *The Guardian* and *The New York Times* have launched their own data websites or teams, or both. In 2009, *The Guardian* launched Datablog (www.theguardian.com/data), dedicated to data journalism and publishing data-driven reports and even datasets. The pioneering Datablog was among the first organisational efforts of the news media to embrace data journalism in the world (a detailed discussion about early influential data-based news articles can be found in Rogers, 2013a). *The New York Times* launched its own website, The Upshot, for data-driven reporting in 2014, after the departure of Nate Silver's data blog: FiveThirtyEight (fivethirtyeight.com) in 2013. With The Upshot, the paper aims to help people understand data stories, as well as to embrace the opportunities offered by big data (Leonhardt, No year). *The Economist* launched its data site, Graphic Detail, in 2015, and turned it into the home of its data journalism in 2018 (*The Economist*, 2018).

As of 2021, the news media beyond the Anglo-American world have also created their own sites for data journalism. Prominent examples include the datanews of Caixin (datanews.caixin.com), the data news of Sohu (news.sohu.com/matrix) and the DataBlog of Netease (data.163.com) (all in China), the Brottspejl of Sveriges Television (SVT, Swedish Public Service Television) (www.svt.se/pejl) in Sweden (Mills, Pidd, & Ward, 2012), Deutsche Welle's DW data (www.dw.com/en/data/t-43091100), and *Die Zeit* (www.zeit.de/datenjournalismus) (Germany), and *El País* (the Data Unit of *El Confidencial*) (www.elconfidencial.com) (Spain). Although data journalism is lagging behind in relative terms in Arabic media (Lewis & Al Nashmi, 2019), journalists at Al Jazeera Labs collaborate with a number of programmers, designers and data analysts to produce data-based news stories (Raseef22, 2017).

Data teams in news organisations are usually small in size, comprising data reporters and sometimes coders too. In the *Hindustan Times*, in India, for example, a team of three data journalists and two programmers was launched in 2016, producing data stories for the paper (Kakade, 2017). In the UK, the data teams of the news media that support the practice of data journalism, such as *The Guardian, The Times*, and *The Daily Telegraph*, usually comprise three or four people. The data team of the *Berliner Morgenpost* (in Germany) has six people (Figl, 2017). *The Economist* had a 12-member data team in 2018. *The Age* (part of the Fairfax newsgroup in Australia - now Nine (Nine Entertainment and Fairfax Media)) also has a small data team (Wright & Doyle, 2018). In addition to producing their data-driven stories, data teams, along with interactive, visuals or development teams, support or collaborate with beat journalists within their organisations.

News agencies such as Reuters, Associated Press, Agence France-Presse (AFP), and the Agenzia Nazionale Stampa Associata (ANSA) (Italy), or regional news agencies, such as dpa (Germany), have also started to support the practice of data journalism. Associated Press founded its five-member data journalism team in 2013. The number of its team members was increased to 11 in 2018 (Hoyer, Minkoff, & Thibodeaux, 2016; AP, 2018). In 2019, Reuters' data team had six data journalists (Reuters, 2018a). In 2017 AFP, ANSA and dpa collaborated to launch the European Data News Hub (EDNH), sponsored by the European Commission, which provides data-based news packages in five languages (EDNH, No year).

Other examples of online news media such as the independently produced online offshoot of the news magazine *Der Spiegel* (Germany), the Internet media company Buzz-Feed, and the financial news service, Bloomberg, have also committed to data reporting. In 2016, *Der Spiegel* set up its data journalism department. As for BuzzFeed, its three-member data team is part of its investigative unit (Sunne, 2016). Bloomberg not only uses financial data to underpin financial market news but also supports a strong data journalism practice. Its 30-member international data journalism team, though named the graphics team, comprises not only data journalists but also designers, researchers, editors and developers (Southern, 2019).

These digital news outlets often combine data reporting with investigative reporting, and they use data journalism to produce exclusives or compelling investigative reports. They usually take on global and national topics and issues, which act as a significant force in shaping debates in national and international arenas. Excellent data-driven investigative reports include Bloomberg's stories on racial biases in Amazon's same-day delivery service (Ingold & Soper, 2016), the changes in the Arctic (Roston & Migliozzi, 2017) and the gender gap (Gu, 2018); BuzzFeed's unsolved shootings (Ryley, Singer-Vine, & Campbell, 2019), Russia's Online Trolls (Aldhous, 2018), China's censorship on WeChat (Silverman, Rajagopalan, Pham, & Yang, 2018), the 'From Russia with Blood' investigation in 2017, and 'Spies in the Skies' in 2016; and *Der Spiegel's* investigation into discrimination against foreign names (Berg & Hamed, 2017) in 2017, in which it collaborated with BR Data (www.br.de/extra/br-data), and the speed limit investigation (Stotz, 2019) in 2018. This is by no means an exhaustive list.

Data reporting can also be found in daily news, especially those in relation to topics such as health, crime, economic and politics. It is extensively used in public interest stories, such as governments' budgets, social inequalities, hospitals, elections and pollution incidents (see further discussions later in this chapter). As of 2021, during the COVID-19 pandemic, data reporting has become an essential part of news stories about COVID-19. The integration of data journalism into daily reporting, which was already noticeable before the pandemic, has been greatly deepened.

As for local journalism, data journalism offers two types of opportunities. First, most open data can be dissected geographically. Therefore, it can provide a rich resource for reporting local stories. Second, interactive data visualisations and data-based news stories about local issues that are at the heart of residents' lives create an opportunity for newsrooms to re-engage with local communities. Small and local newsrooms may not have sufficient resources to support their own data journalism practice. However, they may receive support from their parent company or other organisations, as shown in the case of local data journalism in the UK (see the detailed discussion in Box 5.5). In the US, ProPublica started its Local Reporting Network in 2018 and launched its collaborative data journalism initiative along with the publication of the Collaborative Data Journalism Guide (https://propublica.gitbook.io/collaborative) in 2019, with funds received from the Google News Initiative.

■ BOX 5.5 ■

The case of local data journalism in the UK

As elsewhere, British local newsrooms are struggling financially. The launch of the data unit of Reach plc (previous Trinity Mirror) group, the Shared Data Unit of the BBC, and the Bureau Local (of The Bureau of Investigative Journalism) have contributed significantly to solving the problems of lack of resources and developing local data journalism in the UK.

The data unit of Reach plc, established in 2013 and based in Manchester, daily supports its regional and local titles across the country. Its launch and operations centralise the work of data reporting within the team, which started with two members in 2013 and had grown to 12 members by 2019. Open data and public records data, which can often be broken down by regions and cities, is their primary source of data reporting. Mostly, they use existing open datasets, as well as requesting public records data from government bodies through FOI requests. They conduct both short-term and long-term data projects that suit the needs of local papers. Short-term data projects focus on social issues, such as poverty and crime, education, the NHS, and other issues that are in the public interest and address topics that the public want to know about. They also publish information-based content, such as school guides. Long-term data projects delivered by them include (but are not limited to) gender inequality, the Wigan Pier project and Universal Credit. Since November 2019, they have started producing a local data podcast: The North in Numbers.

Both Bureau Local and the Shared Data Unit of the BBC play a crucial role in integrating data journalism into local newsrooms in the UK. Bureau Local was set up in 2017, aiming to establish 'a network across the UK whose members include regional and national news outlets, local reporters, hyperlocal bloggers, technologists, community-minded citizens and specialist contributors' (Bureau Local, No year). Intending to 'find and tell the stories that matter in local communities', a team of six members at Bureau Local try to help local newsrooms benefit from data reporting. This team has provided a much-needed resource to local newsrooms, which have been experiencing financial deficits and skill shortages. Meanwhile, Bureau Local can make the most of local knowledge to help collect data, conduct investigations and find stories. Its collaborative model is powerful, in terms of data collection, investigations and agenda-setting for nationwide debates on issues such as domestic violence, the deaths of homeless people and councils selling public spaces.

Likewise, the Birmingham-based Shared Data Unit of the BBC, launched in 2017 as part of the corporation's Local News Partnerships project, supports local journalism. The idea is to help local reporters to produce data-based news articles, as well as to develop data journalism skills and expertise. The shared data unit not only collaborates with local titles in terms of data reporting but also by upskilling and increasing the data literacy of local reporters. The unit prepares a 'story pack', which offers local reporters analyses of the data collected from open data sources, and shares data and methodology with them, so that local reporters can use the resources to produce public interest stories and to find their own angles, those that suit their audiences. By 2020, more than 1,000 news stories had been produced and published across multimedia platforms, including print, online, TV and radio.

On the other hand, the Shared Data Unit targets the upskilling of local reporters and aims to bring them into the data world. The unit provides 12 local reporters at a time with secondments lasting for 12 weeks, and these secondment opportunities happen three times per year. By the end of a secondment, the participants should have essential data skills, as well as basic coding and web scraping skills. The unit tries to encourage a collaborative culture among local newsrooms to enable them to cope with the challenges caused by financial difficulties and skill shortages.

The practices of data journalism, however, vary from country to country. Many of the differences depend on factors such as the level of openness of the society in which news outlets operate, newsroom cultures and journalists' data literacy levels. For some news organisations, such as those in China, the practice of data journalism is mostly equated with the use and presentation of numbers and graphics in news articles (Tan, Zhang, & Chen, 2017). However, newsrooms in the US and the UK would expect data journalists to conduct proper investigations and to develop human stories with the assistance of data and data algorithms. Compared to other features of data journalism practices, the use of data visualisations is universal in data-based news stories in different countries. For example, data visualisations are central to *The New York Times'* organisational strategy of attracting an audience, as their news stories need to 'become more visual' (*The New York Times*, 2017). Likewise, Chinese news organisations are also keen to use data visualisations for the same purpose, as exemplified in the First Financial News' data visualisations, showing where people went after they left Wuhan during the start of the COVID-19 pandemic in 2020 (Chen, 2020).

Beyond legacy news media, the emergence of three types of non-profit, independent, or non-government organisations – news organisations, journalism organisations, as well as human rights, environmental and open data organisations – represents a new driving force for data journalism (see Box 5.6). The efforts of these organisations have given rise to a collaborative culture among data journalists. The discussions on the mailing list of the NICAR, for example, illustrate this collaborative culture (see Box 5.3). Important investigative reports involving the extensive use of large-scale data are often collaborative projects. Facilitated by the International Consortium of Investigative Journalists (ICIJ), the Panama Papers and the Paradise Papers are well-known international collaborative data journalism projects. In the UK, in 2018 and 2019, the Bureau Local (of the Bureau of Investigative Journalism) organised local news outlets to collaborate on data journalism projects such as 'Dying Homeless' and 'Sold From Under You'. In 2012, Al Jazeera carried out data visualisations in response to the campaign from Invisible Children, which is an non-profit organisation (Bouchart, 2017). Furthermore, *Der Spiegel* and AlgorithmWatch, which is also an non-profit organisation, worked together in investigating Google search results (Elmer, 2018). The pioneering Italian data journalism collaboration, ConfiscatiBene (Confiscated Goods) (confiscatibene.it) is another excellent example of cross-border collaboration between independent newsrooms and non-profit organisations. African and European non-profit civic technology organisations have also started practising data journalism (see related discussions in Cheruiyot, Baack, & Ferrer-Conill, 2019 and see the collection of articles discussing data journalism in the Global South in Mutsvairo, Bebawi, & Borges-Rey, 2020).

■■■■ BOX 5.6 ■■■■

Three types of organisations that are important for data journalism: non-profit, independent or non-government

The first type is non-profit, independent or non-government news organisations, prominent amongst which are ProPublica (US), The Ferret (Scotland), datajournalism.it (Italy), The Reporter (www.twreporter.org) (Taiwan), the Data Journalism Agency (Texty.org.ua) (Ukraine) and Inkyfada (Tunisia) (inkyfada.com/fr).

Journalism organisations are the second type. The following are some examples: the International Consortium of Investigative Journalists (ICIJ), the Centre for Investigative Journalism (CIJ), the European Journalism Centre (EJC) and its DataDrivenJournalism.net, The Bureau of Investigative Journalism (TBIJ), the Global Investigative Journalism Network (GIJN), the European Data Journalism Network (EDJNet) (which is funded by the European Commission), journalismfund.eu, Hacks/Hackers, Investigative Reporters and Editors (IRE) and its National Institute for Computer-Assisted Reporting (NICAR) and Open Data and Data Journalism (Açık Veri ve Veri Gazeteciliği) in Turkey (www.verigazeteciligi.com). This type of non-profit, independent, or non-government organisation provides support, ranging from funding to technical support and networking for data journalists worldwide. A well-known example is the ICIJ, which played a crucial role in facilitating the Pulitzer-Prize-winning Panama Papers. Organisations such as the Data

Journalism Awards and the International Journalism Festival promote the institutional and international recognition of data journalism.

The third type consisting of human rights, environmental and open data organisations – such as Invisible Children, AlgorithmWatch, Global Witness, Greenpeace and its Unearthed project, the Open Knowledge Foundation – are also endeavouring to advance the practice of data journalism.

What Do Data-Based News Stories Look Like Today?

Today's data reporting and data-based news stories tend to use data visualisations and interactive features extensively. Apart from handling data, data journalists may also use traditional journalistic techniques, like interviewing, to produce data stories. Crowd-sourcing (see Box 5.7), and the collaboration between journalists and experts, such as academics, may be adopted. We can also often see the inclusion of content about methodology and data in data stories, which even occasionally publish the data. Long-form data-based investigative news articles such as ProPublica's 'Color of Debt' (discussed above) are more likely to have all of these features than short-form data stories do.

Short- and long-form data stories

Data-based news articles can be short in length and may mainly report on the findings of the analysis of data. Compared with long-form data-based investigative reports, short-form data stories are less likely to publish data and methodology. Common topics of short-form data stories include health, politics, government, finance, business, crime, education, the environment, wars, sports and social issues. The following are two examples of short-form data-based news articles: 'Find Out How Your Child's School Performed at GCSEs Using Our Gadget' (Miller & Fitzgerald, 2017) and 'The Parts of Cardiff Where Most (and Least) Crimes Are Committed' (Mosalski, 2017), published by Reach plc's local titles (formerly Trinity Mirror, the UK). The series of news articles on school performance, produced by Chris Cook of the *Financial Times* (the UK) between 2012 and 2013, is an early, excellent example. Cook's stories (Cook, 2012) are based on analysis of the National Pupil Database, which contains the longitudinal academic performance of secondary school children in England, broken down by the contextual demographic data. His analysis led to exclusive stories about school performance and the influence of social markers such as poverty and social mobility on children's performance, and this triggered public debates about the issues raised.

To produce data stories, in particular those that are long-form, journalists usually collect and analyse data to identify problems faced by society, or by a particular group of people, and adopt traditional journalistic skills, like interviews, to verify data and find human stories. This practice is partly due to the need to put a 'human face' on a data story but is also due to ethics-related difficulties in practice (Tong, 2020). Typical examples of long-form data stories include the 2019 Herd Immunity story (Howatt & Webster, 2019) in the *Star Tribune* in Minneapolis (the US); 'Antarctic Dispatches', commissioned by *The New York Times* in 2017; and the 'World's Penicillin Problem' in 2017 – a joint data journalism project sponsored by the European Journalism Centre and published by Quartz and Al Jazeera (both international), *Folha de São Paulo* (Brazil), *El Mundo* (Spain), *The Mail & Guardian* and the *International Business Times* (all UK). 'Mafia, la mappa dei beni confiscate Ma spesso lo Stato non riesce a gestirli' (Mafia, the map of confiscated assets, but often the state fails to manage them)' published by *L'Espresso* (Italy) in 2014, and the disparity in black student arrests in North California published by WRAL (in the US) in 2018 (Hinchcliffe & Dukes, 2018), are also good examples.

Data visualisations as key elements

Data visualisations and interactive features have become essential elements of data-based news stories. The data story, 'The Swedes in Paradise Papers' by the SVT (Sweden) shows an excellent use of visualisations to present the findings from the analysis of The Paradise Papers' data (svt NYHETER, 2017). Some news outlets, such as *The Economist* and *The New York Times*, even like to start their articles with visuals, including data visualisations. Data visualisations and interactives enable audiences to click and scroll vertically or horizontally, offering them interactive and immersive experiences. Visualisations can also separate stories into several sequenced segments and act as the summary of main points. For example, in the 2019 election news report entitled 'Scientists and Climate Advisers Condemn Tory Environmental Record' by *The Guardian*, simple and straightforward graphs are used to convey precise meanings that advance the criticisms of the Tory environmental record (Laville & Taylor, 2019). They also function as bullet points for the paragraphs that follow them.

The inclusion of academic elements

Data-based investigative reports commissioned by news organisations such as *The Guardian*, the Bureau Local (the UK), ProPublica, the *Star Tribune* (the US), and Reuters, often involve collaboration between journalists and academics; these reports also frequently publish the methodology used and the underlying data. Some news organisations, such as BuzzFeed and *Der Spiegel*, which prioritise data journalism, may publish methodologies and data on Github – rather than in the coverage – as a supplement to their data stories.

An earlier, classic example, encompassing most of the features of data stories discussed here, is the 'Reading the Riots' project about the 2011 riots in the UK, which was commissioned by *The Guardian* (The Guardian, 2011–2012). In this example, *The Guardian* used data visualisations and interactive features, such as interactive maps, extensively, showing the spreading of rumours on Twitter; this was an outcome of a collaboration between journalists and academics. The paper also published the data and methodology used in order to explain how they carried out the analysis.

━━━━━━━ **EXERCISE 5.5** ━━━━━━━

Choose several data-based news stories published by a news outlet of your choice at different times. Examine whether they present one or more of these features of data stories, and whether and if so, how their features change over time.

━━━━━━━ **BOX 5.7** ━━━━━━━

Crowd-sourcing in data journalism

Crowd-sourcing differs from crowd-funding, which refers to seeking financial support from ordinary people. Crowd-sourcing in data journalism means that ordinary people are invited to contribute or examine data. It is a means of audience participation in data reporting, in particular in data collection and analysis. Crowd-sourcing appears to be an effective way of collecting data and finding stories in data. It can be particularly useful on occasions where data does not exist, or where data journalists cannot get data, for example, from authorities. Crowd-sourcing can thus effectively generate the data that data journalists need to reveal some social issues. Meanwhile, encouraging the public to examine datasets themselves, some of which may be very large, can inform data journalists about what interests the public, as well as increasing the efficiency of data reporting. *The Guardian*'s two data journalism projects: 'MPs' Expenses' in 2009, and 'The Counted' in 2015 and 2016, are excellent examples that illustrate the use of crowd-sourcing in data journalism.

In the **MPs' Expenses project**, crowd-sourcing was used to analyse the data. In 2009, following *The Daily Telegraph*'s exclusive investigation into MPs' expenses files, first published in May, the House of Commons released information about MPs' receipts. The data included '700,000 individual documents contained within 5,500 PDF files covering all 646 Members of Parliament' (Rogers, 2009). This data was massive in quantity. As the documents were in pdf format, they were unstructured and thus difficult to analyse. In addition, the 'key address and personal details are blacked out and impossible to analyse' (Rogers, 2009). It would have been extremely time-consuming for journalists to go through the receipts themselves, one by one. *The Guardian*, therefore, launched a crowd-sourcing experiment, publishing the data on their website and inviting its readers to take a look at that data and then tell the paper what they thought. They crowd-sourced – i.e. *The Guardian*'s readers examined – 458,000 documents, which became the basis of their analysis of MPs' expense claims (Rogers, 2012).

The **Counted project** used crowd-sourcing to collect data about ordinary people who were killed by the police, or by other law enforcement agents in the US, between 2015 and 2016. Killing by law enforcement personnel has been a big problem in the US, often triggering domestic and even global protests, unrest and debates, as seen in the shooting of Michael Brown in 2014 and, more recently, following the death of George Floyd in 2020. Despite the importance of this issue, the US government did not hold records of how many people were killed by law enforcement officers. *The Guardian*, therefore, invited the public to submit detailed information, such as name, age, gender, ethnic background, address, law enforcement agency, when the killing happened, and whether or not the victim was armed, in order to understand who these people were and how they died. After verifying the information provided by the public, the journalists updated the online database. News stories (see Glendinning, Swaine, Laughland, Lartey, & Popovich, 2016) developed from the data revealed the problems, like racism, in law enforcement in the US. In 2016, drawing on the data collected by *The Guardian*, the US government started a programme: the arrest-related deaths programme (Bureau of Justice Statistics, 2016), within which to count the number of people killed by police officers (Swaine & McCarthy, 2016).

Data-based news articles have great potential to reinvigorate the role of journalism in democracy for three reasons. First, they often reveal scandals or make disclosures, triggering public debates and holding powerful interests to account. Second, data-based news articles make the most of both open and big data in order to maintain and even revive the spirit of 'paper and pen' or 'shoe-leather' journalism, both terms referring to old-fashioned news reporting in which journalists relied on paper and pen for taking notes and they walked on foot from one news source to another. Lastly, through the use of data visualisations, and even through fun, interactive gadgets, they offer innovative and entertaining means, such as games, as exemplified by the *Financial Times'* News Games, with which to engage audiences.

EXERCISE 5.6

Choose a data-based news story that demonstrates extensive use of data visualisations. Read the news story and try to think about the role that the data visualisations play in telling stories and engaging audiences. After that, show it to your friends or family members and discuss with them whether, and how, the data visualisations help them to understand what the news story is about, whether they like the news story, whether they like the data visualisations, and what the reasons are for their answers to the previous questions. Then, try to write up to four points to explain the role that data visualisations may play in storytelling and audience engagement.

Challenges for Data Journalism

The practice and development of data journalism can be stalled by a number of factors within newsrooms and beyond. At the top of the list are problems relating to data, the level of openness of a society, data journalists' access to data, and the resources made available to data journalists.

The problems relating to data

The primary problem with data concerns the difficulty in verifying its reliability, no matter whether this is public records data, leaked data or scraped data (for a detailed discussion see Tong & Zuo, 2021). Data is not neutral. The socially constructed nature of data exacerbates this verification problem. For example, data may be influenced by the level of digital technology diffusion in society. Social groups who lack access to digital technologies may be excluded from the data that is collected and published. The structure and content of data may also be influenced by existing social knowledge or schemas. Gender is an excellent example of this. Censuses usually adopt the binary category of male and female, although very recently in some countries, such as the 2021 census in the UK, censuses have been changed to encompass non-binary and inter-sex people. However, some people's gender identity may not be in alignment with their biological sex. The traditional, binary category rules out this possibility. Without fully acknowledging the socially constructed nature of data, data journalists may therefore repeat existing social biases or schemas in their news stories.

The level of openness of a society

The openness of society varies from country to country. While data journalists enjoy the autonomy allowed by the FOI Acts in the US and the UK, their counterparts in other countries may not have this luxury. In particular, countries such as China, Egypt[1] and Russia have low levels of transparency and a poor record on freedom of expression. They are unlikely to provide a fertile environment for data journalism. Even countries in Europe may not have legislation that endows journalists with the same level of freedom of information rights as in the US. Take Germany, for example. The Federal Open Data Act was not adopted until 2017 (data.europa.eu, 2017), which is one of the reasons why data journalism started later in Germany than in the US (Elmer, 2018).

Data journalists' access to data

Even in Anglo-American societies, access to data is not entirely guaranteed. First, not all public records data is made available to the public or can be freely downloaded. Data journalists can submit FOI applications to request the data they need. Their requests, however, may be rejected for many reasons. Common reasons include the costs of processing requests, which may exceed the set cost limit, data being too sensitive, and the need to protect the privacy of individuals and the national security of the country. On some occasions, although journalists receive data, it is provided in paper form. Processing the data would require enormous resources and special skills, which data journalists may not have.

Resources made available to data journalists

The shortage of skills and training opportunities is a second hindrance. Producing data-based news articles requires journalists to combine traditional journalistic skills, like interviewing, with interdisciplinary data techniques. For non-data journalists, the lack of necessary skills, training and the difficulty of learning to use new tools may prevent them from practising data journalism.

Without sufficient institutional support and adequate resources, data journalism is difficult to practise and develop. As for large-scale data, proper data interrogation is time-consuming. Without sufficient time being allowed for analysing data, it is difficult to produce data stories of high quality. In terms of tools, cash-strapped newsrooms welcome free tools. Although there are open-source tools, a lot of quality data tools are still not free, which may limit data journalists' capacity to carry out data reporting.

■■■■■■■■ EXERCISE 5.7 ■■■■■■■■

In a particular country, the development of data journalism may be influenced by many contextual factors, ranging from political systems and cultures to social attitudes toward data disclosure and use, and the resources that are available to journalists. These factors may also change over time. Choose a country and identify the factors that may influence – hold back or facilitate – the development of data journalism in that country. Try to examine the situation over a relatively long period of time. You can consider the state of data journalism in that country a few years ago, have a look at what it is now, and think about what has changed – which factors have influenced the development of data journalism, and in what ways?

Key Academic Debates About Data Journalism

This section will discuss the following three questions addressed by key academic debates in the burgeoning literature about data journalism: (1) Is data journalism better journalism? (2) How do data journalists do their job? (3) How do data journalists see themselves and their work?

Question 1: Is data journalism better journalism?

Overall, the practice of data journalism is seen as enhancing the quality of journalism. Data journalism is seen to be an effective measure through which to 'regenerate' news (Hermida & Young, 2019). It is a useful tool with which to practise investigative journalism and to hold power accountable. Data journalism is even considered to empower marginalised and disadvantaged communities in developing countries and regions such as Afghanistan, Pakistan, Kenya, Kyrgyzstan and the Balkans. Data journalists in these areas have used data to produce stories that contributed to stopping people from going hungry, securing justice for vulnerable people such as abused women and rural labourers, and providing a quality education for children in impoverished areas (Constantaras, 2018).

The optimistic discussion of data journalism partly results from the use of statistics, which is seen to improve accuracy, impartiality and objectivity in news articles (see, for example, Hammond, 2017; Parasie & Dagiral, 2012; Tandoc & Oh, 2017). However, other scholars (see, for instance, Parasie, 2015; Bradshaw, 2014) who pay attention to the problems that are associated with the messy nature of data, argue that data journalism may not necessarily be more accurate than traditional journalism. Tong and Zuo (2021) call for an awareness of the socially constructed nature of data journalism and argue that objectivity is inapplicable to data journalism. For them, it is more appropriate to see data journalism as public journalism, and the centre of its principles should be to serve democracy and the public interest (rather than objectivity). Due to concerns over the quality of data and the socially constructed nature of data journalism, it is crucial to endeavour to verify data, to use data within its context, and to increase the transparency of the data-based reporting process.

The belief that data journalism produces journalism of a better quality also stems from the idea that the adoption of crowd-sourcing, interactives and visuals in data journalism can help to engage audiences and to tell compelling stories. Nevertheless, this belief has been criticised as potentially illusory. For example, the design of interactives may still be author-driven and come from a paternalistic approach (Appelgren, 2017). Additionally, both the use of the interactive features of data-based news articles on the websites of news organisations and the interest of audiences in complex interactivity may be quite limited. The level of interactivity in the data reports published by *The New York Times* and *The Washington Post* in the first half of 2017, for example, was actually low (Zamith, 2019). As a result of these limitations, data journalism may not necessarily be better journalism, if judged on the basis of its interactivity.

Question 2: How do data journalists do their job?

There are three aspects to this question about the actual practices of data journalists: (1) the distinctions between data reporting and traditional news reporting; (2) the approaches to data reporting; and (3) restricting factors for data reporting.

The distinctions between data reporting and traditional news reporting

Earlier studies (see, for example, Coddington, 2015) view data stories as being about numbers and consequently do not think that data journalists need traditional journalistic methods such as interviews, but that they will rely mainly on examining data for their data reporting. Therefore, for them, data reporting should be clearly distinguished from traditional news reporting. More recent studies (see, for example, Tong, 2020), however, identified the continuing importance of traditional journalistic techniques, such as interviews, to data reporting, along with the increasing integration of data journalism into daily reporting. The expertise of data journalists is supplementary to traditional journalistic expertise in telling a story. This means the distinction between the two may not be that clear. As discussed above, especially for long-form data stories, the importance of putting a human face on data stories may even diminish the presentation of data (analysis) in these stories.

Data journalism practitioners are also inclined to integrate data reporting into traditional reporting and see the former as on a continuum with the latter. Take the knowledge of data and data sources for example. In news organisations where the practice of data journalism has been (or is being) incorporated into daily newsroom work, data journalism practitioners have begun to treat data as a vital supplement to traditional human news sources. Just as reporters need to know who they can talk to and what questions to ask of their human sources, data journalists need to have good knowledge of data sources – what data exists, and where can we find it – and a clear idea of what to get from the data. The importance of the two types of knowledge is summarised by the phrase 'data state of mind', a term coined by MaryJo Webster, data editor at the *Star Tribune* in Minneapolis (the US) (Webster, 2016). Using this phrase, she argues that it is necessary for data journalists to have a good knowledge of what data is available, and where to find it, and how to interrogate the data with prior prepared questions. When reporters have questions to ask, it may be even more helpful to ask the data the questions than to ask the human sources. This phrase, stressing the equal importance of the knowledge of data and data sources to news reporting, encompasses the development of integrating data reporting into traditional news reporting and their convergence.

The approaches to data reporting

Overall, two main approaches to data reporting have been identified: data-driven or hypothesis-driven (Parasie, 2015). The data-driven approach requires journalists to stay open minded and thoroughly explore their data to identify stories. Journalists may not know what stories they can eventually develop from the data beforehand. This approach allows journalists to find the overall, and most intriguing, patterns in the data. However, this approach is very time-consuming, and journalists may get lost because too many patterns emerge from the iterative data exploration. As for the hypothesis-driven approach, which means journalists developing clear, prior hypotheses to guide their exploration of datasets, it can significantly save the time of journalists and may be better suited to the aim of the reporting. The downside of this approach is that it may only reveal to journalists what they want to find, rather than what is in the data.

Being time-efficient, the hypothesis approach may become a more popular approach to data reporting than the data-driven approach. Having specific purposes in mind, data reporters can fit their work well into the newsroom news cycle. By so doing, without wasting time in restlessly exploring data, they can make news stories from data within reasonable time spans. Nevertheless, this hypothesis-driven practice may apply typical news values in selecting data sources and story angles, which would imply the continuing influence of organisational cultures on the practice of data journalism.

If the hypothesis-driven approach is taken, the 'design subjectivity' of data journalists may also have a more substantial influence on data reporting. 'Design subjectivity' refers to the subjectivity involved in the process of a journalist designing a data journalism project (Tong & Zuo, 2021). Following a hypothesis in order to design a data reporting project may intensify the impact of the journalist's subjective choices on the data stories that they will finally produce, as deciding hypotheses results from their subjective choices made at the beginning of the reporting project.

Tensions and challenges for data reporting

Prominent among tensions and challenges identified are (a) the epistemological tensions and ambiguity as recognized in related studies (see, for example, Barrowman, 2018;

Borges-Rey, 2017; Coddington, 2015; Lewis & Westlund, 2015; Parasie, 2015; Parasie & Dagiral, 2012; Splendore, 2016), (b) challenges relating to the processing of data and approaches to data analysis, and (c) the influence of organisational factors.

The epistemology of data journalists is about how data journalists know what they know, which happens in a process of journalists deciding what is true and verifying information and absorbing it as part of their knowledge of things. Traditional journalists' knowledge forms in their investigations based on observation, interviews or research. An environmental journalist, for example, may understand an environmental issue through observing the environmental conditions of a place, from personal experiences, or reading related materials such as academic articles and government reports and interviewing experts. However, data reporting is different as the findings of journalists' own data analysis play a vital role in influencing their understanding of a reporting topic, although traditional journalistic methods such as interviews may also be used. Computational and statistical methods and approaches are essential for data reporting, which indicates different ways of knowledge formation. This difference is the main source of the epistemological tensions and ambiguity. However, traditional journalistic approaches such as observation and interviews continue to enjoy a privilege in newsroom. For example, in the context of the UK and the US, data and data reporting skills and techniques, which journalists may not be familiar with, were considered to be epistemologically less trustworthy than the more traditional journalistic techniques that may be, such as interviews (Lewis & Waters, 2018). While practising data journalism, journalists, therefore, may be pulled in two directions by their journalistic thinking and computational thinking.

As discussed earlier in this chapter, there are challenges relating to the processing of data and approaches to data analysis. Prominent among these challenges are the problems surrounding data and data access, the difficulties in verifying data and the pros and cons of different approaches to data analysis. Adopting the above-discussed hypothesis approach can help mitigate the epistemological tensions and the challenges regarding approaches to data analysis. Continuing to use traditional journalistic methods such as interviews and cross-checking contributes to addressing the challenges in relation to the quality and verification of data.

Organisational factors such as resource allocation, the level of newsroom acceptance of data journalism, the organisational structure and its norms and values play a role in influencing and even restricting data reporting. Well-resourced, 'elite' newsrooms such as The New York Times are likely to give data journalism more support than local, poorly off newsrooms (Ali, 2014). Compared with their counterparts in the wealthy West, newsrooms in the Global South such as Pakistan, Bangladesh and Thailand, may just be starting to pick up data journalism practices which are still in their infancy (see the discussion about data journalism in these countries in Jamil, 2021; Islam, 2018; and Thienthaworn, 2018). In addition, frictions at the organisational level, for example with respect to organisational structure, have been identified as acting as an obstacle to collaboration between data journalists and beat journalists to facilitate knowledge exchange and combine expertise within newsrooms. Collaboration is a prominent feature of today's data journalism practice and at the heart of data journalists' work in most newsrooms (see discussions about collaboration in different contexts in Hermida & Young, 2019; Borges-Rey, 2016, 2017; Stalph, 2020; Lewis & Usher, 2014; and Tong, 2020). Low recognition of the importance of data journalists' work, however, may stop beat journalists from collaborating with data journalists.

Question 3: How do data journalists see themselves and their work

Despite the integration of data reporting in newsrooms and the adoption of journalistic methods such as interviews in data reporting, the involvement of extensive data processing in the news reporting process means that the work of data journalists is different from that of traditional journalists. Skills and work tasks required in the whole data processing process – data collection, cleaning, analysis and visualisation – have gone beyond the scope of traditional journalistic work. It is common for a data reporter to know and use a programming language, such as R or Python, or for them to work closely with coders or statisticians. The blurring of the boundaries between journalists, coders and statisticians may mean challenges to the professional identity of data journalists and their perception of what journalism is, and what journalists do in their job, although, as discussed above, data journalists tend to still see themselves as journalists practising journalism. Therefore, it is necessary to strengthen the professional identities of data journalists (Appelgren, 2016).

As for how data journalists see their role, there are some cross-country variations as a result of the influence of contextual factors and journalism's historical roles in these contexts. With a watchdog journalism tradition, data journalists in US newspapers value the importance of nurturing democratic citizenship through conversations with audiences, and display a willingness to shoulder their social responsibilities (Boyles & Meyer, 2016). UK data journalists recognise their classic public service role (Anderson & Borges-Rey, 2019). However, Arabic data journalists see their 'dominant loyal-facilitator role' as a significant obstacle to the development of data journalism in the Arab region, where journalism is dependent on the authorities (Lewis & Al Nashmi, 2019).

Summary of the Chapter

Data journalism is an important new form of journalism that has emerged since 2008. This chapter explores its concepts, history, development, state and practices against the backdrop of both big data and open data. Examples from different countries have been used to enrich the discussion. The key academic debates surrounding data journalism are also discussed in this chapter. The next chapter will focus on algorithms, automation, and journalism.

━━━━━━━━ **END OF CHAPTER EXERCISE** ━━━━━━━━

Select a recent data-based investigative report. Try to identify the data (analysis) elements in it and understand the role played by them in the story. Think about how the reporters created the story. Look for related methodology and data, if there is any. You may find such information is published on other online media, such as Medium or Github, or even on social media sites such as Twitter. Based on your observation of this example, use your own words to define what data journalism is, as compared to traditional journalism.

━━━━━━━━ **FURTHER READING** ━━━━━━━━

Coddington, Mark (2015). Clarifying journalism's quantitative turn. *Digital Journalism, 3*(3), 331–348. Coddington's article compares computer-assisted reporting, data journalism and computational journalism – three forms of journalism that use quantitative data extensively. He discusses journalistic epistemology, professional values and journalistic practices, and introduces a typology with which to distinguish one from another.

Hermida, Alfred, and Young, Mary Lynn (2019). *Data Journalism and the Regeneration of News.* London and New York: Routledge. This book examines the professional identities, tools and practices of data journalists and how data journalists deal with the issues emerging in the digital world, such as misinformation and disinformation, and the challenges posed by audience participation.

Tong, Jingrong, and Zuo, Landong (2019). The inapplicability of objectivity: understanding the work of data journalism. *Journalism Practice.* Online first: https://doi.org/10.1080/1751 2786.2019.1698974. This article unpacks the work of data journalism and discusses the factors that may influence the epistemology of data journalists in the data reporting process. It argues that data reporting is a knowledge construction process and draws our attention to the importance of 'design subjectivity' in data journalism practices.

Gray, Jonathan, and Bounegru, Liliana (2012) *The Data Journalism Handbook 1. (2018) The Data Journalism Handbook 2.* European Journalism Centre and Google News Initiative. Accessible at https://datajournalism.com/. The two books introduce examples of excellent practices in data journalism and showcases successful data-based news articles from around the world.

Note

1 In 2017, *Egypt Today* reported on 'Egypt's first freedom of information law to come to light', https://datajournalismhandbook.org/index.php?p=handbook/two (accessed 25 April 2019). However, no news has been reported on the launch of FOI in Egypt since then.

SIX

ALGORITHMS, AUTOMATION AND JOURNALISM

KEY QUESTIONS

- What is an algorithm?
- What is automation of news writing/reporting?
- What is computational journalism?
- What are robot journalism, automated journalism and algorithmic journalism?
- How and to what extent are algorithms changing journalism?
- What is algorithmic accountability?
- What ethical and legal challenges are there surrounding the use of algorithms and automation in journalism?
- Who is the author of automated news?

KEY CONCEPTS

algorithm
automation of news writing/
    reporting
computational journalism
robot journalism

automated journalism
algorithmic journalism
algorithmic accountability
authorship
legal liability

Algorithms have become universally pervasive in our society. From governments to financial services, algorithms are used to assist and automate the work of humans. Journalism and news media are no exception; the use of algorithms features in today's news work. Following the previous chapter on data journalism, this chapter discusses how, and to what extent, algorithms and automation are changing journalism. It will start with a discussion about the concept of the algorithm, before examining three ways of using algorithms in journalism. The last part of this chapter will look at the implications of these changes for journalism from four perspectives: (1) journalism labour and craft; (2) the work and quality of journalism; (3) algorithmic accountability and ethical challenges; and (4) authorship and legal liability.

What Is an Algorithm?

An algorithm refers to a series of steps designed to complete a job. *The Oxford Dictionary*, for example, explains that an algorithm is 'a set of rules that must be followed when solving a particular problem' (The Oxford Dictionary, No year). By this definition, quite a lot of things in our everyday life can be seen as algorithms, such as the steps we take in tooth-brushing, cooking from recipes and making tea. In the context of journalism (and in this book), the term is used as it is in computing, that is, to refer to a well-defined set of instructions, which are implemented on a computer or computational device for solving a problem. Algorithms running on computers are known for their accuracy and speed. Making use of computer algorithms (shortened to algorithms in this book) can thus increase our ability to fulfil our needs.

The world we are living in is full of algorithms and the data that algorithms need to use. Algorithms bring search results for us on Google. Algorithms rank news on Facebook. Algorithms detect trends on Facebook and Twitter. Amongst other vital things, we need them to operate markets, run political campaigns, offer social and health services, identify target consumers, and understand human behaviour. Algorithms are everywhere and have become embedded in our daily lives.

Algorithms need data to be functional, and, meanwhile, they also collect data from devices on which algorithms run. GPS (satellite navigation) and Fitbit devices are two good examples of this. A GPS device requires sufficient data to calculate routes, and at the same time to generate data about the driving records of a car. Likewise, a Fitbit device needs data about its users, such as their age, weight, height and gender, motion data and GPS data, in order to calculate the steps, distance and calories burned. In the meantime, Fitbit users generate new exercise log data, which is simultaneously collected by the device.

A close look at contemporary news work will reveal that the extensive use of algorithms has gradually changed journalistic work. Within newsrooms, journalists have started to employ algorithms in their news production process such as data gathering, analysis, storytelling and news dissemination. Beyond newsrooms, news feed algorithms have changed how news articles are accessed, disseminated and consumed.

Three Ways in Which Algorithms Have Influenced Journalism

This section will discuss the algorithmic influence on news writing, data processing and news distribution. The penetration of algorithms into these three aspects of journalism is considerable, with profound implications for the occupation of journalism.

Using algorithms to write news: the rise of 'robot reporters'

Globally, big news organisations have started to adopt algorithms to produce news articles, such as *The Washington Post*'s Heliograf, Bloomberg's Project Cyborg (see Box 6.1) (Mullin, 2016), the Automated Insights' platform that has been adopted by The Associated Press, and Tencent's Dreamwriter (China). Other news outlets have followed suit, although not all newsrooms are using news-generating algorithms. For example, in 2016, the *Financial News*, a local news outlet in Korea, started to use a robot reporter, named IamFNBOT, to report on Korean stock market prices and other data (Son, 2016). In 2019, the Jewish Telegraphic Agency tested its robot reporter: Bert Cyberg (Silow-Carroll, 2019). In the same year, *The Guardian*'s Australian edition published its first report generated by an experimental automated news reporting system: ReporterMate (ReporterMate, 2019; Peiser, 2019b). This global trend of adopting algorithms to automate news stories in different languages has been facilitated by the development of natural language generation (NLG), which is a subfield of artificial intelligence (AI) and a process in which algorithms automatically generate national language from structured data. Using artificial intelligence and computational linguistics techniques, NLG systems can automatically produce comprehensible texts in human languages such as English.

These latest developments in the news industry suggest that robots (algorithms), rather than human writers, have started to write news with (presumably) impeccable accuracy and at an unprecedented speed. This form of journalism has been given different names, for example, 'automated journalism', 'robot journalism' and 'algorithmic journalism'. With slightly different emphases, these names refer to the same thing: 'automated journalism', a term that is adopted in this chapter to refer to the use of algorithms (termed 'robot reporters' in this chapter) to automate and convert data into news text by following particular formats.

Originating from reporting on weather forecasting in the 1960s (Glahn, 1970; Graefe, 2016), algorithms, which are automated news writing systems, can be very useful in generating short and simple news items from data provided. These algorithms function similarly: they quickly analyse data which has been fed into the system and use templates to rapidly produce short and simple news articles, and all of these steps are repetitive. *The Guardian*'s ReporterMate, for example, is a system that can automatically transform input data into templated stories. Robot-generated reports are able to break news stories very swiftly. For example, the *Los Angeles Times* was the first newspaper to break the news of an earthquake in California in 2014. Its news about the earthquake was automatically generated and published online within about three minutes (The BBC, 2014).

Robot reporters are particularly useful in reporting on finance, sports, weather and traffic news. *The Washington Post*, for example, used Heliograf in the coverage of high-school football, creating a new model for hyperlocal coverage (WashPostPR, 2017). Heliograf was also employed to cover the 2016 Rio Olympic Games and the 2016 US elections. Yahoo!Sports has used Automated Insights' Wordsmith (natural language generation) platform to generate over 70 million reports (Automated Insights, No year). Since 2014, through automating news stories, The Associated Press has even increased its Minor League Baseball coverage (AP, 2016).

BOX 6.1

The Cyborg Project of Bloomberg

Bloomberg launched its Cyborg Project in 2016. Its aim was to form a ten-person team to develop the use of automation in news writing and reporting to produce 'smart automated content' (SAC) (Kelly, 2016; Mullin, 2016). In 2019, it was reported that the Cyborg system produced about one-third of the news content (mainly business and financial news) commissioned by Bloomberg News. The Cyborg system can analyse a financial report when it appears and immediately generate a news story that contains the most relevant information. While human business reporters may moan that this kind of reporting is boring, the Cyborg system does not complain (Peiser, 2019b).

The views of practitioners and academics are split over the impact of robot reporters on journalism. One view sees the automation of writing news articles as cutting costs and helping journalists deal with their increasingly heavy workload. Practising automated journalism costs less than paying a real person to write news stories. Especially for repetitive reporting, like that in the sports or financial domain, it is cheaper to get it done by automation programs. Nick Evershed, the editor of *The Guardian*'s Reporter-Mate, explained that their initiative to launch this algorithm came from the need to save journalists, whose number had been dwindling, from numerous work tasks and from writing formulaic stories (Evershed, 2019). With pre-formulated newsworthiness judgement and selection criteria applied, algorithms automate the selection of information, and this works well in tackling the challenge posed by the need to quickly process large amounts of data, as The Associated Press argued (Automated Insights, No year). From a dataset, algorithms can even generate stories in different languages and from various angles, increasing the personalisation potential to suit individual readers (Graefe, 2016). The fact that algorithms don't complain also makes them easier to manage than human reporters. Automated journalism is also thought to be profitable, reducing journalists' workloads and generating new business opportunities, such as *The Washington Post*'s Arc XP (formerly Arc Publishing), which offers clients AI products to increase their digital experience including automated content generation. A study conducted 42 surveys with decision-makers in 24 newspaper companies in South Korea, and concluded that the use of robot reporters is considered to have promising business prospects and to result from a strategy of cutting the number of human journalists (Kim & Kim, 2017). Additionally, breaking news may quickly improve the news organisation's prominence in online search results and thus enlarge its readership. By offering quick and accurate news articles, algorithms thus increase the competitiveness of news organisations and provide them with a new way to engage audiences and broaden their audience base.

However, another set of views recognises the limitations of automated journalism. Although 'robot reporters' can work well in reporting financial information, sports, emergency events and disasters, such as earthquakes, most robot reporters are only able to write simple, short and structured hard news stories. At least at the moment it is not feasible for them to write anything complicated, as Natural Language Generation (NLG) systems may only be capable of generating simple text, mainly comprising elements such as what happened, when and where. The reporting ability of algorithms is thus limited by developments in artificial intelligence (AI) technologies. Much still needs to be done to improve the effectiveness of NLG systems. On top of being limited by the technology, the effectiveness of NLG systems may also be restricted by the level of cleanliness of structured data. As the availability of data is the prerequisite for using algorithms to automate news, and algorithms cannot properly function without pertinent databases and data, NLG systems do not necessarily perform well with messy or unstructured data.

Being inflexible in actual situations, pre-formulated formats and selection criteria may limit the diversity of the topics covered and the angles taken by the news articles generated. A study of robot writing identified six limitations of automated journalism: (1) its dependence on single-sourced, disconnected data; (2) its reliance on merely one dimension of that data; (3) the difficulties of interrogating that data; (4) the absence of human tones in the generated texts; (5) the need to follow a pre-given template to produce texts; and (6) the diminution of creativity in the templating process (Thurman, Dörr, & Kunert, 2017). These six limitations summarise the shortcomings of automated journalism well. Additionally, automated journalism may mean the loss of the critical ability of journalists, as it is possessed by humans rather than machines, and also lead to an over-reliance on fellow journalists who specialise in programming (Linden, 2018).

As for audience acceptance, automated news items are seen as more objective and credible, but more boring and less readable than those produced by human writers (Graefe, Haim, Haarmann, & Brosius, 2018). However, variations were observed between countries. For example, a comparative study revealed that US users liked news stories produced by human journalists and the traditional media more than the Chinese users did (Zheng, Zhong, & Yang, 2018). Another study found that European news audiences saw the content made by humans, automated algorithms, and a combination of humans and algorithms as having an equal level of credibility. However, for sports news, automated content was seen as more trustworthy than that produced by humans (Wölker & Powell, 2018). Two studies carried out with audiences from North America suggest that audiences saw news with a human reporter as its author as more credible than the news that was credited to an algorithm (Waddell, 2018). In the context of South Korea, both the public and journalists thought news attributed to an algorithm was more credible than that attributed to a human journalist (Jung, Song, Kim, Im, & Oh, 2017). Dutch audiences perceived automated and human-made news to be equally credible and Dutch journalists, by contrast, saw human messages as more credible than automated news items (van der Kaa & Krahmer, 2014).

As a global trend, automatically generating news items from data, propelled by the availability of data and technologies, has changed the journalism landscape. However, it is too early to conclude that robot reporters will replace human writers. Their potential to increase profits by lowering financial costs and increasing efficiency, has to be weighed against the technological limitations as well as the acceptance and reading habits of audiences.

Using algorithms in data processing (collection and analysis)

Apart from automated journalism and robot reporters, journalists have increasingly used algorithms to collect and analyse data as part of a 'quantitative turn' in journalism (Coddington, 2015). The term 'quantitative turn' describes the shift from computer-assisted reporting through data journalism to computational journalism. In spite of their differences, these three types of journalism all use computing algorithms to handle data to meet journalists' needs. Algorithms are needed in every step of the reporting process. They facilitate the collection, aggregation, cleaning, analysis, visualisation and sharing of data.

For the reporting purpose, algorithms can be used on two levels, or in other words, there are two potential scenarios in which algorithms are used: one is individual use, and the other is organisational use. In terms of the individual use of algorithms, journalists who are able to program may write code in the programming languages of their choice, such as Python, R or Java, creating a series of algorithms that are designed to meet specific needs by following a particular procedure. For those who do not have programming skills, they have existing – sometimes free, open-source – tools at their disposal to accomplish their reporting needs. Among these tools are Google Sheets, Scraper, Excel, OpenRefine and Google Flourish.

On the organisational level, algorithms may be developed and adopted to help journalists' output in a way that engages the audience. News organisations have begun to use algorithms – powered by the technologies of artificial intelligence and machine learning – to identify trending topics for reporting. For example, Bertie, the content management system of *Forbes*, recommends real-time viral topics on which to report, as well as advising on how to make headlines more attractive and selecting relevant images to go with the coverage (Dans, 2019).

Providing computational platforms or tools for users, including journalists and non-journalists, to process data is another form of using algorithms in data processing, which is classified as computational journalism by Coddington (2015). Prominent examples include the BBC's Juicer; DocumentCloud, which was established by former journalists of *ProPublica* and *The New York Times*; and the International Medical Devices Database, the Offshore Leaks Database and Datashare developed by the International Consortium of Investigative Journalists (ICIJ). These platforms have two common aspects: (1) sharing data, and (2) enabling users to use algorithms to identify patterns in, and to extract information from, data. The International Medical Devices Database of the ICIJ, for example, provides users including journalists with data and machine learning algorithms to identify problems relating to medical devices so that journalists can report on these problems (Díaz-Struck & Carvajal, 2018). With this institutionalised support for using algorithms in news reporting, more journalists, and even non-journalist users, who cannot code themselves, can benefit from state-of-the-art technologies, such as artificial intelligence and machine learning.

The availability of these algorithms and platforms potentially contributes to augmenting the ability of journalists to process data and to conduct data-based news reporting. For example, artificial intelligence technologies can help investigative reporters to explore data and identify investigative story ideas. However, there are also limitations, which will be discussed later in this chapter.

The role played by algorithms in distributing and ranking news

In the context of journalism, another important use of algorithms is related to the distribution and ranking of news. The rise of search engines, news feed algorithms, and organisations' newsbots have dramatically changed the way in which news is distributed and selected by the audience to consume, as well as which news is ranked as important and relevant. Humans no longer entirely decide which news or information is important and relevant, but computer algorithms do.

Search engines help us to navigate the sea of abundant information on the Internet. The most popular search engines include Google, Bing, Yahoo! and their counterparts or competitors in other countries, such as Baidu and Soso (in China), Naver and Daum (in South Korea) and Yandex (in Russia). Google and Yahoo! are also popular in non-Western countries, such as Japan and South Korea. Search engines crawl, identify and index websites, web pages and online content and save related information, such as index and search results, in their enormous background databases. When users search in their databases, the algorithms of these information companies generate and present search results for readers. Google, for example, uses its algorithm, PageRank, to rank the importance of web pages, the results of which determine the order of the information displayed on its results pages.

Commercial Internet companies, such as Google, Yahoo! and Facebook, also aggregate, rank, distribute and feed news to users, acting as news aggregators. Prominent among others are Google's news ranking algorithms and Facebook's News Feed algorithms. The algorithms of these information companies feed and deliver news to readers. Ranked by their news search algorithms, news items are returned in specific orders in the search results. Even when using the same dataset, the different algorithms used by tech giants such as Google, Facebook and Twitter may produce differing rankings. With their news feeds and search engines, these companies enable users to browse and read the news that is most important and relevant to them.

These tech giants allow their users to personalise their news selection. In Google News, for example, users can personalise what they want to receive and read. As for Facebook, its News Feed algorithm decides what appears in the news feeds of users. However, it works differently in terms of recommending content for them. It determines which stories appear first, not only by the relevance of stories, but also by how many likes, comments and forwards they have received. Friendship becomes a vital factor that influences the selection values of Facebook's News Feed.

Newsbots, mostly offered by news organisations, are another type of algorithm, aggregating, selecting and disseminating news content for users – both journalists and readers. As well as automatically generating and distributing news to audiences, they also help journalists monitor the publication of particular stories and engage with readers. Prominent examples are ChatBot from the Australian Broadcasting Corporation (ABC), the PEACH project of the European Broadcasting Union (EBU), and the BBC's Chatbots. A case study of the ABC (Australia Broadcasting Corporation) newsbot reveals that the new generation of newsbots mediates the relationship between journalist and audiences (Ford & Hutchinson, 2019).

■■■ EXERCISE 6.1 ■■■

Take a look at a newsbot of your choice and use it for several days. Based on your own experience as a newsbot user, think about how the extensive use of newsbots, and other algorithms in news distribution, could change the concept of journalism and the relationship between journalists and audiences.

The Implications of Using Algorithms for Journalism

In the wake of extensively using algorithms, journalists have become more dependent on technologies than ever. A new human–machine relationship is forming in journalism, one where human journalists and algorithms work together to co-practice journalism. So, what does it mean for journalism and for the nature of its work and for the occupation of journalist?

Transforming journalistic labour and craft

There are three concerns in relation to journalistic labour and craft. The first is the fear of job losses. Generally, a long-standing concern has existed over the possibility that automation, or robots, in the workplace will eliminate the number of human jobs. In human history, in general, and the history of journalism, in particular, there have been examples where machines have replaced humans, and some occupations, such as switchboard operators, who were largely replaced by automated phone systems, have even vanished following the introduction of new technologies. The popularity of computers led to the disappearance of typists and typing pools from offices. At a time when news organisations have been reducing job costs but expanding coverage, a question naturally arises as to whether the use of robot reporters may lead to more job cuts in the news industry. Some scholars (see, for example, Latar, 2015, 2018) even believe that automated journalism brings with it a bleak future for human journalists, who may be replaced by robots.

In parallel, a rosier view of automated journalism is evident. For example, both audiences and journalists in South Korea were in favour of news generated by algorithms (Jung et al., 2017). In the US, the homicide news project, an early automated journalism project run by the *Los Angeles Times*, was perceived positively by journalists, who saw the algorithm as improving – rather than taking over – the work of crime reporters (Graefe, 2016; Young & Hermida, 2015). Automation is also thought to save journalists from doing repetitive reporting tasks, thereby allowing them more time to investigate more complicated and interesting topics (Jung et al., 2017; Van Dalen, 2012; Young & Hermida, 2015). It has been noticed that more new jobs, such as 'news robot trainers, API (Application Programming Interface) editors or algorithm editors', have appeared in newsrooms in the wake of automated journalism (Linden, 2018: 237).

Algorithms are most useful in producing news based on available, structured data. Without structured data, or data of good quality, it is difficult to practise automated journalism. This limitation dramatically mitigates the threats posed by robot reporters to human journalists' jobs. Although algorithms may take over repetitive and simple news production, human verification and investigation are still needed for reporting. Human journalists, in particular those who are involved in in-depth, analytical or investigative reports, are unlikely to be replaced by robots. A study examining South Korean journalists, for instance, reveals that in contrast to robots being seen as a supplement to journalists' news reporting, human journalists were considered to be able to engage with investigative reporting more closely (Jung et al., 2017).

The second, acute concern is about the craft of journalism: to be successful, what essential knowledge and skills should journalists possess? Knowledge and skills are at the heart of journalistic labour. The nature of essential journalistic skills and toolkits has changed along with the extensive use of algorithms in journalism. The potential of algorithms to replace human reporters in accomplishing simple, repetitive and routine reporting based on structured data makes the skills of investigation, the knowledge of data and computational thinking as well as the skills of handling data and using computers and algorithms, extremely important. Under the impact of automated journalism, the qualities of a good journalist have changed from an emphasis on being factual, objective and able to write simple sentences or conduct speedy reporting, to an ability to analyse and write linguistically complicated sentences, alongside an emphasis on the personality and creativity of individual journalists (Van Dalen, 2012). Overall, journalism itself has shifted from descriptive to interpretive reporting, and journalists have changed from being observers to being analysts (Albæk, 2011).

The third concern relates to the extension of the function of journalism from covering news to providing a service. As discussed earlier in the book, the rise of computational journalism and data journalism may mean journalism is starting to act as a service, through fact-checking and verifying information and producing and synthesising databases for ordinary users to use (Webb, 2016). Although it may result in new financial opportunities for the news industry, journalism as a service would change the concept and role of journalism profoundly. Not only will the outcome of journalistic practices be expanded from news stories to other products, such as databases or platforms, but also the target users of journalism will be extended from news audiences to other user groups, such as businesses that want to gain insights from related data. This service is akin to providing business intelligence and consultancy and extends the traditional function of the trade press.

EXERCISE 6.2

Can you identify up to three changes that the use of algorithms will bring to journalistic labour and craft? Discuss whether, and to what extent, these changes are opportunities or threats to journalism?

The work and quality of journalism

Algorithms increase the ability of journalists and editors to fulfil their journalistic tasks. The availability of algorithms enables computer-assisted journalism, data journalism and computational journalism. Nevertheless, the use of algorithms in journalism may not necessarily enhance its quality, as discussed in the previous chapter. The employment of automated algorithms to generate news may even impair media pluralism and the originality that is exclusive to humans (Ombelet, Kuczerawy, & Valcke, 2016a).

Additionally, algorithmic practices by tech giants have been found to reconfirm existing personal biases and exclude the opposite arguments (Bozdag, 2013). Concerns have arisen over the threats brought about by algorithms, such as those that act as news recommenders, to democracy. For example, automated journalism that helps to deliver personalised news to news consumers may further fragment public opinion (Graefe, 2016).

A prevailing academic view sees editorial judgement as having been swayed – or even weakened and overtaken – by algorithmic judgement. The (false) assumption of algorithmic objectivity leads to a belief in the superiority of algorithmic judgement over journalistic judgement (Carlson, 2018a). This means that editorial judgements concerning news-worthiness and a news story's success have become subordinated to the decisions made by algorithms, such as news aggregation and ranking algorithms. In their news selection process, news organisations and journalists may prioritise what is ranked as important and relevant to readers by algorithms, despite the fact that it is likely that they may only have a limited idea of how algorithms work. In addition, when journalists do online research for news reporting, results returned from the searches may subtly influence journalists' understanding of the world and therefore shape the reports they produce. This subtle influence is one of the main ways that the 'invisible hand of the unaccountable algorithm' of Google, Facebook and other information companies has changed journalism (Brake, 2017).

Although the move toward (news consumption) personalisation is a solution provided by online information intermediaries, like Google News, to solve the problem of information overload, these information companies have partly replaced traditional news outlets and become gatekeepers who influence – if not decide – what news audiences will consume. In addition, deep personalisation in news consumption raises concerns over the impact of audience metrics on editorial decisions and users' information exposure. In the contexts of European and Australian public service media, for example, the adoption of algorithms in news production and recommendations has brought about challenges for striking a balance between popularity and uniqueness and for maintaining users' diverse exposure to news content (Sørensen & Hutchinson, 2018).

Search Engine Optimisation (SEO) practice, a means of maximising appearances and prominence in search results, has become common in newsrooms around the world and among independent journalists. As a result of the widespread adoption of SEO in newsrooms, there has been a trend towards following SEO, rather than journalistic rules, in news production (see further discussions about SEO in Chapter 8). In the wake of the prevalent use of search engine algorithms, for example, news producers pay much more attention to news headlines and the tags used in their reports in an attempt to make their news articles search engine friendly.

Along with the changes in the craft, labour and work of journalism, the concept of journalism has changed. For example, the broad adoption of automation algorithms, such as news chatbots in journalism, suggests the emergence of conversational journalism, which means content is delivered through chats (Jones & Jones, 2019). Not only have the originator of the content – humans or machines – and the skills that they should have on the job altered, but also the concept of authorship has changed, which will be discussed later in this chapter.

Algorithmic accountability and ethical challenges

Another acute, increasingly growing concern is around the opacity of algorithms. The 'black box' surrounding algorithms leads to journalists' fear of losing control of their work. This fear originates from knowing the existence of algorithmic biases yet not knowing what these biases are or how they influence the outcomes of using algorithms. Having biases, and possibly making mistakes, algorithms are not as objective as they were assumed to be. Instead, they are socially constructed and laden with social and cultural values. Algorithms are affected by the subjective judgements and decisions of their makers, e.g., programmers. They may be influenced by the interests of the organisations employing programmers and the ontology and epistemology of those programmers (Lewis, Sanders, & Carmody, 2019). Algorithms used in generating news, collecting and analysing data and the news dissemination process are thus all subject to the particular subjective judgements of their designers, including both organisations and programmers.

Value-added decisions that are shaped by prior bias are embedded within the design of algorithms. For example, capitalist ideology shapes the algorithms of search engines. The products of Facebook serve its business interests and desire for revenue. One piece of empirical evidence for this is that during the Arab Spring, fearing the retaliation of political authorities, Facebook itself censored the posts by those protestors who were based in Arab countries via its algorithms (Tufekci, 2017).

Influenced by algorithmic biases, algorithms prioritise, classify, associate and filter information and content. The search engine and news ranking algorithms of Google rank information and news according to rules that remain unknown to most of the users. With algorithmic biases, an algorithm-based recommendation system may unfairly influence users' media exposure.

The ways in which algorithms make decisions and by which criteria they do so lacks transparency and remains enigmatic. Users may not know of the existence of algorithms, which often work subtly, let alone be informed about how the algorithms work. Although tech giants such as Facebook and Google have started to publish the mathematical formulae behind their algorithms, not everyone can understand them. Besides, other crucial information – for instance the procedures through which an algorithm is written and built, actual human judgements, and other factors such as the organisational cultures that have shaped the forming of an algorithm – are still shielded from the public eye. This obscurity raises academic awareness of the importance of algorithmic accountability, a term referring to exposing the issues surrounding the outcomes of using algorithms for decision-making under the influence of algorithmic design. Using 'reverse engineering'– knowing how algorithms are made – and traditional reporting techniques such as interviews and document reviews are thought to be able to provide a potential solution to practising algorithmic accountability reporting (Diakopoulos, 2014).

Journalists have started investigating the problems associated with algorithmic biases and discrimination. Influential investigative reports include: 'Machine Bias Investigating Algorithmic Injustice', commissioned by ProPublica; 'Websites Vary Prices, Deals Based on Users' Information', published by *The Wall Street Journal*; the exposure of racial inequality in Uber's service (Stark & Diakopoulos, 2016) by *The Washington Post*; and the investigation of the use of child abuse data by councils (McIntyre & Pegg, 2018) by *The Guardian*. The publication of these journalistic investigations shows that journalists are increasingly aware of the problems that are related to algorithms, algorithms' creators and the datasets used by algorithms.

Algorithmic judgement is considered to fundamentally challenge journalists' professional news judgement, shaping news and influencing the legitimacy of journalism (Carlson, 2018a). Subjectivity embodied in algorithms will subtly influence news stories. Further, data is itself subjective and socially constructed, and may also contain errors. The problems with data may have significant implications for the objectivity and accuracy of news articles that are produced based on that data. Thus the accuracy of automated journalism cannot be guaranteed, because doing justice to data also requires data to be pre-verified and interpreted appropriately within contexts, which algorithms may not be able to do. Whether algorithms can generate quality news in terms of more objective and accurate news articles than humans do is therefore open to considerable debate.

Given the problems existing around data and algorithms, transparency is particularly important for automated journalism. While transparency is becoming a fundamental principle of journalism ethics, it is crucial to have practical guidelines for achieving algorithmic transparency, which means the disclosure of information about algorithms so that algorithms can be monitored, checked, criticised or intervened in where necessary. Such practical guidelines, however, are largely absent at the moment.

Another important issue surrounding automated journalism is that of responsibility. On the occasions when algorithms make mistakes, who should shoulder the responsibility? Should we blame algorithms or their designers or users for these mistakes? Should journalists be held legally responsible for the errors made by algorithms? Who – the program, the journalist who uses the algorithm, the news organisation, or the algorithm – is the author of automated news content? This point is related to what will be discussed below in the section on 'authorship and legal liability'.

Authorship and legal liability

Who are the authors of automated news articles? Humans or machines? In the context of algorithms, the idea of authorship is controversial. The controversy mostly comes from the inevitable involvement of humans in algorithmic works. Although algorithms automatically generate news from data, the involvement of human work, or 'human agency' cannot be ignored (Uricchio, 2017). Human work can be seen in the generation, collection and curation of the data. It can also be found in the design, creation and use of the algorithms. Due to this human work, the authorship of an algorithm can sometimes be attributed to the user, yet on some occasions programmers or news organisations are considered to be the authors of automated content (Montal & Reich, 2017).

The authorship of algorithms also depends on whether this work is original and creative, and if it is made intentionally (Montal & Reich, 2017). Algorithms mostly produce pre-designed, simple news articles, rather than complicated, insightful journalistic pieces. Algorithmic works are thus hardly original, creative or made with intention and, therefore, algorithms cannot be seen as the authors. However, along with the advances in technologies, algorithms have had deeper involvement in the creative process. In this sense, they can be regarded as the authors (Uricchio, 2017). In the Belgian context, for example, the algorithm is seen as an employee working for a news organisation and thus it has authorship conferred on it (Ombelet, Kuczerawy, & Valcke, 2016b).

Associated with ambivalent authorship is the question of legal responsibility. Who should bear legal liability if something goes wrong? Can we really expect algorithms to be held liable? Or, perhaps, should the programmer, the journalists who are the users of the algorithms, or the news organisations, who are the employers of the algorithm, take the blame and shoulder the responsibility? If the programmer, journalists or news organisations are seen as the authors, the answer is probably 'yes'. In the Belgian context, for example, news organisations are expected to take on the legal liability, as they are held responsible for checking the content before it is published (Ombelet et al., 2016b). But if news organisations are not held to be the author, should they bear the blame if something goes wrong?

The use of robot reporters in journalism thus raises questions about liability, for which new laws and regulations are urgently needed. The possible use of erroneous, detrimental or illegal content in the process of automating news may lead to the production of libellous news content by algorithms (Lewis, Sanders et al., 2019). The problem of legal liability is severe in the current communication environment, where the online prevalence of fake news (see Box 9.5 in Chapter 9) has become a big headache for content producers and users. Fake news is not a new phenomenon. In the history of journalism, it has been a problem that has been particularly identified and associated with coverage by sensational tabloids. However, today, the unprecedented popularity of social media and the advent and affordances of digital technologies have made this problem worse. Artificial intelligence (AI), natural language generation and news-automation algorithms, for example, can be used to produce authentic-looking fake news or even 'deepfakes', whereby deep learning, a type of artificial intelligence technique, is used to fake images of people or events in still or moving images, as shown in the deepfake alternative Queen's Christmas speech delivered by Channel 4 in 2020 (in the UK) (Channel 4, 2020). In a world of information overload, it becomes increasingly difficult to tell genuine from fake news.

There have been efforts to mitigate the fake news problem. Machine learning and artificial intelligence techniques are also utilised to recognise and remove fake news. Some news organisations, such as Bloomberg, have begun to use AI to detect fake news. Technology start-ups, such as the UK's Fabula AI, have joined legacy news media in endeavouring to develop new technologies, such as Fabula's Geometric Deep Learning, for this purpose. Some universities or companies have tried to build up datasets containing textual statements and claim to be able to tell fake from genuine news. Sponsored by Amazon, Fever is a good example, in which researchers have introduced a dataset 'for fact extraction and verification'. But none of these measures is entirely effective. Globally, fake news is still posing an immense threat to the health of public communication.

For the news media, the fake news phenomenon has posed a dilemma in terms of covering hot topics online. They cannot afford to overlook what goes viral online. Their coverage of trending topics on the Internet, identified by news ranking algorithms, satisfies the interests of users. In addition, information collected by their data scraping algorithms is used as a source of news. Meanwhile, however, news automation algorithms cannot verify the related information and there have been cases of algorithms failing to identify fake content. In 2016, several days after removing human editors from the role of Trending curators, Facebook's Trending News algorithm promoted a fake story claiming Megyn Kelly, a Fox News anchor, had been fired by Fox News. Although Megyn Kelly did not intend to sue Facebook for libel (Weber, 2016), this case has implications for legal issues surrounding the use of algorithms in journalism. If what is used in news articles is fake and inaccurate, news stories will even contribute to endorsing and disseminating fake news. In addition, if that happens, the possibility that the news media will have to shoulder the legal liability for the circulation of fake news poses a danger to their survival in the data era.

▄▄▄▄▄▄▄▄ **EXERCISE 6.3** ▄▄▄▄▄▄▄▄

Try to identify arguments supporting and opposing the statement that journalists and newsrooms should be legally liable for defamatory and libellous content that is produced by algorithms.

Summary of the Chapter

After introducing the concept of algorithms, this chapter discusses three ways of using algorithms in journalism. It then explores how the algorithmic practices of journalism have changed it and have raised ethical and legal challenges to journalism and the news industry.

▄▄▄▄▄▄▄▄ **END OF CHAPTER EXERCISE** ▄▄▄▄▄▄▄▄

Consider this statement: journalism can benefit from algorithms. Try to think about the pros and cons of this proposition. You can consider different aspects of journalism – for example, journalistic labour, work, ethics and legal liability. Please identify up to three arguments for either side of the statement. You can select and discuss some examples to support your arguments.

▄▄▄▄▄▄▄▄ **FURTHER READING** ▄▄▄▄▄▄▄▄

Brake, David (2017). The invisible hand of the unaccountable algorithm: how Google, Facebook and other tech companies are changing journalism. In J. Tong & S.-h. Lo (Eds.), *Digital Technology and Journalism: An International Comparative Perspective* (pp. 25–46). Cham: Palgrave Macmillan. Brake's chapter addresses an important and pressing issue that is being faced by journalism – the subtle influence of big tech giants such as Facebook and Google on journalism through the ways in which journalists collect information and understand the world.

Lewis, Seth C., Sanders, Amy Kristin, and Carmody, Casey (2019). Libel by algorithm? Automated journalism and the threat of legal liability. *Journalism & Mass Communication Quarterly*, 96(1), 60–81. This article discusses the legal liability challenges posed by automated journalism. It draws our attention to the risks that algorithms may generate due to the publication of defamatory news content.

Montal, Tal and Reich, Zvi (2017). I, robot. You, journalist. Who is the author? Authorship, bylines and full disclosure in automated journalism. *Digital Journalism*, 5(7), 829–849. This article discusses the way algorithmic authorship is shown on bylines and in full disclosure, related policies and the perceptions of it. The study that is reported on in the article portrays a detailed picture of the perceptions of authorship, attribution policies and the actual authorship credit systems in the news organisations in question.

SEVEN

ENTREPRENEURIAL JOURNALISM

KEY QUESTIONS

- What is entrepreneurial journalism?
- Why does journalism need entrepreneurialism?
- What does entrepreneurial journalism mean for journalism and its role in democracy?
- What are the concerns and issues surrounding the practice of entrepreneurial journalism?

KEY CONCEPTS

entrepreneurialism

entrepreneurial journalism

niche market

blurring advertising-editorial boundaries

crowd-funding

sustainability

In 2005, The Huffington Post was launched by Arianna Huffington, Kenneth Lerer and Jonah Peretti with the help of Andrew Breitbart. It started as an independent news site, offering free news and commentaries to users and relying on advertising for revenue. The site has grown into a news organisation, particularly since it was sold to AOL for US$315 million in 2011 and later to BuzzFeed in 2020. In 2016, Jason Calacanis launched Inside as a set of email newsletters providing news on the topics of business, technology and venture capital, generating revenue from subscriptions and sponsorship. It had a revenue of US$1.1 million and 750,000 active subscriptions in 2018 and raised US$2.6 million from investors in 2019 (Schmidt, 2019). In the United Kingdom (UK), as of 2021, over 100 hyperlocal online news sites, such as Ray Duffill's HU12 Online, supply local communities with local news. These stories suggest that entrepreneurial journalism has come to prominence in today's news arena.

Following the discussions about algorithms and journalism in the previous chapter, this chapter explores entrepreneurial journalism. It discusses the concept of entrepreneurial journalism, the idea of entrepreneurialism and the reasons why journalism needs it, as well as the implications of practising entrepreneurial journalism. The chapter will also examine the differences between entrepreneurial journalism and freelance journalism, and how entrepreneurial journalism has benefited from the prevalence of digital technologies and the emergence of new funding models, such as crowd-funding, sponsorship, and even venture capital. The last section of this chapter will discuss the extent to which the rise of entrepreneurial journalism may change the concept of journalism.

What Is Entrepreneurial Journalism?

Entrepreneurial journalism should not be confused with business journalism, which covers business, economic or financial stories. Instead, it refers to a new way of practising journalism, in which individual journalists launch their own – usually Internet-based – news outlets, and thus create jobs, primarily for themselves, but sometimes also for other journalists. Such online news outlets are not only journalism projects but also business operations.

Entrepreneurial journalism came to the public attention after the turn of the 21st century when, globally, a range of journalism start-ups, such as Rafat Ali's paidContent (in 2002, US), became successful. Rafat Ali, a former journalist, launched paidContent as a news blog, developed it into a news website and later sold it to *The Guardian* for a disclosed US$30 million in 2008 (Kiss, 2008).

It is common for journalists to work on a freelance basis for news organisations at some points in their careers, meaning that rather than being directly employed by news organisations, they sell their stories to them and are paid for the stories they produce. Some journalists may have ongoing relationships with particular news outlets, such as serving as 'stringers' for a newspaper or news agency in an overseas or regional location. However, entrepreneurial journalists differ from freelance journalists in three ways. First, entrepreneurial journalists are the owners of their own businesses, although they are not media moguls such as Alfred Harmsworth or Rupert Murdoch. They own (online) journalistic start-ups, seeking new platforms and markets for journalism. Second, through their news outlets, entrepreneurial journalists either supply news content to their audiences directly or provide content to partner companies. Third, entrepreneurial journalists are more than just news reporters. Most of the time, individual journalism entrepreneurs need to take on an all-encompassing role. That means, apart from producing news content, they also have to play the roles of entrepreneurs, owners and decision-makers for their own business. They need to produce journalistic content, manage the business, look after technology and finance, design their websites, and market and promote their content and brand. For small-scale journalism start-up companies, these roles may be shared among a limited number of people. Entrepreneurial journalists, therefore, need to learn a wide range of skills in most, if not all, related areas, including journalism, marketing, management, technology, finance and design, so that they can play multiple roles in their businesses.

In a nutshell, practising entrepreneurial journalism means individual journalists use the platform of the Internet to launch independent news media outlets. Entrepreneurial journalism de-institutionalises journalistic practice and is usually small-scale, individual or takes the form of a small partnership. Entrepreneurial journalism projects usually have one, or multiple, types of income, such as advertising, donations, sponsorship or membership. They may or may not be able to develop their news outlets into bigger digital news organisations that hire more people.

Why Entrepreneurial Journalism?

The importance of entrepreneurialism

Entrepreneurialism is at the heart of this type of journalism. This concept refers to the entrepreneurial spirit, which encourages acting in an entrepreneurial manner, employing entrepreneurial thinking, serving customers well, celebrating innovations, being competitive, and taking performance-based and market-based approaches (Milakovich & Gordon, 2009). The pursuit of entrepreneurialism results from the transformation of social and economic systems into the entrepreneurial society, where entrepreneurship acts as a driving force for economic growth and the economy's competitiveness in international markets. In the United States (US), for example, the Clinton administration advocated this idea of entrepreneurialism by calling for the formation of an entrepreneurial government that encourages the generation of change from the bottom up (Milakovich & Gordon, 2009). Entrepreneurialism is seen as vital for advancing the capability of organisations to innovate and improve performance. Today, entrepreneurship penetrates almost all aspects of our society. Among others, Apple, Facebook, Google, Twitter, TikTok and Uber serve as living, successful examples of embracing creativity and entrepreneurialism.

Entrepreneurialism is thought to be crucial for journalism's survival in a digital world. This is a time when the revenues of traditional news media are in decline, with limited job opportunities for journalists, especially for those who are new to journalism and those whose career prospects in big legacy news organisations look bleak. Meanwhile, in the data age, new digital technologies carry on emerging and rapid changes in people's lifestyles and in capital markets continue to occur. In the media ecosystem transformed by digital technologies there are spaces for innovative, creative and entrepreneurial mindsets to flourish. To survive and thrive, both news media and individual journalists need to quickly adapt to such changes. Taking full advantage of entrepreneurialism can help them make the most of the data age. Media experts such as the Tow-Knight Center's Jeff Jarvis (Townend, 2009), Clique Media Group's Katherine Power (Bryant, 2016) and *The Washington Post*'s editor Martin Baron (Albeanu, 2017) have started encouraging journalists to develop an entrepreneurial mindset and to be entrepreneurial within or beyond news organisations. Changes in big legacy newsrooms such as *The Washington Post* are hailed as 'revolutionary' for their embrace of digital technologies and for adapting their business models to the digital world. Journalists have made good use of crowd-funding to start their journalism enterprises; for example, Tortoise Media, an online journalism start-up, launched in 2018, following a successful £75,000 fundraising effort (Mayhew, 2018), to publish slow news – news stories that take time to produce – and to open up journalism as a response to the information overload and power imbalance problems of our time.

Journalism educators have also started picking up and incorporating the idea of 'entrepreneurialism' into journalism curricula that prepare future journalists, as it is crucial for journalism students to learn entrepreneurial techniques and skills in order to succeed in the increasingly complex media environment. In the Spanish context, for example, the students surveyed showed an increasing interest in entrepreneurship (Casero-Ripollés, Izquierdo-Castillo, & Doménech-Fabregat, 2016). In the context of Taiwan, there has been a call to set the boosting of journalists' interest in 'social entrepreneurial practices' as one of the principal goals of journalism education (Liu, Chang, Liang, Yin, & Liang, 2019).

Entrepreneurial journalism as a potential solution to digital disruptions

Entrepreneurial journalism is deemed to be an innovative way of reinventing journalism. Its emergence suggests that journalists are taking up the opportunities that are provided by digital technologies and embracing entrepreneurism in order to survive and flourish. In the past, creating and owning a media outlet required considerable investment in order to buy or lease facilities, ranging from newsrooms to printing presses, and secure distribution channels. Digital technologies have significantly brought down the costs of developing and running a media outlet. Through understanding and using the technological affordances of digital technologies, along with embracing entrepreneurialism and acting and thinking like entrepreneurs, journalists will have good opportunities to practise journalism.

Entrepreneurial journalism is thought to be a potential solution to digital disruptions and a promising example of journalism evolving to adapt to the changing media ecosystem, which has led to the financial crisis faced by the news media and the crisis in quality journalism (see detailed discussions of these crises in Chapter 3). Entrepreneurial journalism has three advantages in dealing with the two crises facing journalism: (1) opportunities to adopt new business models; (2) the potential to revive local journalism; and (3) the possibility of offering quality, niche, but diverse content. Entrepreneurial journalism outlets are seen as 'forerunners' that are promoting a culture of much-needed 'hybrid journalism' and 'hybrid engagement' with audiences (Ruotsalainen & Villi, 2018).

(1) Adopting new business models

Entrepreneurial journalism has new, diverse business models, which may include advertising, crowd-funding, grants, sponsorship, donations, subscriptions and membership. Such outlets may work as an infomediary, which is a mediator between information producers and consumers, by collecting and selling information, data and data analysis, as shown in the case of How India Lives (India) and the ProPublica (US). These kinds of outlet may also be financially supported by venture capital and may benefit economically from platform capitalism (see a discussion about the concept of platform capitalism in Box 7.1), brokerage or the holding of live events (see examples of business models in Box 7.2).

BOX 7.1

Platform capitalism

Platform capitalism refers to the capitalisation of digital platforms, such as Google, Facebook, Twitter, Amazon, YouTube, Uber and Airbnb (Gillespie, 2010). It has become an outstanding feature of the contemporary economy, with key attributes such as the role of data as a crucial business asset. Spurred by platform capitalism, changes in society are not only economic but also political and cultural. The social consequences of platform capitalism are, however, controversial. Under the influence of the capitalisation of digital platforms, the interests of the audience may be geared to pursuing entertainment, and content producers may prioritise revenue over journalistic values, as shown in the case of China, which is discussed in Chapter 9 (also discussed in Tong, 2017a).

BOX 7.2

Examples of business models adopted by entrepreneurial journalism projects

Entrepreneurial journalism projects have adopted various business models. For example, Tortoise raised its funds through first crowd-sourcing and later membership. As of 2021, it has 85,000 members who pay a yearly fee of £80 (Edmonds, 2021). BuzzFeed is a successful example of attracting venture capital investment. Pando is a product of a journalism start-up with a focus on Silicon Valley and tech start-up companies. It was founded by Sarah Lacy, a technology journalist, in 2012. It has attracted a little short of US$4 million in investments from people in the tech industry. In 2015, Pando adopted a membership/subscription model ($10 per month) (pando.com).

Crowd-funding is one of the main business models for entrepreneurial journalism. The Ferret, based in Scotland, is a good example. A group of freelance journalists launched this investigative journalism platform, relying on crowd-funding as well as subscriptions. In 2013, US$1.7 million was raised in crowd-funding by Rob Wijnberg and Ernst-Jan Pfauth for De Correspondent in the Netherlands (Reid, 2014). Likewise, FactWire was established in 2015 in Hong Kong, after its organisers crowd-funded HK$4.75 million.

Another outstanding example is Hong Kong Free Press, the first crowd-funded English online news outlet in Hong Kong, launched in pursuit of press freedom. In 2015, it raised HK$150,000 through the FringeBacker website in just two days (Sala, 2015). It has survived since with hybrid funding models, ranging from crowd-funding and donations to advertising, products, books and even a deal with NordVPN.

Grants are another major source of funding for entrepreneurial journalism. In the US, for example, between 2009 and 2017, journalists received over US$235 million from the Knight Foundation for Innovation. From 2007 to 2014, the Knight News Challenge provided over US$37 million to fund 111 projects (Centre for Community Journalism, 2017).

A data-journalism-centred and Delhi-based journalism start-up – How India Lives – was founded in 2012, benefiting from 'grant money, partner capital and service revenue'. One of the founders received US$16,000 from the Tow-Knight Center for this entrepreneurial journalism project. What is interesting is that How India Lives also provides services to help clients to handle data (howindialives.com).

Govindraj Ethiraj, a former journalist in India, has founded three entrepreneurial journalism projects with a focus on data journalism. IndiaSpend (founded in 2011) relies on donations to stay independent. FactChecker.in also depends on funds and donations, while BoomLive is subscription-based (both launched in 2019).

■■■■■ EXERCISE 7.1 ■■■■■

Identify one or two entrepreneurial journalism projects and examine their funding models. Try to compare them with the traditional revenue models of the news media and then identify up to three advantages and disadvantages of each.

---

(2) The potential to revive local journalism

As discussed in Chapter 3, in the Anglo-American context, one ramification of financial difficulties is the decline of local journalism in the wake of the closure of local media outlets and the loss of local reporting and editorial roles. The rise of entrepreneurial journalism has given local journalism significant hope in regard to reviving local news content and jobs. Quite a lot of digital media outlets launched by journalism entrepreneurs target local communities, both in and outside the US and the UK. On the US side, Mike Orren's Pegasus News (launched in 2006), Tracy Record's West Seattle Blog (launched in 2005) and Evan Smith's The Texas Tribune (launched in 2009) were successful examples in the first decade of this century (see further, Briggs, 2012). Among others, more recent examples include Detroit-based Outlier Media (launched in 2016), The Tyler Loop (launched in 2017) and The Oaklandside (launched in 2020).

In the UK, typical local and hyperlocal Internet-based news sites include Ray Dufill's HU12 Online (launched in 2009), Mark Gorton's Heswall Today (launched in 2016), West Leeds Dispatch (launched in 2017) and Cheltenham Post (launched in 2020). The members of the Cardiff-based Independent Community News Network (ICNN) increased from 70 in the launch year of 2018 to 125 in 2021 (ICNN, 2021). In Australia, Carol Altmann's The Terrier was launched in 2018 to serve the local communities in Warrnambool, Victoria. With their public interest value, hyperlocal Internet-based news outlets are thought to be important to citizens' and local communities' participation in social and political life.

Beyond the Anglo-American countries, entrepreneurial journalism is emerging too. A good example is Mandara Online, a local news portal from Upper Egypt (www.mandaraonline.com). This journalism start-up is funded by institutes supporting entrepreneurial journalism, such as the Vienna-based International Press Institute. It serves the local community in Upper Egypt and is run by local journalists and bloggers. In the context of Greece, four entrepreneurial journalistic projects (Efimerida ton Syntakton–Efsyn, Alterthess, The Cricket, and Flash FM) are contributing to boosting the public's trust in media and rebuilding community (Siapera & Papadopoulou, 2016).

(3) Offering quality, niche, but diverse content

To succeed, entrepreneurial journalism will have to produce quality – and innovative – news, engage audiences and build its own brand. Moving from mass to niche markets and audiences, as well as supporting particular social values, are two common strategies that are being adopted by journalism start-ups.

In terms of targeting niche markets, quite a lot of journalism start-ups focus on investigative journalism or data journalism, as exemplified by The Ferret, introduced in Box 7.2, and The Shift News, which will be discussed later in this chapter. Some journalism start-ups focus on particular issues. A good example of targeting niche markets by attending to environmental issues is Inside Climate News. It is aimed at the niche market of environmental news, intending to contribute to stopping climate change. David Sassoon and Stacy Feldman started Inside Climate News as a blog in 2007. It then received financial sponsorship from NEO, a philanthropic organisation. It won the 2013 Pulitzer Prize in national reporting for its report on an oil spill in the Kalamazoo River. TechCrunch is also a good example of targeting a niche market. In 2005, its founder, Michael Arrington, started it as a blog to write about (Internet) tech people and companies. Quickly, TechCrunch attracted massive page views and the attention of entrepreneurs and venture capitalists. In 2006, after TechCrunch was the first to cover the news of YouTube's acquisition by Google, it became a completely news-focused outlet.

In terms of promoting social values, the above-mentioned Inside Climate News is an example of promoting environmentalism. Mediapart is another example of using values – press freedom, independent reporting and the pursuit of truth – as resources (Mediapart, 2017). These values polish up their brands, differentiate them from other content providers and build their own community of loyal followers.

Is It Still Journalism?

Questions, such as who can be seen as journalists, what is journalism, and what should journalists do, have been at the heart of our understanding of journalism. Traditionally, journalism refers to an occupation that is attached to media organisations, which hire journalists to produce credible and accurate news items. Professional routines, conventions and norms set the standards for ethical journalism practice. Journalists are expected to serve the public interest and democracy. A clear separation of advertising operations from editorial operations should be made, so as to guarantee the quality and impartiality of journalism, as the latter should be preserved and protected from the power of the markets.

Entrepreneurial journalism is both different and similar to traditional journalism (see Table 7.1 for a comparison). The practice of entrepreneurial journalism has almost completely changed the relationship of these journalists to organisations and the nature of their work. The professional role of entrepreneurial journalists moves them away from being attached to news organisations and towards becoming individual and independent. The fact that entrepreneurial journalistic outlets may only be run by one, or a small number, of individual journalists suggests a deinstitutionalised tendency for the workforce, in which journalistic work is individualised. As discussed earlier in this book, one significant aspect of this data age is that work and jobs have become more individualised and flexible than they were in the industrial era. The emergence of entrepreneurial journalism is part of this individualised and flexible work-related trend.

That journalist entrepreneurs may take on multiple roles, ranging from being reporters to marketing, rewrites the concept of journalism in relation to what journalists can and

Table 7.1 Comparison between entrepreneurial journalism and traditional journalism

Comparison	Entrepreneurial journalism	Traditional journalism
Differences	Journalists need to take on multiple roles such as content production, distribution, marketing, brand building and promotion, fundraising and website building and maintenance	Journalists take on a single role as content producers and distributors
	Journalists practise both journalism and business	Journalists practise journalism
	Blurred boundaries between editorial and business operations	Clear boundaries between editorial and business operations
	Journalists need to learn multiple skills in areas ranging from journalism to marketing, fundraising and website building	Journalists need to learn skills mainly in journalistic production, such as writing, making videos and audios, and editing
	Journalists and their work are individual and deinstitutionalised	Journalists and their work are attached to employers' news organisations
Similarities	The role of journalism in democracy and society; serving the public interest	

should do. The roles of creating and disseminating content and generating revenue have converged. The division between advertising and editorial roles has blurred, in particular, in cases where news outlets are run by one or two people, who thus have to look after all aspects of their business. This may cause ethical problems for entrepreneurial journalism, such as the boundaries between editorial operations and advertising becoming unclear (which will be further discussed later in this chapter). When journalism start-ups become successful and reach a certain size, such as BuzzFeed and TechCrunch, however, they may be run in the same way as traditional news organisations would be.

At the same time, traditional journalistic practices and ideals continue in entrepreneurial journalism. Although entrepreneurial journalism is often seen as innovative and atypical, entrepreneurial journalists may practise journalism in conventional ways. Entrepreneurial journalists have been found to have an unchanged desire to practise quality journalism in a traditional sense. In the French context, for example, an examination of the French journalism start-up, Mediapart, reveals that its operation strengthens rather than challenges a classic understanding of journalism (Wagemans, Witschge, & Deuze, 2016). In the context of India, some journalism start-ups – especially those with 'guardian' social identities – are still trying to preserve or save the role of journalism as a guardian of democracy and of the public interest, and to stick to established news values (Harlow & Chadha, 2019). In another study examining the manifestos of ten for-profit digital news start-ups in the US (Carlson & Usher, 2016), however, journalism start-ups are found to be clarifying both their commitments to, and criticism of, traditional practices, while they try to show they are excellent at innovation.

▬▬▬▬▬ EXERCISE 7.2 ▬▬▬▬▬

Examine an entrepreneurial news outlet of your choice, such as a hyperlocal news site, and compare it to a traditional news outlet, such as *The Guardian*, CNN or the BBC. Try to identify the similarities and differences in their journalism. Think about the crises of journalism, discussed in Chapter 3, and try to answer the following questions: Can entrepreneurial journalism provide quality journalism that traditional journalism may not be able to offer? Can practising entrepreneurial journalism fix the crises of journalism?

Concerns and Issues Surrounding Entrepreneurial Journalism

The practices of independent and innovative journalism start-ups and their ability to cope with the crises in journalism have been explored in the academic literature (see, for example, Bruno & Nielsen, 2012; Simons, 2013; Coates Nee, 2014; Cohen, 2015; Vos & Singer, 2016; Singer, 2018; Mutiara & Priyonggo, 2020). Three interrelated concerns arise in the literature over the practices of entrepreneurial journalism: (1) the blurring of the boundaries between the editorial and business sides; (2) the tricky balance between serving the interests of the funders and the public interest; and (3) sustainability.

(1) The blurring of the boundaries and (2) the tricky balance

The first two issues concern the multiple roles taken on by journalism entrepreneurs, which may impair the commitment of journalism to democracy. The boundaries between the editorial and advertising sections are blurring in entrepreneurial journalism, particularly in those projects that involve selling advertising to raise money. Tensions exist between the 'public mission and social role' of journalism and 'profit and individualism' (Siapera & Papadopoulou, 2016: 178). Attracting funding from donors is seen as actually 'selling' the audience to them, which turns the audience into 'consumers' (Hunter, 2016). A study of crowd-funded journalism projects in four European countries – Germany, Italy, the UK and the Netherlands – and the US reveals that accountability and transparency remain ethical issues in these projects (Porlezza & Splendore, 2016). In addition to these tensions, for journalists who have sought crowd-funding, their awareness of the need to be responsible to their funders, suggests a danger that crowd-funding may impair objectivity and result in advocacy journalism (Hunter, 2015). This particular method of getting funding will thus make journalists prone to – and even advocate for – the interests of its patrons, no matter whether they are individuals or organisations.

The fundamental question thus is: whether, and to what extent, entrepreneurialism is in tension, or is even incompatible, with journalism's democratic role? Supporters (see, for example, Manfredi & Artero, 2014) argue that the practice of entrepreneurial journalism is beneficial to democracy, as entrepreneurial journalists can be free from the influence and interference of news organisations in their journalistic work. Successful stories, such as the role played by the Drudge Report in revealing the Clinton-Lewinsky scandal (see Box 2.5 in Chapter 2), demonstrate entrepreneurial journalism's potential to speak out using its independent voices, and to take social responsibility that the legacy news media have presumably failed to fully shoulder. By targeting (hyper-)local audiences, the practice of entrepreneurial journalism can also help to revive (hypo-)local journalism.

However, opponents (see, for example, Rottwilm, 2014) believe that entrepreneurial journalists still encounter restrictions. In addition, the fact that they need to take on a wide range of roles, ranging from marketing to fundraising and project management, may compromise – or even sacrifice – journalistic principles and journalism's commitment to serving the public interest. The need to seek financial sustainability may potentially compromise independent and quality editorial practice. In the German context, for example, in 12 digital entrepreneurial outlets, the journalistic autonomy of the founders and editorial staff was limited by their struggles to secure funding and their dual duties to practise journalism and raise funds (Heft & Dogruel, 2019).

(3) Sustainability

Journalism practitioners invent their own jobs by launching digital entrepreneurial journalism projects. These projects, making the most of Internet-based platforms and resources, can help ease the problem of job losses in the news industry. The sustainability of these entrepreneurial journalism projects, however, is an unresolvable, persistent problem. Although its creation and running costs may be relatively low, an

Internet-based media outlet still requires a substantial financial income to keep going. Entrepreneurial journalists thus must find viable funding to survive and succeed. Online journalism start-ups, however, often have financial difficulties (particularly) in their early years (see, for example, the cases discussed in Briggs, 2012 and Wagemans et al., 2016). Although crowd-funding may liberate journalists, some journalists may be reluctant to carry out business duties (Chadha & Koliska, 2016). They may only have limited entrepreneurial skills and inadequate knowledge of the market. With a limited understanding of business, they may not excel at – or even be unfamiliar with – starting and running a business (Buschow, 2020; Price, 2017; Wagemans et al., 2016).

Many journalism projects, therefore, have failed or are unsustainable. *Contributoria*, for example, was backed by The Guardian Media Group and was 'a service for making independent journalism' (www.contributoria.com). Starting in January 2014, it experimented with 'community-funded collaborative journalism' – a funding model mainly relying on membership for journalism community members and other types of funding sources, such as crowd-funding and sponsorship. It published 787 articles and brought in over £26,000 for its authors (Albeanu, 2015). However, it closed in September 2015. Another example of failed journalism projects is The Correspondent (the English language platform), an online, ad-free platform for 'unbreaking news'. Following a successful crowd-funding campaign in 2018 it was launched in 2019 and relied on membership subscriptions. With a significant number of membership cancellations in late 2020, the membership-based journalism outlet was not financially sustainable. It stopped publishing in January 2021, due to 'financial setbacks' (The Correspondent, 2021).

Associated with these three concerns are some key problems faced by entrepreneurial journalism, including enormous stress and psychological costs, the problem of credibility, and the risk of facing expensive lawsuits. The labour involved in crowd-funding and campaigns can be quite extensive and increase workload and stress (Hunter, 2016). Central to the crisis of credibility is the quality of writing. Such criticism can be dated back to the mass media era when most independent media were criticised for being sloppy with journalism basics such as spelling, punctuation and quotations (Lowenstein & Merrill, 1990). In traditional newsrooms, the news is published after going through a whole process of writing, fact-checking, editing and subediting. The shortage of human resources in independent news start-ups means that they may skip the process of checking, and thus the quality and credibility of their content may be reduced. The editorial integrity and quality of independent entrepreneurial news outlets is thus questionable.

Journalistic entrepreneurs may also be vulnerable to lawsuits. Big media houses hire their own legal teams to do pre-publication checks and provide post-publication services. However, for independent small-scale entrepreneurial news outlets, if it comes to lawsuits, they may not be able to afford costly legal fees, let alone their own legal teams. Filing a lawsuit against the media is not new. Laws such as libel, privacy, copyright, fraud, sedition and obscenity have been used to censor or punish the media (Lowenstein & Merrill, 1990). In many cases, by using legislation, plaintiffs want to force the media to give up, because they cannot afford the expensive legal costs; this type of lawsuit is called a Strategic Lawsuit Against Public Participation (SLAPP) (Kakar, 2018).

Independent media outlets are thus threatened by an increase in the number of libel lawsuits, imposing enormous financial penalties against them. In 2017, The Shift News, a small-scale Maltese investigative journalism outlet, for example, was facing a SLAPP lawsuit threat from Henley and Partners, a company that wanted them to withdraw an article about its suspected involvement in a scandal in Grenada (Hyvarinen, 2018; The Shift Team, 2017). In 2018, European MEPs urged the European Commission to protect independent media against SLAPP lawsuits that were being brought and used by powerful private parties to intimidate and silence these outlets (Kakar, 2018).

Summary of the Chapter

This chapter discusses the key aspects of entrepreneurial journalism. It starts with an introduction to the concept of entrepreneurial journalism and the idea of entrepreneurialism. It then addresses why journalism needs entrepreneurialism before examining its implications for journalism, as well as the challenges faced by it.

END OF CHAPTER EXERCISE

As discussed in the chapter, in traditional journalism, a clear distinction between editorial and advertising departments lies at the heart of ethical journalism practice. In other words, to remain independent, journalism should stay distant, and protect itself, from the commercial interests of news organisations and advertisers. However, when it comes to entrepreneurial journalism, entrepreneurial journalists may need to take on multiple roles, including seeking and securing funding for their start-ups. Will this need to perform various tasks across both business and journalism mean that there are compromises in relation to journalists' commitment to serving democracy? Can journalists turn themselves into entrepreneurs without sacrificing their democratic conscience? Think about these questions and try to develop your answers to them by examining two or three entrepreneurial journalism projects of your choice.

FURTHER READING

Rafter, Kevin (Ed.). (2018). *Entrepreneurial Journalism*. London and New York: Routledge. This book offers a detailed account of the concept and practice of entrepreneurial journalism and the ethical issues that surround its practices.

Rafter, Kevin (Ed.). (2016). Special issue of *Journalism Practice*, *10*(2) on Entrepreneurial Journalism. This special issue is composed of papers examining entrepreneurial journalism from different angles, including media discourse, ethical issues, business models, the job satisfaction of entrepreneurial journalists and journalism education.

EIGHT

UNDERSTANDING THE AUDIENCE

- Why do we need to study the audience?
- How has the concept of the audience changed in the data age?
- How has the relationship between journalism and its audience changed?
- What do these changes mean for journalism?
- How do news organisations understand and measure audiences and their news consumption behaviour?
- How does the use of audience metrics by news organisations influence journalism and newsrooms?

---

audience	prosumer
the active audience	audience metrics
the passive audience	news consumption
the diffused audience	sharing
the elusive audience	Social Media Optimisation (SMO)
produser	Search Engine Optimisation (SEO)

With audiences able to choose, create and disseminate content, not only the concept of the audience has changed but also a new relationship has emerged between audiences and journalists. This chapter, aimed at outlining the shifting dynamics of audiences in the data age, will start with a discussion of the importance of studying audiences for understanding journalism. It then briefly addresses the characteristics of the audience in the past before discussing their features in the data age. After that, the chapter will examine the implications of these changes for understanding the relationship between journalism and audiences. It will also explore the audience measurements used by news organisations, and their possible impact on journalism and newsrooms. The final part of the chapter will look at news organisations' social media audience engagement strategies.

Why Study Audiences?

It is vital to study audiences not only because journalists and audiences are two necessary parts of communication, but also because audiences are a crucial determinant of media revenue. Traditionally, audiences pay for journalism content, while advertisers pay for the audiences of journalism. In this sense, audiences are the lifeblood of journalism. Without audiences, journalism cannot thrive or even survive. Understanding and connecting to audiences has become tremendously important for news organisations in the wake of their persistent financial difficulties, as knowledge of audiences is an essential premise for effectively reaching target audiences and engaging with them as citizens and subscribers.

The dramatic changes in audiences' news consumption behaviour also make it crucial to study audiences. As we have discussed in previous chapters, along with the popularity of digital technologies, audiences can choose, produce and disseminate content and interact with journalists. Accordingly, the news consumption behaviour of audiences has undergone unprecedented changes. These changes are partly the result of the digitisation, digitalisation and datafication of social lives. They are partly caused by shifting social dynamics, such as the formation of the network society (see Box 2.1 in Chapter 2) and the emergence of ephemerality (see Box 2.8 in Chapter 2) as a characteristic of post-modern consumption and economies. Understanding audiences' news consumption behaviour in the data age enables us to comprehend the potential impact of audiences' everyday lives and tastes on journalism and the operation of newsrooms in the digital world.

━━━━━━━ **EXERCISE 8.1** ━━━━━━━

Before proceeding to read the remainder of the chapter, ask yourself the question: if you were going to write a news article, who is this news story for, and who is your target audience? As a student journalist, would you consider who your audiences are and change your writing style to suit different groups of audiences? Would your consideration of the interests of audiences influence your decision on the selection of story topics and angles? After having finished reading this chapter, you can have another look at your answers to these questions. Think about how the changes in audiences and the relationship between journalism and audiences influence journalism.

What Is the Audience?

Denis McQuail, a communications scholar, gives a classic definition that the 'word *audience* has long been familiar as the collective term for the "receivers" in the simple sequential model of the mass communication process (source, channel, message, receiver, effect) that was deployed by pioneers in the field of media research' (McQuail, 1997: 1, italics in original). While McQuail's explanation well captures the idea of the audience as the receivers of messages, however, the concept of the audience is not that straightforward. The audience are the receivers and consumers who consume the products of the news media, and, meanwhile, they are 'products', sold by the news media to advertisers (Smythe, 1977). The concept of the audience is also increasingly related to, and entangled with, that of 'publics', whose participation and civic engagement and actions are central to a democracy. Its concept is thus entwined with that of 'citizens', whose votes in elections should ideally be well informed by the news media.

The concept of the audience has been transformed in tandem with the changes in society and communication (technologies). It has first shifted from being a passive audience to being an active audience. Later, more diverse concepts of the audience have appeared, such as the 'diffused audience' and the 'elusive audience' (both concepts will be discussed later in this chapter). Fuelled by the proliferation of information communication technologies and social transitions, audiences have become increasingly individualised, privatised and fragmented.

Audiences before the data age

In their book *Audiences: A Sociological Theory of Performance and Imagination*, sociologists, Nick Abercrombie and Brian Longhurst discussed the three types of audience – 'the simple audience, the mass audience and the diffused audience' (Abercrombie & Longhurst, 1998: 39). With this typology, they nicely described how the concept of audience has changed in the mass-media age, in particular, the television period. From the simple audience through to the diffused audience, the power of audiences increases, the relationship between audiences and performers changes, and media consumption becomes more privatised and fragmented.

Traditional 'simple audiences' refer to a group of individuals who gather in public areas, such as theatres or ceremonies, to consume (listen, watch or read) a particular form of the media together. They physically co-locate with performers. They are individuals who decide to view the media with others at the same time and in the same place. There is direct communication between audiences and performers (Abercrombie & Longhurst, 1998).

With the popularity of mass media, such as books, newspapers, magazines, radio, TV and cinema, this traditional understanding of the audience has been replaced by the concept of the mass (media) audience. Although still voluntarily consuming media content, the mass audience is larger in size and more dispersed and privatised than the simple audience. Production time and space are also separate from reception time and space. Moreover, performers and audiences no longer locate in the same place when media consumption takes place. Mass media consumption fits into everyday lives and activities and may happen at the same time as other daily activities. When it comes to news media and journalism, the relationship between journalism and audiences is asymmetric as the role played by the audience is limited to selectively receiving the information offered by journalists.

The shift from the simple to the mass audience happened against the background of the formation of mass society. Modernisation, industrialisation and urbanisation propelled this change. People who moved from their home villages or towns to urban cities were uprooted and lost contact with their original communities. The introduction of mass production machines reduced working time and increased leisure time for workers. All of these changes created needs for media consumption in mass society. Afterwards, fragmented markets and consumption behaviour emerged as a result of further changes in society, such as the collapse of the Fordist model of mass production, the rise of a flexible system of production (see Box 8.1 in Chapter 8), and the cultivation of consumers' ephemeral tastes and interests (see Box 2.8 in Chapter 2 for a discussion of ephemerality). These developments in the broader environment are an integral part of the process in which the diffused audience, and later audiences in the data age, appear.

▬▬▬▬▬ BOX 8.1 ▬▬▬▬▬

A shift from Fordist to flexible production

The Fordist model of mass production (and consumption) prevailed in the post-war world. However, it encountered a crisis after the 1970s. A major reason for this crisis was the rigidities of Fordism. Flexible production – a new system of the organisation of production and consumption – has emerged along with the advent and popularity of digital technologies. In this system, a typical scenario, for example, is that (flexibly) contracted workers use computerised machinery to fit together products in order to meet the rapidly shifting tastes of consumers. Such flexibility is reflected in labour processes, labour markets, products and consumption. See the detailed discussions in Ankie Hoogvelt's *Globalisation and the Postcolonial World* (Chapter 5: 'From Fordist to flexible production') (Hoogvelt, 1997: 90–113).

The idea of the 'diffused audience' describes a state in which media penetration and consumption is omnipresent and thus becomes woven into everyday life. No longer limited to being present in a particular time and space, being a member of the audience is part of the daily experience (Livingstone, 2005). In other words, mass media have become part of everyday life and are always on in the background. Another aspect of the concept of the 'diffused audience' is that the pervasiveness of the media turns audiences into an 'audience and performer at the same time' (Abercrombie & Longhurst, 1998: 68–69). The heavy consumption of the media makes them constitutive of the everyday life of the audience member. Audiences' zeal in recording and publishing their daily life and in being looked at makes their life 'a constant performance'. With the concept of the 'diffused audience', these authors (e.g. Abercrombie & Longhurst, 1998 and Livingstone, 2005) believe that media consumption has become part of everyday experience, audiences are active, and the boundaries between audiences and producers are blurred.

The term the 'elusive audience' refers to the predicament faced by media institutions in the wake of the increasing individualisation and fragmentation of audiences. This concept arose in discussions about the crisis in the measurement of the television audience as a result of the magnitude of viewing choices made available to them by communication technologies such as the videocassette recorder (VCR) and the proliferation of TV channels (Ang, 1991). Since then these choices have only proliferated with the advent of catch-up and streaming services. The debates about the death of the audience in the Internet age (see, for example, Livingstone & Das, 2013) resemble discussions about the disappearing TV audience. On top of these concepts is the trend towards supplanting the notion of 'audiences' with that of 'users' (see, for example, Lievrouw & Livingstone, 2002).

The conceptual shift of audiences, discussed above, signals the paradigmatic change from the passive audience to the active audience. The passive audience means that audiences sit at the receiving end of mass communication and are passively influenced by the media's strong effects. Famous experiments, like 'The War of the Worlds' radio programme in 1938 (see Box 8.2), and Bandura's Bobo Doll Experiment (see Box 8.3), confirm such strong media effects.

Later on, scholars (see, for example, Katz, Blumler, & Gurevitch, 1973 and Hall, 1980) from both sides of the Atlantic began to pay more attention to what audiences choose to consume, how they make their choices and how they actively interpret what they see and hear, as shown in Uses and Gratifications Theory (see Box 8.4) and in Encoding and Decoding Theory (see Box 8.5). These new concepts of the audience: the diffused audience, the elusive audience, and audiences as users advance the idea of the 'active' audience.

BOX 8.2

'The War of the Worlds' radio programme in 1938

'The War of the Worlds' radio programme was broadcast in 1938. In the radio show, it was announced that Martians were invading the Earth. The radio drama created a panic among the American population, and some people even fled their homes. This programme is seen as an example of strong media effects, i.e., the media casting a strong influence on audiences.

---- **BOX 8.3** ----

Bobo Doll Experiment

Bandura and his colleagues designed the famous Bobo Doll Experiment to test whether children would copy the physically aggressive actions shown on a film in real-life situations. The results of the experiment were interpreted as confirmation that children were likely to imitate the violence they see on the screen (Bandura, Ross, & Ross, 1963). This experiment is seen as a classic study confirming strong media effects (also see Chapter 4 in Bryant, Thompson, & Finklea, 2013, for further discussion). However, there has been criticism about whether the children's imitative behaviour can be interpreted as aggression (see, for example, Tedeschi & Quigley, 1996).

---- **BOX 8.4** ----

Uses and Gratifications Theory

The advocators of Uses and Gratifications Theory argued that the media compete with other sources to gratify the needs of audiences (Katz et al. 1973).

---- **BOX 8.5** ----

Encoding and Decoding Theory

In the UK, one of the most famous and seminal theories about the active audience is the Encoding and Decoding Theory that was advanced by Stuart Hall (Hall, 1980). He argued that media practitioners encode messages according to dominant ideologies, and therefore these messages contain 'dominant or preferred meanings'. Audiences decode the messages and may respond in three different ways: (1) 'dominant reading' – audiences accept the preferred reading, although it may or may not have been the intention of the author(s); (2) 'negotiated reading' – audiences partly accept, but partly resist or change the preferred reading, and their opinions, values and backgrounds influence their resistance or negotiation; and (3) 'oppositional reading' – audiences reject the preferred reading, although they understand it (Hall, 1980).

The next section will discuss the features of audiences in the data age. In this era, the individualisation and fragmentation of audiences, observed by scholars in the late 1990s and early 21st century, have been significantly heightened and deepened.

Audiences in the data age

The data age has taken the individualisation, fragmentation, privatisation and interactivity of audiences to a new level. Audiences, ceasing to exist as collectives, become fragmented individuals in the networked world. The content they consume is diverse and individualised. In theory, they can decide what content to read and when, and in which order; they want to do so without limitations – although, in practice, their ability to choose may be influenced by contextual factors, such as their living environment and the financial affordability of related technologies. While 'broadcast' audiences have dissipated, 'narrowcast' audiences – which are small, niche audiences – have appeared under the sway of the rise of the individualisation and personalisation of their consumption behaviour.

Audiences subscribe to news feeds or apps that deliver news to their mobiles (see Chapter 4 for a discussion of app-based news delivery). Portable electronic devices and news apps enable them to access subscribed content anywhere. The customisation features of news websites or apps on their mobile devices allow them not only to consume content of interest but also to ignore other content. The proliferation of content providers has also led to the unprecedented diversity and multiplicity of media content. Content providers include the broad spectrum of TV channels, subscription-based content providers, like Netflix and Amazon Prime, news aggregators, like Google and Yahoo!, social media platforms, like YouTube, Facebook, Twitter and Instagram, and even independent digital journalism websites. Audiences can choose content that is related to their interests but may not necessarily be news stories.

Sharing is a distinctive feature of audiences' news consumption behaviour in the data age. Audiences are networked, getting used to receiving news and links from family and friends. They receive news stories from those they know and read news articles based on the recommendations of people they trust. News organisations, of course, can benefit from such social recommendation to extend their audience reach. However, by drawing each other's attention to particular topics, the audience's sharing habits may circumvent the agenda-setting of the news media and journalists. Influenced by the 'echo-chamber' effect (see Box 8.6), sharing may lead to the further fragmentation of audiences. For this reason, the popularity of sharing – social (media) recommendation – will further undermine news organisations' established business models, which are based on their ability to deliver large, aggregated audiences to advertisers.

━━━━━━━━ **BOX 8.6** ━━━━━━━━

The 'echo-chamber' effect

The 'echo-chamber' effect refers to a phenomenon in which like-minded users share information with each other. This effect may strengthen the existing values and opinions of users and thus facilitate the formation of polarisation on the Internet and of segmentation in society. There are, however, counterarguments in the literature, which reject the existence of the 'echo-chamber' effect. You can find the related discussion in the next section.

In the data age, audiences can participate in public communication mainly through two means. First, by producing content on the Internet, audiences have become content producers. Some – but not all – of them are seen as practising citizen journalism or grassroots journalism. Second, with their content incorporated into the news by professional journalists, users who generate such content are seen as participating in news production. Their participation – although the inclusion of their content is subject to journalists' selection – is labelled participatory journalism or participatory news. By creating their own content, sharing and reacting to news content, for instance by pressing 'like' or making comments, audiences have become content producers, as well as promoters of news content. However, in most cases, their labour for doing so will not receive any financial rewards (although some users who publish content on the Internet, such as vloggers (video-bloggers), may receive enormous financial rewards through carrying advertisements on their programmes when they become popular).

The participation of audiences in online communication can be described with some old and new concepts. These concepts are similar and all refer to the joint efforts of people sitting on either side of the communication process and the blurring of the previously clear division between these two groups of people – content producers and audiences. The idea of the 'produser' refers to a combination of producers and users in producing media content (Bruns, 2008b). A similar term 'prosumer' is an older concept referring to a mixture of producers and consumers emerging in the third wave of the information society (Toffler, 1980). Likewise, the idea of 'productive consumption' has emerged to describe the dynamic collaborations between producers and consumers (Laughey, 2010: 110). The concept of 'pro-ams' describes the combined efforts of professionals and amateurs in producing news content with the aim of changing our society. These concepts nicely portray the ubiquitous public participation in communication that is facilitated by digital technologies, such as Web 2.0 tools and portable electronic devices.

Therefore, today's audiences are no longer just audiences in the passive sense but a group of people who find, produce, 'remix', verify and distribute content (see the discussion about remixing and remixability in Chapter 2). The asymmetry between journalism's 'performance role' and audiences' communication receiver role, discussed above, abates with journalism losing its monopoly of communication to the audience. The latter now has more power to create their own content. Being digital endows audiences with a high degree of autonomy in deciding what to consume and enables them to enter a collaborative relationship with content producers. Crowd-sourcing, as used in cases such as that of the 2009 MPs' expenses scandal in the UK (discussed in Chapter 5), for example, turns audiences into collaborators with journalists. Furthermore, audiences may become sponsors or funders in crowd-funding projects for entrepreneurial journalism (discussed in Chapter 7). No matter whether audiences support journalism through subscribing to memberships or making donations to sponsor a single entrepreneurial journalism project, crowd-funding moulds the relationship between journalism and audiences into that of journalism and funders.

EXERCISE 8.2

Critically evaluate the impact of the collaboration between audiences and journalists on journalism. Does this collaboration influence the content journalists produce, and thus weaken the cultural authority and legitimacy of journalists? If so, why, and to what extent? (Discussions about cultural authority and legitimacy can be found in Chapter 10.)

Three issues relating to audiences: homophilous, disoriented and apolitical

Audiences in the data age tend to be homophilous, disoriented and apolitical. **Homophily**, a concept bearing a resemblance to that of the 'echo-chamber' effect (see Box 8.6), refers to the phenomenon in which people like to connect with those who share similar beliefs, rather than with those holding different or even opposing viewpoints.

The existing studies on audiences, however, have contrasting arguments about whether they have become increasingly homophilous or heterogeneous. One side of the debate views each of the fragmented audience groups as comprising like-minded people, separated from each other with no, or few, interactions (Sunstein, 2007). Audience segmentation started from before the data age. In the data age, however, the Internet has worsened the situation. Political echo chambers are formed on the Internet of those who like to connect and interact with others who share a similar political ideology (Boutyline & Willer, 2017). Audiences tend to stay in the zones of like-minded media, which become echo chambers reflecting and amplifying the same views, suggesting the tendency to polarisation and homophily in audiences.

On the other side of the debate, scholars have also found evidence that does not suggest audience segmentation and homophily. The echo-chamber theory (see Box 8.6) is criticised for being overstated. Variations and diversity have also been found in audience segregation (Gentzkow & Shapiro, 2010). Researchers have also found that overlaps between audience groups exist (Webster & Ksiazek, 2012). Such overlaps mark the recognisable interactions between different audience groups. Although inclining to be increasingly exposed to opinions that are similar to their own views, American audiences may not necessarily avoid contact with opposing viewpoints (Garrett, 2009). In the UK, a survey-based study has found that due to the complexity of the media environment, only a tiny proportion of the whole population discover themselves in 'an echo chamber' (Dubois & Blank, 2018).

Disorientation, the second issue, is about audiences' attention and comprehension. In the data age, audiences may be headline readers with short attention spans and no genuine interest in long reads. Although potentially engaging readers, providing them with more background details and enlarging the information space infinitely, the prevalence of hypertext and non-linear reading (see Box 4.4) on the Internet may create a problem of disorientation. Audiences, navigating through web pages or apps, may be distracted from what they had planned to read. The distraction problem describes the potential of a user to become lost in hypertext when reading it, as they need to make additional efforts to stick to their original reading plan. Hypertext may create incoherence, divert the focus of readers and confuse their comprehension.

The third issue identified for audiences in the data age is making them **apolitical** – a multitude of entertainment content has the potential to distract audiences from consuming topics of social importance. Online audiences' apolitical appetite for sensational and entertaining content may lead to the decline of serious journalism, and to a sharp rise in tabloid-type media, including sports and celebrity journalism. However, in some cases, entertainment content may also be able to contribute to the construction of the public sphere. For example, in the context of Rwanda, although they are apolitical, entertainment websites are seen as still able to create 'a digital youth public' (Grant, 2019).

EXERCISE 8.3

In Exercise 2.1, you were invited to record your media consumption habits. In this exercise, why not have another look at your records completed in Exercise 2.1, carry out a critical reflection on how you consume media content and what types of media content you consume, and ask if, and to what extent, they illustrate the three problems discussed in this section.

Journalism and Audiences

This section will discuss the implications of the changes in audiences for journalism in relation to four aspects: (1) the emergence of a shared relationship between (news) producers and audiences; (2) the changing journalistic practices and shifting concept of the news; (3) news organisations' efforts to understand audiences; and (4) engaging audiences on social media and the consequences of such engagement.

(1) The emergence of a shared relationship between (news) producers and audiences

The above-mentioned concepts of 'produser', 'prosumer' and 'pro-am' suggest that the level of activity and the interactivity of digital audiences have eroded the distinction between (news) production and consumption, as well as between producers (the author) and audiences (the reader). This erosion started from an early stage of online communication since audiences have been able to write, publish and distribute online content to other fellow Internet users. News of events, especially emergencies, such as earthquakes, tsunamis and protests, are likely to break on the Internet. Ordinary people have been hailed as 'grassroots journalists' and 'we the media' (Gillmor, 2006). In this sense, the idea of the author of the first draft of history has been rewritten. As soon as journalists started to incorporate user-generated content (UGC) into professional news programmes, audiences began to enter into a collaborative relationship with journalists in news production.

The traditional journalistic gate-keeping process is thus 'opened' up. Traditionally, news organisations sent out trained professional journalists to gather information, produce news stories and send them back to the editor's desk to be edited through the editorial hierarchy, published and disseminated to audiences. After the publication of news stories, selected but limited audience feedback may be published. Today, however, media outlets open up their 'gates' by welcoming the participation of ordinary users in getting news stories and interacting with journalists. These changes in the gate-keeping process indicate a more shared relationship between reporters and their audiences, and suggest that news is becoming a conversation, rather than a lecture (Bruns, 2008a). In addition, the user-driven circulation of the news on social media further changes the relationship of journalism with audiences by reducing journalistic authority in deciding what the public should know, and when they should know about it (Hermida, Fletcher, Korell, & Logan, 2012).

(2) The changing journalistic practices and shifting concept of the news

In compressing the news cycle to hours or even shorter periods of time and pressurising editors about what to report and when, the rise of social media and UGC has fundamentally changed the way news is broken. For news organisations, competing with Internet users to break the news has turned out to be an unwise thing to do. The job of journalists has moved towards interpreting and analysing, rather than describing events (Albæk, 2011). In addition, along with the proliferation of fake news in recent years, social media users increasingly agree that news broken on social media should be fact-checked and verified by the traditional news media (Sparkes, 2014), which offers some positive prospects for journalism, as this means journalism is still much needed. A focus on verifying and curating information about particular emergent events is thus a more sensible approach.

In the meantime, news is required to be always-on on the Internet, as a response to the appearance of an ongoing information system on social media, i.e. the prevalence of social media platforms makes information always available to ordinary users. Despite providing fragmented information, Twitter, for example, has become an ambient system where users receive an ongoing flow of information from both established media and their fellow users and become aware of the occurrence of news and events in the world (Hermida, 2010). The emergence of this ambient system has triggered some changes in news and journalistic practices.

The birth of live blogs (or live blogging) (discussed in Chapter 4) is a prominent example of journalism adapted to the need to be always-on on the Internet. The creation of live blogs is the result of news organisations trying to incorporate content that is generated by users and to make the best of the activity and interactivity of audiences. However, this form of dissemination turns news into an open and ongoing process, and an endless news hole that has to be filled all day long and that will involve continuous contributions from audiences.

This ambient information system also provides journalists with enormous news sources for their news stories where they may quote related social media posts published by users who are involved in an event, or who happen to be on the scene when an event occurs. In addition, the fact that the online activities of Internet users will leave a (data) trail means that the Internet becomes an enormous archive of data, on which journalists can draw for their investigations (see the discussion about data and journalism in Chapter 5).

(3) Moving from ignoring audiences to trying to understand audiences: audience analysis and measurements

Conventionally, although advertising departments might be eager to understand audiences in terms of their demographics, income and consumption behaviour, editors and journalists have difficulty – or more precisely reluctance – in understanding their audiences, with little knowledge of audiences and little attention paid to audience feedback (Turow & Draper, 2014). They have been criticised for ignoring the audience, being obsessed with self-reference and having an 'in-group orientation', which means that their journalistic peers or key national news media rather than the audience have the most influence on what is seen to be news (Deuze, 2008; Donsbach, 2004). In his seminal book *Deciding What's News*, Gans (1979: xviii–xix, and 230) noted:

> [M]ost journalists still shun audience research, pay little attention to the characteristics of their actual audience, and continue to see themselves and people like them as audiences they seek to reach.

> I was surprised to find, however, that they [journalists] had little knowledge about the actual audience and rejected feedback from it. Although they had a vague image of audiences, they paid little attention to it; instead, they filmed and wrote for their superiors and for themselves, assuming, as I suggested earlier, that what interested them would interest audiences.

Gans' quote accurately reflects the classic mentality of journalists – especially those working in quality newspapers – towards their audience, which is that journalists should decide what is in the public interest and, thus, what audiences should read. Meanwhile, they do not care much about what audiences want.

In the data age, with algorithm-facilitated audience measurements, journalists' attitudes towards, and understanding of, audiences have fundamentally changed. Behind this radical change is news organisations' determination to measure and understand audiences, making crucial the algorithms that underlie audience measurements. Most audience measurement methods record the online activities of Internet users, or the information that is typed in by themselves; the data collected can be used to measure the audience. Audiences are measured by the frequencies, time-duration or actual content of their activities, such as hits and ratings. Site or web-based analytics measure things, such as the number of unique visitors, page views (per visit), the amounts of time spent on the site, online traffic, traffic source/access locations, and search terms (see Webster, Phalen, & Lichty, 2014 for a systematic and detailed introduction to audience measurements and analytics).

The use of audience measurement analytics has impacted upon journalistic practices and newsroom cultures. For example, the use of web analytics by online journalists in the US influenced the news production process, including their processes of decision-making; by this means editorial judgement is influenced by audience preferences (Tandoc, 2015). The process of gate-keeping is, thus, changed by web analytics, as web metrics become the determining criteria of news selection and judgement (Tandoc, 2014).

The impact of audience measurements on journalism varies. Interviews with journalists in Austria, for example, disclosed variations in the influence of audience analytics on journalistic norms, practice and culture caused by contextual factors such as journalists' hierarchical positions, organisational cultures and the different platforms' influence on news making (Hanusch, 2017). Likewise, a study of Al Jazeera English Online revealed the decisive role played by the institutional culture of the news organisation in influencing journalists' use and understanding of audience metrics (Usher, 2013).

Scholars have been highly critical of the use of audience metrics in journalism, being primarily concerned with the consequences of audience metrics on news values, selection, gate-keeping and journalists' professional norms (see, for example, Lee, Lewis, & Powers, 2014; Tandoc, 2014, 2015; Vu, 2014; Welbers, van Atteveldt, Kleinnijenhuis, Ruigrok, & Schaper, 2016). Data collected about audiences – including their demography, online presence, the time spent on visiting web pages and reading particular posts, and even the tracking of their eye movements while they are exploring online content – gives news organisations a good idea of their audiences. However, this knowledge may drive news organisations towards catering to audiences' interests and influences their decisions about which stories to report and how to cover them (Mitchell & Rosenstiel, 2011). Audience measurements may influence news judgement by pushing journalists to take into account what audiences want, as shown in numbers such as the click rates that certain types of news stories receive (Anderson, 2011). In addition, evaluating news stories' impact by looking at the quantity of Internet traffic, or online hit rates will result in pursuing the interests of audiences instead of the public interest.

Therefore, web analytics may make journalism more prone to the influence of the market, as the success and quality of news articles may be judged mainly by the amount of viewers, page views or forwarding on social media. An online survey with 358 news journalists in Australia, for example, found that journalists' exposure to audience feedback through web analytics was associated with their perceptions of the importance of market and consumer orientation (Hanusch & Tandoc, 2019). Allowing web analytics to guide news selection may also impair the cultural authority of journalism in making a judgement on newsworthiness and selecting news for audiences (see more discussions about journalistic authority and legitimacy in Chapter 10). For example, an interesting ethnographic study of a Reuters newswire bureau in Kenya finds that the introduction of audience metrics suited the institutional need to boost profits and enabled managers to more efficiently control and influence journalists. The adoption of audience metrics meant that the resulting dynamics even changed the concept of who counts as a 'good journalist'. As a result, the culture of the newsroom moved away from 'professional values' towards 'profit motivations' (Bunce, 2019).

The heavy reliance on audience data may also create a trend to personalisation, threatening the capacity of the news media to connect with different social groups. While news organisations progressively use algorithms to understand the content preferences of audiences, news websites – for example, those in the US and the UK (Thurman, 2011; Thurman & Schifferes, 2012) – are increasingly personalised and customised. That is to say, the technological features of the websites enable news media to deliver news content to individual users to suit their preferences. Personalisation arguably restrains the relevance of the gate-keeping of journalists, as what audiences receive and consume is no longer decided by journalists but by the algorithms of websites. Personalisation may shape the information flows on the Internet in a way that diminishes diversity. This is because delivering news content according to audiences' preferences means they may only receive the content that they are interested in, while having little chance of being exposed to other types of news content and worldviews.

Scholars (see, for example, Kormelink & Meijer, 2018; Tandoc & Thomas, 2015) call for a critical assessment of the use of user metrics in news work so that journalists can retain their autonomy and maintain the 'communitarian role' of journalism. News workers have also expressed criticism and scepticism in relation to metrics and have come to appreciate that metrics cannot accurately explain the genuine interests of audiences, an understanding of which requires more in-depth and qualitative research with audiences. For example, journalists have been found to be sceptical about whether the figures collected by metrics can show the success of a journalism project, as exemplified in the study of data journalists in the US (Fink & Anderson, 2015).

EXERCISE 8.4

In terms of using audience metrics in news work, do you think this is essential for today's newsroom? How should newsrooms use audience metrics? What consequences might their use have on journalism? Will it enhance the quality of journalism? Will it bring journalists closer to audiences? Will it mean journalists lose control of their work? Will it mean audiences have more power in influencing journalism and the news produced by journalists?

(4) Engaging audiences on social media, and its consequences

In addition to the use of audience metrics, discussed above, social media strategies for content promotion and audience engagement are particularly important for news organisations, or entrepreneurial journalists (see Chapter 7), who want to enhance their reach to audiences. Social Media Optimisation (SMO) and Search Engine Optimisation (SEO) are two common practices. SMO aims to optimise and increase the publicity for news stories on social media. Audiences are encouraged to like, make comments and share the story links across social media sites. The practice of SEO by news organisations, or by entrepreneurial journalists, is undertaken to increase the chances of stories being found in searches on social media and by search engines. The resulting changes have appeared in news writing and the main components of news stories, as news content has to be compelling to its target social media users, and also has to be search engine friendly. To increase SEO, for example, newsrooms have extended the essential elements of a news story to include:

- the page title – words that appear in the title bar at the top of the browser. This is often the same as the story headline but longer, with more keywords;
- the headline – this should stand alone. Never rely on an image to explain a headline;
- the first paragraph of body copy;
- the last paragraph. (Hill & Lashmar, 2014: 209)

These elements are necessary because search engines and social media search algorithms read them. What search engines and social media search algorithms actually read is the related content (tailored to be compatible with search engine indexing and page rank algorithms) contained in the HTML code of a web page. Such content may be the same as, but may be different but similar to, that appearing on the web page (see Table 8.1). In this sense, the key elements that can influence a news article's searchability on search engines are actually hiding in the HTML code of the web page where the article appears.

The need to engage audiences on social media and the strategies employed to do so may further accelerate audience segmentation, individualisation and personalisation. If readers visit different news sites, discrepancies exist in the topics that they encounter. In the online world, however, the extensive use of algorithms tailors news content to suit audiences' preferences and personalises the news audiences receive, which depletes the possibility of being exposed to different news content and values.

Table 8.1 An example of elements of a news article published by *The Guardian* (Elgot & Allegretti, 2021) on the web page and in the HTML code of the web page

Elements on the web page	Elements in the HTML code of the web page
Page title: 'Tory rebels await Speaker's decision on bid to restore aid pledge | Foreign policy | The Guardian' Headline: 'Tory rebels await Speaker's decision on bid to restore aid pledge'	\<title\> Tory rebels await Speaker's decision on bid to restore aid pledge | Foreign policy | The Guardian \</title\>
Topics: 'Foreign policy House of Commons/ Conservatives Aid/Commons Speaker/ Andrew Mitchell/Theresa May/news'	\<meta property= 'article: tag' content = 'Foreign policy, House of Commons, Politics, Society, UK news, Conservatives, Aid, Global development, Commons Speaker, Andrew Mitchell, Theresa May'\>

The influence of the social media strategies of news organisations and entrepreneurial journalists on their business is double-edged. Although these strategies have the potential to help engage and reconnect journalists with their audiences so as to boost revenue, they may also further disturb the incomes of legacy media. This is because legacy media's heavy use of social networking sites may advance the popularity of these sites, and the latter will snatch away more revenue and put traditional news organisations under further financial strain (see further discussion about the financial crisis of the news industry in Chapter 3).

Summary of the Chapter

This chapter discusses the changes in (the concepts of) audiences and their implications for journalism and newsrooms. The transformed relationship between audiences and journalism in the data age is also explored. The discussion in the chapter enables us to understand what the new forms of journalism examined in previous chapters mean for journalism through the lens of the audience. As the changed journalism–audience relationship is one important factor influencing the autonomy and legitimacy of journalism, this chapter also lays the foundation for the discussions in the following two chapters about journalistic autonomy and legitimacy.

■■■■■■ END OF CHAPTER EXERCISE ■■■■■■

By now, you have read about news organisations or entrepreneurial journalists endeavouring to understand and engage audiences in the data age. Think about the following questions: What do they do to achieve this aim? Is it necessary for them to do so? And what impact might their efforts have on journalism, in terms of the quality, practices and cultures of journalism?

FURTHER READING

Abercrombie, Nicholas, and Longhurst, Brian J. (1998). *Audiences: A Sociological Theory of Performance and Imagination*. London, Thousand Oaks, CA, and New Delhi: Sage. This classic book on audience studies nicely encompasses the transition of the audience from the simple audience to the mass audience to the diffused audience. It also discusses the importance of spectacle and performance to the concept of the diffused audience. Although focusing on audiences before the data age, the discussion in the book offers some useful concepts for understanding audiences today.

Loosen, Wiebke, and Schmidt, Jan-Hinrik (2012). (Re-)discovering the audience. *Information, Communication & Society, 15*(6), 867–887. This article discusses the shifting concepts of the audience and the relationship between journalism and its audience, which has been transformed under the influence of technological, organisational and institutional changes.

Hanusch, Folker (2017). Web analytics and the functional differentiation of journalism cultures: individual, organizational and platform-specific influences on newswork. *Information, Communication & Society, 20*(10), 1571–1586. This article addresses the impact of web analytics on journalism cultures and news work. It discusses different levels of influences from individual journalists, organisations and platforms on how journalists and newsrooms interpret and use web analytics in their day-to-day work. The impact of the use of web analytics on the roles, values and norms of journalism is also explored.

NINE
JOURNALISTIC AUTONOMY

━━━━━━━━━━ **KEY QUESTIONS** ━━━━━━━━━━

- What is journalistic autonomy?
- How do digital technologies influence the autonomy of journalistic practice?
- What changes are there in media (self-)regulation and control in the data age? What implications do they have for journalistic autonomy?

━━━━━━━━━━ **KEY CONCEPTS** ━━━━━━━━━━

journalistic autonomy	media regulation
media systems	self-regulation
the power of technology	censorship
media control	self-censorship
the interference of the state	
the power of the market	

Up to now, we have discussed the changes in journalism and its environment under the influence of digital technology. What do these changes mean for journalistic autonomy? Are journalists enjoying more autonomy in their practice and beyond because of these changes? This chapter will explore the transformation of journalistic autonomy in the data age on two levels – the level of journalistic practice, and that of media freedom and journalistic independence (from the state and the market). It will address the concept of journalistic autonomy in the first part before going on to discuss how changes in the communication environment and in journalism, such as the heavy use of web metrics in newsrooms discussed earlier in this book, have influenced the autonomy of journalistic practice. The chapter will examine the implications for journalistic autonomy of the latest developments in media (self-)regulation in democratic countries, and media control in authoritarian societies. Three cases – the UK, the US and China – will be discussed in order to illustrate the main points.

What Is Journalistic Autonomy?

Journalistic autonomy refers to the freedom accorded to journalists to exert control over their practice. It allows journalists to independently carry out their duties of informing citizens, monitoring governments and those in power, and/or advocating certain social values. Gaining journalistic autonomy enables individual journalists to oppose influences coming from within their media organisations and beyond. If conceptualised at the level of media systems, journalistic autonomy is associated with the political domain and is similar to media freedom. The degree of journalistic autonomy at the media-system level can also influence the autonomy experienced by journalists within organisations and in their practice.

At the media-system level, most restrictions journalists experience come from the state and the market. In different media systems (see Box 9.1) journalists experience different levels of autonomy and state interference. Generally speaking, in Western democracies, such as the United States (US) and the United Kingdom (UK), the news media and journalists enjoy relatively high levels of autonomy and mostly comply with media self-regulation and/or regulation. However, in authoritarian countries, such as China and Cuba, the state significantly interferes in the work of the news media, severely restricting journalistic autonomy. In Arab countries, like Egypt and Sudan, laws are even used to limit the freedom of journalism and to intimidate journalists (Amin, 2002).

================== BOX 9.1 ==================

Different models of media systems

Scholars (see, for example, Curran & Park, 2000; Hallin & Mancini, 2004; Siebert, Peterson, & Schramm, 1956) have identified diverse models of media systems at the national level in different regions in the world. These media systems have different levels of state

JOURNALISTIC AUTONOMY | 137

interference in the performance and operation of journalism, and, thus, varying levels of journalistic autonomy and media freedom. State interference is exercised through various means, ranging from self-regulation and regulations to media control. The activity level of the market also varies from one media system to another.

An early and classic typology is the four theories of the press (Siebert et al., 1956). In this model, judged by how different they are from the classic liberal model of a neutral watchdog press, which is free from state interference, the media systems of the world were categorised into four types: authoritarian, libertarian, social responsibility and Soviet Communist. This classification fits the then cold war framework. Western liberal (US) and parliamentary (European) democratic countries had libertarian or social responsibility media systems. Authoritarian media systems can be found in most of the developing and pre-democratic countries. The media systems in the Soviet Union, and in other Communist countries, were Soviet Communist. This model is criticised for being normative, and it is out-of-date today.

In 2000, in the name of de-Westernising media studies (Curran & Park, 2000), global media systems were divided into two opposites, according to the political structures of the countries: authoritarian and democratic political systems. Their economic structures further subdivide each of these oppositions into neoliberal and regulated economic systems.

More recently, three models of media systems in Western Europe and North America have been introduced (Hallin & Mancini, 2004). A polarised pluralist model is featured, with the integration of the media into party politics, weak commercial media and a strong state. In a democratic corporatist model, commercial media exist side-by-side with the media that are attached to social and political groups, with the state playing a small but active role. In a liberal model, the media operate based on the principles of the free market, without formal connections with politics and with little state interference.

The market is often considered to be liberating for journalism, enabling it to oppose the power of the state. Inactive, weak and under-developed media markets will prohibit journalism from developing and being independent. For example, the lack of material resources, investments in journalism and training for journalists have constrained the development of African journalism, which became vulnerable to political and economic pressures (Ronning, 2005). By contrast, highly commercialised and developed media markets will prompt the birth of a diverse press. The commercialisation of the media in the US, providing fertile soil for the free press, played a significant role in the shift from a partisan press to objective journalism (Kaplan, 2002). In the 1990s, the introduction of the market diversified the news media and created certain levels of journalistic autonomy in India (Thussu, 2005). Likewise, in China, well-developed and active media markets stimulated the development of journalism and facilitated the plurality and diversity of journalism at the beginning of media marketisation (Lee, 2001).

Nevertheless, with the deepening of media marketisation, instead of remaining a liberating force, the market has instead become a factor that limits the autonomy of journalism. In the case of Chinese journalism, for example, a state-capitalist model appeared in which the market, collaborating with the state, became another force constraining journalism (Lee, He, & Huang, 2006). Likewise, after an initial period of increased media freedom following the fall of the People's Democracies – a term referring to Eastern European countries ruled by Communist parties such as Bulgaria, Hungary and Poland – in 1989, journalistic autonomy and editorial independence in Central and Eastern Europe were reduced under the influence of media marketisation, as the media became deeply intertwined with political and economic systems (Stetka & Örnebring, 2013).

Worries have mounted over increasingly converged media ownership which compromises the democratic promise of journalism. The political stance and interests of media owners, as well as their relentless pursuit of profits, may give rise to tabloid journalism – or even paparazzi journalism – and lead to the decline of serious and quality journalism, such as investigative journalism. A prominent example of this is the revelations made by Peter Oborne, a British journalist, in 2015. The UK's *Daily Telegraph* allegedly censored its coverage of the HSBC scandal to avoid offending the bank group, which was a big advertiser in the paper. Oborne also expressed his grave concerns over the interference of the Barclay brothers, the owners of *The Daily Telegraph*, in the paper's editorial independence (Oborne, 2015). Nevertheless, *The Daily Telegraph* responded by calling the statement of Oborne an 'astonishing and unfounded attack, full of inaccuracy and innuendo' (The BBC, 2015). In the light of the increasing concentration of media ownership, critics (see, for example, Benson, 2016; Mancini, 2018; Moreira & Oller Alonso, 2018) also warn of the instrumentalisation of journalism as one danger of commercial censorship, which means journalism is used as an instrument by media owners to achieve their political goals.

The Influence of Digital Technologies on Autonomy in Journalistic Practice

Can digital technologies empower journalism to gain more autonomy in practice? If so, to what extent? On the surface, the arrival of digital technologies and the proliferation of data can give journalists the technical means to take control of their work and gain more autonomy in it. At the beginning of the new millennium, for example, an observation-based case study of four converged news organisations in the US found that although there were some doubts about convergence, most journalists interviewed regarded newsroom convergence as expanding the space for expression, providing audiences with news in different, often innovative, ways, and enabling them to obtain reporting resources (Singer, 2006). The availability of digital technologies, such as videophones used for covering live events, enables war reporters to create narratives that may be different from the official accounts of events offered by the combatant governments. In authoritarian countries, such as China (see further discussions in Tong & Sparks, 2009; Xin, 2010) and Egypt (Amin, 2002), digital technologies, such as the Internet and broadcasting networks, have contributed to freeing journalists from state interference, particularly in the first decade of the 21st century.

New communication platforms and channels also endow journalists with more autonomy to do what they cannot do otherwise. This empowerment is particularly true when it comes to entrepreneurial journalism, for the practice of which the availability of digital platforms is crucial (see the discussions about entrepreneurial journalism in Chapter 7). A study of entrepreneurial journalism projects in Germany found that although financial pressure may restrict the autonomy of the founder(s) and journalists, the embrace of entrepreneurialism boosted the perception of autonomy at the individual and organisational levels (Heft & Dogruel, 2019). Moreover, the digitalisation of our daily lives provides journalists with copious amounts of data, which are rich resources for news stories and facilitate new ways of reporting to hold power accountable, as exemplified in data-driven investigative news articles, such as the Panama and Paradise Papers investigations (see Box 5.1 in Chapter 5).

However, a closer look into the current situation can reveal that recent changes in journalism and its environment have actually degraded journalistic autonomy. Scholars (see, for example, Anderson, 2011; Nikunen, 2014; Nygren, 2012; Phillips, 2010; Tong, 2017a) have suggested that such a degradation of journalistic autonomy results from the intertwining of economic and technological imperatives – i.e., the joint influence of the need for financial sustainability and that of embracing the affordances of digital technologies.

Take the tracking of audience data by using digital technologies, such as audience metrics. The extensive use of audience data in newsrooms comes from news media's desire to understand audiences through making the most of digital technologies so that they can bolster revenue. This is, however, at the centre of academic concerns. As discussed in the previous chapter, an overwhelming attention to audience data gradually influences the once prevailing journalistic value of autonomy, even taking away from journalists the freedom to make news judgements. The increasing adoption of web metrics and other technologies, such as automation, in the news production process, lessens journalistic autonomy in making decisions about news to an extent that journalists can no longer entirely control their own work. The understanding of audience behaviour that is gained from audience data thus makes newsrooms more vulnerable to their desire for profitability.

In addition to the over-reliance on audience metrics, the burgeoning of native advertising (see Box 10.2 in Chapter 10), a sign of journalism succumbing to news organisations' business needs, is also diminishing journalistic autonomy, as advertising materials invade editorial space, blurring their boundaries with journalism content. The transformation of media labour in the digital age, such as outsourcing, using unpaid or low-paid labour and automation in newsrooms, leads to job precarity for journalists and diminishes the professional status and prestige of journalism in the job market, which may undermine journalistic autonomy.

The rise of bloggers, citizen journalists and other Internet users who create and disseminate content (user-generated-content (UGC)) and comment on journalists' work challenges the authority and autonomy of journalists in controlling and defining journalistic norms and telling the truth (see further discussions about the influence of UGC on journalistic legitimacy in Chapter 10). 'Crowd-criticism', one of the new ways of monitoring media accountability and journalistic performance, refers to the criticism voiced by Internet users over media performance through online means, such as emails, social media or the commentary functions of the websites of the news media (Fengler, 2012). The Internet – in particular, blogs and social media – facilitates this newfound critical ability of users, which has emerged along with allegedly unsuccessful and insufficient media self-regulation. Bloggers even monitor and criticise the performance of journalists as 'watchdogs on the watchdogs' (Singer, 2007). Audiences who make comments – particularly those that are negative and critical – on the performance of journalists pose a potential challenge to journalistic authority and autonomy. On some occasions, hostile comments on social media even pose threats to (the safety of) journalists (O'Neill, 2020).

For other scholars, however, the situation is not so bad. Some studies (see, for example, Tandoc, 2017) found that analytics had little influence on autonomy. Journalists who sought crowd-funding for their projects, also developed contradictory feelings. They believed that journalists should retain journalistic autonomy but, meanwhile, felt it was necessary to be responsible to their funder(s) (Hunter, 2015). A study undertaken with Australian journalists shows that although in the longer term journalistic and audience news values might be realigned under the influence of web analytics, news values and journalists' ability to make news judgements remained untouched (Hanusch, 2017).

<hr>

EXERCISE 9.1

Give some thought to your own views on the influence of digital technologies on journalistic autonomy at the level of journalism practice. Do you agree or disagree with one of the perspectives discussed in this section? Are these perspectives still relevant or are they obsolete?

<hr>

Media (Self-)Regulation and Government Interference in Democratic Contexts

In democratic contexts, apart from being under severe financial strains (discussed in Chapter 3), the news media and journalism face increasing pressure and scrutiny from governments, policymakers and regulators. Recent developments in media (self-) regulation and control suggest that journalistic autonomy – at the level of media freedom and journalistic independence – is at risk. This section will address the situation in democratic contexts in which the news media abide by media self-regulation and regulation, while the following section discusses the situation in authoritarian societies and societies in transition, where direct media control is practised. Regulations can contribute to maintaining the practice of high-quality journalism. For example, media regulations are one reason behind the diversity of Europe's media (Irion & Valcke, 2015). Nevertheless, regulations may limit journalistic autonomy. Historically, the self-regulated news media have received continuous threats from the state to regulate them. Today, more indirect media governance – or even state interference – has become evident and present. The issuing of new regulations may gag the press and pose a menace to journalistic autonomy. The news media have to make changes to their self-regulation in order to cope with legal threats.

The democratic contexts have seen a tendency to pressurise the news media and journalists to self-regulate and pass more media regulations potentially limiting the autonomy of journalism. Well-known examples include the publication of the Leveson Report and the struggle between the British government and the press over the self-regulation of the press in the UK (see the discussion later in this chapter). New regulations and laws that have been passed in the name of increasing data security and protecting privacy or national security may also limit the autonomy of journalism. Prominent among these is the 2017 General Data Protection Regulation in Europe and the UK; the Counter-Terrorism and Border Security Act 2019 in the UK; the 2017 Netzwerkdurchsetzungsgesetz (NetzDG) law (the Network Enforcement Act) in Germany; the 2012 Finkelstein Report, the 2015 metadata laws and the National Security Legislation Amendment (Espionage and Foreign Interference) Act 2018 in Australia; and the Telecommunications (New Regulatory Framework) Amendment Bill (2018) in New Zealand.

This trend is the result of three factors. First, the changes in the news media, journalism and the communication environment, such as media convergence and fake news (Box 9.5), have created new challenges to the existing systems of regulations or self-regulation. Media convergence, for example, challenges inflexible standards and regulation and potentially leads to 'regulatory convergence' – i.e., the convergence of regulations suitable for all platforms (Fielden, 2016). When it comes to fake news, not only technologies but also solutions on the legal and regulatory levels are needed to tackle this problem.

Should more laws and regulations be introduced, they may, however, also be used to censor content on the Internet and pose a threat to journalistic autonomy (Andorfer, 2017). In Singapore, which has a parliamentary democracy but with authoritarian features in its politics and society, for example, its fake news law – the Protection of Online Falsehoods and Manipulation Bill (POFMA) – that came into effect in 2019 is seen as potentially giving the government much more power to censor online content and silence political dissidents, social media companies and news media (Agence France-Presse, 2019). In the context of Australia, the passage of new national security laws opens up the discussion about the balance between the freedom of the press and national security (Brookes, 2018).

Second, recent events and developments in public life draw public attention to media accountability and have driven regulators to rethink media regulation and self-regulation. Among other factors are the surge of fake news and mounting threats to state security triggered by events such as the WikiLeaks and Snowden revelations, and the Facebook-Cambridge Analytica data scandal (Box 9.6). Although suggesting the perils of powerful state surveillance, WikiLeaks (Box 9.2), Snowden (Box 9.3) and Manning (Box 9.4) give rise to worries about the potential harm of leaked documents to national security. These events justify the necessity to keep a closer eye on journalism and information security. The case of WikiLeaks, for example, reveals a vacuum in regulation, and it triggers concerns about regulations and journalistic ethics (Brevini & Murdock, 2013; Dunn, 2013). Countries such as the UK, Australia and New Zealand as well as various European nations, have investigated the practices, ethics and cultures of the news media and journalism since then. Scholars and journalism practitioners (see, for example, Brevini, 2017; Brookes, 2018; Lashmar, 2017; Ponsford, 2014) are concerned that not only new government policies and laws, but also state surveillance may threaten the freedom of the press. For example, as you will find below in the discussion of the case of the US, the Trump administration secretly seized journalists' phone and email logs.

Third, the latest changes in politics and in the relationship between (right-wing and populist) politicians and journalism, fuelled by the resurgence of populism across the globe, have implications for the endeavours of related politicians and authorities to discipline journalism and the news media and to limit media freedom and journalistic autonomy. Their efforts are exemplified in the hostility of Trump to journalism and news outlets. After coming to power in 2017, Donald Trump often used 'fake news' and 'bad journalism' to label journalism practised by the news media, in particular *The New York Times*, which heavily criticised his policies (see further discussion in the case study of the US below). The 'fake news' accusations made by Trump led to an increase in public distrust in journalism and news organisations, de-legitimating journalism (Lischka, 2019). In Latin America, leftist presidents have also viewed the news media as their enemy, and their disdain for the media limits media freedom (Kellam & Stein, 2017).

To summarise, along with the rise of populist politics, the recent developments discussed above have raised public awareness of problems such as 'fake news', privacy and national security, fuelling public distrust in journalism and pressing media regulators and authorities to increase control of journalism and the news media. In the remainder of this section, the cases of the UK and the US will be explored in order to illustrate the main points discussed here. Over the recent decade, media freedom and journalistic autonomy have significantly receded in both countries. In the index provided by the Reporters Without Borders' survey of press freedom, the US fell from No. 32 in 2013 to No. 44 in 2021, while the UK dropped from No. 29 to No. 33 (Reporters Without Borders, 2021). The two cases reveal a picture of UK and US regulators and authorities making efforts to regulate and control journalism and the news media, threatening the journalistic value of autonomy and independence.

BOX 9.2

WikiLeaks

Founded by Julian Assange in 2016 as a whistleblowers' platform, WikiLeaks publishes leaked documents and information, particularly about the operations of governments and influential politicians, which would not otherwise be published. From Daniel Arap Moi (former Kenyan President) to Icelandic banks, WikiLeaks discloses documents that reveal corruption or other wrongdoing by those in power. WikiLeaks has collaborated with the news media, such as *The Guardian* and *The New York Times*, in order to maximise the publicity and influence of these leaks (Rusbridger, 2011). The most famous leaks include the Guantanamo operations and the Afghan and Iraq war logs. These revelations resulted in 'the largest data breach in US military history' (*The Guardian*, 2019). The case of WikiLeaks is associated with debates about transparency (openness), disclosure (secrecy), privacy and national security. For more discussion about WikiLeaks and its implications for journalism and democracy, you can read *Beyond WikiLeaks: Implications for the Future of Communications, Journalism and Society*, edited by Benedetta Brevini, Arne Hintz, and Patrick McCurdy (2013).

BOX 9.3

Snowden

In 2013, former US National Security Agency (NSA) contractor, Edward Snowden, disclosed documents that revealed the digital surveillance conducted by Western governments, in particular, the NSA and the UK Government Communications Headquarters (GCHQ). The Snowden leaks exposed 'mass surveillance' by governments in the digital age, targeting ordinary people's daily communication (Bowcott, 2014; Dencik & Cable, 2017).

BOX 9.4

Manning

Chelsea Manning is a whistleblower who was serving in the United States Army, and who leaked government (military) documents to WikiLeaks. One of her leaks, for example, revealed that US aircrew shot Iraqi civilians and two employees of Reuters. She was sentenced to 35 years in jail for her leaks in 2013 but this sentence was commuted by Barack Obama in 2017.

BOX 9.5

Fake news

Fake news is not a new phenomenon. In the era of traditional media, it was used to describe news stories containing false facts and fake accounts of events. However, this phenomenon has become exaggerated in the online environment, in particular, on social media. In the context of social media, fake news refers to mis- or dis-information circulated on social media. The prevalence of the Internet in general, and, in particular, of Web 2.0 technologies and social media platforms, breaks down the monopoly of journalists on the creation and mass dissemination of information. The freedom to produce and send information online, however, creates difficulties not only for ordinary users, but also for journalists themselves, in checking the credibility of information and detecting misinformation. Not only the social media practices of ordinary Internet users, but also the use of bots – algorithms that automate tasks on the Internet such as automatically generating and disseminating content – accelerate the spread of fake news. Fake news has been accused of having played a crucial role in important political events, such as the 2016 US presidential election and the 2016 UK's EU membership referendum (see related discussions in Dewey, 2016; Grice, 2017; Parkinson, 2016; Shao, Ciampaglia, Varol, Flammini, & Menczer, 2017; Silverman, 2016).

BOX 9.6

The Facebook-Cambridge Analytica data scandal

Cambridge Analytica bought Facebook data created by tens of millions of users without their knowledge. It allegedly used the data to help the electoral victory of Trump in the 2016 US presidential election. Since it was revealed in 2018, this scandal sparked campaigns for a global boycott of Facebook among users and raised widely shared concerns over user privacy.

The case of the UK: the Leveson Inquiry and Snowden leaks

Overall, journalistic autonomy in the UK is under threat. As of 2020, Boris Johnson, the Prime Minister, tried to limit, for example, journalists' access to information and officials by banning some journalists from No. 10 Downing Street, and by moving daily briefings from the House of Commons to Downing Street (Mason & Sparrow, 2020; Mayhew, 2020; Reporters Without Borders, 2020). He has even hired his own in-house photographer to take favourable photographs at the taxpayer's expense. The passage and implementation of the General Data Protection Regulation in 2018 (in the EU but extended to the UK as it was a member at that time) significantly restricts the autonomy of journalism, as, under this regulation, the value of journalistic autonomy must be balanced against other public values, such as privacy and security. In 2020, the Cabinet Office launched a Freedom of Information Act (FOIA) 'clearing house' to deal with FOIA requests to avoid disclosing sensitive or embarrassing information. After news media such as openDemocracy and *The Guardian* raised concerns, the government endeavoured to justify its practice and denied that they handled journalists' FOIA requests differently (The Cabinet Office, 2021).

The Leveson Inquiry was called in the wake of the exposure of the News International phone-hacking scandal in 2011. This was a landmark event with the potential to transform the regulatory framework of British journalism, as arising from the Leveson Inquiry came the launch of new regulatory bodies and legislative changes in press regulation (Woodhouse, 2018). In 2011, *The Guardian* was the first to reveal the scandal: the Murdoch-owned *News of the World* regularly hacked the phones of royals, celebrities and even ordinary people, such as the missing and murdered girl Milly Dowler and the relatives of British soldiers killed in Iraq and Afghanistan as well as the 7/7 London bombing victims. Facilitated by the affordances of digital technologies, the tabloid conducted these totally disgraceful practices in pursuit of exclusives, thereby gaining larger market shares. In the wake of the scandal, readers boycotted the *News of the World*, and Murdoch closed the tabloid, which had been successful for 168 years. Given the severity of this event and its influence on the Murdoch empire, the phone-hacking scandal is a scandal of Watergate proportions. It later became clear through more investigations and civil actions launched by the victims that rival tabloids such as the *Mirror* had also engaged in phone-hacking (Greenslade, 2020).

The exposure of this hacking scandal raised public awareness of the issue of privacy and triggered a reflection on media regulation and laws and on journalistic principles, such as accuracy and fairness. It fuelled debates on whether, and to what extent, the invasion of privacy can be justified in the public interest, how to strike a balance between press freedom and privacy, and which media ethics principles the news media and journalism should obey.

The scandal shifted the focus from 'deregulation' onto the news media's ethical behaviour. Attention was drawn to addressing several gaps in media regulations and policies in the UK, such as those in relation to the growth and competition in the media markets. The British press had been self-regulating their conduct under the supervision of the Press Complaints Commission (PCC). However, the phone-hacking scandal led to a call for the establishment of an improved regulatory or self-regulatory system amid concerns around the dysfunction of the PCC (Brock, 2012). As the news media's self-regulatory practices were increasingly seen as not being operated in the public interest, reforming the news media's ownership structures was deemed necessary (Freedman, 2012). In addition, that the Press Complaints Commission (PCC) was considered to be a failure also suggested that there was a need to impose stricter media regulations.

Press reform debates started, following the revelations of the phone-hacking scandal. The British government asked Lord Justice Leveson to chair an inquiry into the 'culture, practices and ethics of the British press'. The Leveson Report was published in 2012, triggering discussions on how to balance press freedom and media accountability. There have since been bargains and negotiations between the press and policymakers in relation to journalistic autonomy. In the post-Leveson era, new self-regulatory bodies have been introduced. Following Leveson's recommendations, British newspapers have been asked to establish a system of 'supervised self-regulation' to balance public interest and privacy (Levi, 2014: 910). In 2013, political leaders such as David Cameron, Nick Clegg and Ed Miliband agreed to a Royal Charter with which to establish a new press regulator. The Royal Charter was approved by the Queen in the same year. The regulator would have powers to fine UK publishers and request corrections (The BBC, 2016). British newspapers strongly opposed this proposal and opted not to sign up to any statutory regulator established under the Royal Charter. Instead, in 2014, they created their own regulator: the Independent Press Standards Organisation (IPSO), a new self-regulatory body. IPSO, which refused to seek the Royal Charter's recognition, was accused of 'failing as a regulator', although it was competent as a complaints handler (Ponsford, 2015). IMPRESS, the Independent Monitor for the Press was formed in 2016 and in the same year applied for recognition from the Royal Charter (Barnett, 2016).

The Leveson approach to media regulation in the UK was seen as threatening British journalism's values of autonomy and media freedom (Levi, 2014, 2015). In the aftermath of the Leveson inquiry, the British press coverage of the Snowden leaks also led to the state's interference in journalism. For example, after *The Guardian* covered its Snowden stories (*The Guardian*, No year-b), the Metropolitan Police started investigating the role of *The Guardian* in the leaks (Boyle, 2013; O'Neill, 2013). Julian Smith, a Tory MP, called for the prosecution of *The Guardian* if the paper refused to submit a decryption code to enable the security services to read the related files (Owen & Kiss, 2013). The UK police conducted a years-long investigation into the journalists who were involved in reporting the Snowden leaks (Gallagher, 2015). They were even forced to destroy hard drives containing leaked files (Balkin, 2014; Borger, 2013). In 2013, Alan Rusbridger, the then editor-in-chief of *The Guardian*, remarked that the police's investigation into *The Guardian* and treatment of Guardian staff, such as keeping journalists in a Heathrow transit lounge for a long time and interrogating journalists in *The Guardian* offices, are evidence of the real, growing threat to journalism (Auletta, 2013; Guardian staff, 2013; Rusbridger, 2013).

Meanwhile, the news industry has been fighting for press freedom. After the Leveson inquiry, Section 40 of the Crime and Courts Act 2013, implementing some of the recommendations made by the Leveson Report, would have forced newspapers that had refused to join IMPRESS – the Royal Charter approved regulator – to pay both sides' legal costs in a lawsuit, posing a novel threat to journalism (Levi, 2017). Journalists thus urgently required a legal shield in order to protect their sources in the face of the alarming effect of such new threats to journalism from the UK government (Bradshaw, 2017). The newspaper industry strongly opposed the introduction of Section 40 and called for its repeal. In 2017, the May government revealed its intention to abandon the second stage of the Leveson inquiry into press standards (Leveson 2) and Section 40, and scrapped them in 2018 (Sweney, 2018a).

Although Leveson 2 has not been implemented, the influence of the Leveson inquiry is profound, like a stone thrown into a lake triggering ripples on the surface of the water. Given the international reach of the news media, developments in the UK have also had implications for the news media in other countries, such as the US, and vice versa.

The case of the US: national security and surveillance

In the US, press freedom is inscribed in its constitution and is protected by the First Amendment. However, in recent years, journalistic autonomy has been endangered as a consequence of events, such as the 9/11 attacks, the WikiLeaks, Snowden and Manning revelations, and the hostility of Trump to the news media. More media regulations have been passed and implemented, which the news media must abide by, while direct state interference in journalism has been increasingly noticeable. In 2018, the US was even ranked as a dangerous country for journalists for the first time (Reuters, 2018b).

In the 2000s, it was the 9/11 attacks that were first used to justify state surveillance and restrictions on the journalistic disclosure of governments' activities. Consequently, exposing the secrecy of the state, the revelations of WikiLeaks, Snowden and Manning, raise questions as to whether, and to what extent, state surveillance can be justified in the name of national security. Meanwhile, however, such events made governments worried about the potential of leaks to jeopardise national security. The use of the Espionage Act and the passage of new or extended regulations and laws are seen to potentially threaten the freedom of the press that had previously been enjoyed by American journalism (see related discussions in Freedom House, 2018; Froomkin, 2014; Gallagher, 2013; Human Rights Watch, 2014). Amongst these regulations and laws are the US Patriot Act in 2001, Section 701 of the FISA (Foreign Intelligence Surveillance Act) Amendments Act in 2008, the FISA Amendments Reauthorization Act of 2017 (the reauthorization of Section 702 of FISA until 2024) and the Clarifying Lawful Overseas Use of Data Act (or CLOUD Act), both in 2018.

The principles of freedom of expression have been weakened by the passage of new regulations and by government practices. Censorship and self-censorship are imposed through state regulations, which have shifted from targeting individuals and institutional news organisations to focusing on Internet intermediaries and digital networks. In the aftermath of the WikiLeaks revelations and the Snowden leaks, laws and regulations passed by governments have resulted in the collaboration of the state with private entities, such as Internet companies and digital networks, to tighten surveillance and control of freedom of speech. Internet giants like Google and Facebook are allegedly aiding the surveillance endeavours of governments (Balkin, 2014). These controls are not beneficial to the watchdog role of the American press, which was already in decline as a consequence of the severe financial losses faced by commercial media.

Additionally, political attitudes to the press have become extremely hostile in recent years. The crackdown on journalists and whistleblowers, using laws like the Espionage Act, started from the time of the Obama administration but became worse in the Trump administration (Committee to Protect Journalists, 2018; Risen, 2016). Despite promising and encouraging transparency, as exemplified in the launching of the data.com portal, the Obama administration embarked on an approach of tightening surveillance, controlling information and the news media (Downie & Rafsky, 2013). Governments spied on journalists and their sources by monitoring their digital communication records. For example, in 2013, the government secretly obtained two months' worth of the phone records of Associated Press reporters and editors (The Associated Press, 2013). In the same year, Fox News' James Rosen was investigated for his reports about likely nuclear tests in North Korea. His emails were obtained by the Justice Department with the assistance of Google (Findley, 2013). In 2021, the Biden administration revealed the Trump administration's secret seizures of the phone logs of reporters working for top US newspapers, such as The New York Times and The Washington Post, and the phone and email records of a CNN reporter (Savage & Benner, 2021; Barrett, 2021). As using digital technologies leaves digital trace data that governments are able to get their hands on, in this sense, digital technologies actually enhance the capability of governments to monitor and control the news media, journalists and their sources.

From coming to power in 2017 to stepping down in 2021, Donald Trump had a poor relationship with the US news media. He has been a target of the news media's investigations, as exemplified in *The New York Times'* investigations of his fortune (Barstow, Craig, & Buettner, 2018), ties to Russia (Shane & Mazzetti, 2018) and racism (Shane & Mazzetti, 2018). In the face of Trump's assaults on the press, much of the news media not only discredited the frequent false accusations made by him, but also branded him as a threat to free journalism and democracy.

Trump made great efforts, and used various means, in particular Twitter, to bring the news media into disrepute. Declaring a war with the media, Trump called journalists 'among the most dishonest human beings on earth' and denounced the news media as 'the enemies of the people' (Grynbaum, 2017; Remnick, 2018). While still being a candidate, he had already threatened to change libel laws in the US to enable him to sue news organisations for libel (Gold, 2016). In 2020, during the Black Lives Matter protests, which were triggered by the killing of George Floyd, American journalists were attacked by the police and even some protesters, as a result of Trump's persistent denigration of and contempt for the news media (Smith, 2020).

Most populist rulers seek to limit press freedom (Kenny, 2020). The presidency of Donald Trump, who is a populist,[1] fits this pattern. Trump has been criticised for undermining press freedom and for being responsible for its decline in the US (Finer, 2017; Freedom House, 2019; Simon, 2017). Trump's assaults on the press were compounded by a chronic erosion of the four pillars supporting press freedom as a whole, including 'financial strength', 'protection from the courts', 'public support' and an 'interdependent relationship with government officials' (Jones & West, 2017). That is to say, US journalism is losing its ability to resist the assaults of political actors at a time when the news media face market decline, when regulations and laws pose new threats, when the public is developing distrust in and even antagonism towards members of the news media and when journalists rely too heavily on government officials for news sources.

Trump left office to his successor Joe Biden as president in 2021. Overall, the US news media were joyous over his departure, but it is too early to conclude whether, and if so, to what extent, the Biden administration will prove a blessing to press freedom in the US.

■■■■■■ EXERCISE 9.2 ■■■■■■

Compare the situations in relation to journalistic autonomy and media freedom in the UK and the US. Identify similarities and differences between the two cases and try to answer the questions why, and how, the UK and US governments attempt to control journalism and limit its autonomy. Think about the implications of these changes for democracy.

Tightening Media Control in Authoritarian Regimes or Regimes in Transition

While journalistic autonomy is under threat in the UK and the US, authoritarian regimes, like China and Russia, or regimes in transition, like Egypt, have tightened media control and have squeezed the space for press freedom and journalistic autonomy. The tightening of media control is the result of four interconnected factors. The first comes from the state's fear over losing control. The second is the remaining (or even growing) connection between media owners and the state. The third is that the state is making the most of digital technologies to exercise control over journalism and the news media by various means, such as regulations or surveillance, and thus it has the upper hand. The final factor is that the news media lack the financial strength and legal protection to oppose the interference of the state.

Digital technologies, in particular the Internet and mobile devices, have played their liberating parts in the development of events, such as the Arab Spring and the Egyptian 2011 revolution. Tightening state control of the media is a natural response of governments to social unrest and conflicts, as well as the potential of digital technologies to facilitate political disruption. The state retains sole, or part, ownership of the media in some of these countries, such as China, Russia, Tunisia and Egypt. In Russia, the Putin administration effectively controls the media and has destroyed media freedom by damaging private media ownership, trying to take back the ownership of the media and interfering in media work (Howard & Hussain, 2011; Lehtisaari, 2015). In Tunisia, in theory, the passage in 2011 of related laws – the Decree-law 115 and the Decree-law 116 – offers legal protection for journalism, which sparked some hope for press freedom at the beginning of the post-revolutionary period. However, this hope has proven to be false. Several factors – including the continuity of authoritarian rule, domestic chaos in politics and religion, and the wish to use the media to win political struggles – have further undermined the level of media freedom in this region (see further discussions about press freedom in Tunisia in El Issawi, 2016; Farmanfarmaian, 2017; Joffé, 2014). The situation in Egypt is similar. Although the Egyptian Constitution in theory protects the freedom of the press, media freedom and journalistic autonomy is greatly restrained (see further discussions about press freedom in Egypt in Abdulla, 2016; El Issawi & Cammaerts, 2016; Lohner, Banjac, & Neverla, 2016).

If the news media are privately owned, they may depend on the state for political favours and support. As a result, there is often a close connection between media owners and the state in these countries. In post-communist Ukraine, for example, media ownership has increasingly been concentrated into the hands of several media oligarchs, who have become allied with politicians in exchange for political favours (Ryabinska, 2011). In these countries, connections with politicians and dependence on political support for business have become a significant obstacle to press freedom (Ryabinska, 2011).

Apart from traditional news media, the state also seeks to harness the Internet in these countries. Websites and individuals' IP addresses are blocked, and Internet content is filtered and policed. In addition to direct censorship, the issuing of regulations, such as Internet policies, to support state control and surveillance, is an effective way for states to exert tight control over the media and journalism. In countries like Russia and China, the states have passed regulations and laws to impose Internet censorship and surveillance. Moreover, there are no media laws to protect journalists.

Russia, for instance, has been embarking on a 'dictatorship-of-the-law' approach to Internet policies, and its Internet governance is moving toward digital sovereignty

(Nocetti, 2015). The Russian government sees the Internet as detrimental to its rule, with the potential to enable citizens to get around the state's control over the news media. In 2014, for example, the Federal Law (on information, information technologies and information security) amendments allowed governments to ask social media, such as Facebook, YouTube and Twitter, to remove certain content or to restrict access to it. In the wake of the Snowden leaks, the Putin administration has tightened Internet censorship, enhanced surveillance and passed new regulations and laws, such as the 2014 Federal law #242-FZ, and the 2016 anti-terrorism Yarovaya law. The anti-terrorism laws require Internet providers to store personal data for a period of six months and to allow the Federal Security Service to read encrypted communication data. This requirement is thought to constitute an attack on freedom of speech, citizens' privacy and civil conscience (Nechepurenko, 2016).

China has never had constitutional laws to protect media freedom and journalistic autonomy. While retaining its ownership and censorship of the media, China has passed regulations and policies to limit media and Internet freedom. The Internet was introduced to China in 1994. Since very early on, the well-known 'great firewall of China' has played a crucial role in filtering content and limiting users' access to content. In more recent years, more indirect or subtle means of Internet and expression control have been used for media constraint and surveillance purposes, which have become more and more data-driven. Internet companies such as Google and Yahoo! are (were) forced to comply. Google eventually quit China in 2010 over the country's censorship. In 2013, under the new Internet guidelines, Internet users may be put behind bars for the posts and comments they make online (The BBC, 2013). The cybersecurity law, passed in 2016, requires Internet companies and service providers to support the authorities for the purposes of Internet control and surveillance. Since 2014, enabled by new digital technologies, China has built a data-driven Social Credit System, a system of judging citizens' trustworthiness and credits by considering all aspects of their life, such as their posts on social media, to monitor individuals and organisations. An activist who opposes the Chinese government may not have good enough social credit records to buy train tickets because their dissent labels them dishonest and not trustworthy. The use of digital technologies is at the centre of social and media control, while freedom of expression is hugely limited since Xi came to power in 2012. Artificial intelligence tools are used to trace people's activities for the sake of surveillance. Furthermore, the surveillance measures introduced from 2019 to track and trace the virus, such as the apps developed during the COVID-19 pandemic, may be here to stay. Observers believe that China is on its way to becoming a 'digital totalitarian state' (Qiang, 2019).

Worsening the situation, the financial losses of the news media are contagious and have infected the news industry in these countries. In Russia, media profits have been in decline since the financial crisis commenced in 2008 (Lehtisaari, 2015). Likewise, news media in China started to suffer losses from around 2012 (Tong, 2017a). Their financial difficulties are unhelpful for them in terms of resisting the interference of the state in media work. The case of China discussed below epitomises the combined influence of digital technologies, state interference, media ownership and financial difficulties on journalistic autonomy.

The case of China

Chinese news media and journalism achieved certain levels of media freedom and journalistic autonomy in the process of media marketisation, starting from the early 1980s. In particular, the proliferation of commercial media outlets helped release some manoeuvring space for journalism and the news media. The newly gained media freedom, however, has receded in the wake of the tightening of media control and severe revenue losses in the most recent decade, which the prevalence of digital technologies does not help.

Before the 1980s, all of the news media were financially supported by the state and operated as party organs. From the 1980s, most of the news media lost these financial subsidies and had to look for revenue from the market. Meanwhile, with the economic marketisation, advertising in China was growing rapidly, alongside the economy, with great potential for revenue. Consequently, a large number of commercial news media were launched across the country, and governments even requested the news media to form media groups to accommodate the need to run commercial news media. A newspaper group, for example, would usually include one party organ and several commercial newspapers launched by the party organ. The introduction of the market into the news industry enabled journalism to gain some media freedom. Though remaining state-owned, commercial news media had more freedom to choose what they wanted to report on than party organs did. Prominent changes included a significant increase in people-centred content and the rapid rise of critical and investigative journalism. Although media control continued, journalists had achieved some autonomy with which to push boundaries in terms of practising critical, investigative reporting.

However, over recent years, particularly since 2012, a combination of technological, commercial and political factors has empowered the authorities to restrict media freedom, with journalistic autonomy greatly diminished and media (self-)censorship significantly increasing. Shortly after coming to power in 2012, Xi Jinping noticeably tightened political control of the news media and journalism, starting both media crackdowns and an online 'purge'. The press was silenced. Those news media that did not follow the instructions from the government were subjected to crackdowns. Their journalists, and even high-ranking editorial staffers, were removed. Media ethics were used as a powerful weapon to discipline the news media and to undermine their legitimacy and authority. After several cases in which journalists were found guilty of accepting bribes, or where there was alleged corruption, such as the 2013 case of Chen Yongzhou who confessed to inventing false negative stories about a commercial company for money, an image of 'unethical' journalism was successfully constructed about the journalism practised by commercial news media – in particular, critical and investigative journalism. This type of journalism was once seen as China's conscience and as helping ordinary people gain justice. An image of being unethical is thus a lethal blow to the credibility of Chinese journalism.

Commercial news media in China were hit hard by revenue declines around a decade later than their Western counterparts. Chinese news media's market failures started from 2012 but from 2016 the situation became particularly severe and grave. Since then, they have lost huge amounts of advertising revenue to the Internet, and their subscriptions have shrunk dramatically. They have thus been forced to take up government subsidies and collaborate with the government for financial support. Following the market failures of the news media, their capability to resist the state's control has evidently been in decline. Quite a number of news outlets have been shut down across the country. At the same time, there has been an exodus from the news industry of journalists with expertise in investigative and critical journalism to other areas such as public relations and digital commerce.

Digital technologies have worsened the situation for journalism. The flourishing of content-based digital platforms has lured a significant part of the audience away from consuming quality journalism. Apolitical, entertaining, and even voyeuristic, content prevails on these platforms and attracts the attention of audiences. Advertising revenue follows audiences to digital platforms. In newsrooms, the priority given to the interests of audiences has affected the criteria of news values. The need to engage audiences pushes journalists to report on topics that may be trending on social media and that have gone viral online in a bid to attract people's attention. These topics are unlikely to be about serious social and political issues with potential political consequences. In this sense, the popularity of digital technologies helps restrict journalists from freely choosing which topics to cover.

In summary, in the data age, journalism in China is losing rather than gaining autonomy under the combined influence of technological, economic and political forces, while the discussions above suggest that digital technologies have not turned out to be an empowering force for Chinese journalism (see a detailed discussion in Tong, 2017a).

Summary of the Chapter

This chapter discusses the concept of journalistic autonomy and how it has changed in the data age. It explores this topic at the levels of journalistic practice and media freedom in both democratic and authoritarian countries. It concludes that, on balance, digital technologies appear to be detrimental to quality journalism, and, consequently, journalistic autonomy has suffered because of, rather than been enhanced by, these technologies. Although not being the sole cause of these changes, digital technologies have played a significant role in influencing the situation for journalism. They affect journalistic autonomy partly because of the use of web analytics in newsrooms, and partly because of the transformation of the media ecology and related media policies or controls.

The above discussion of the changes in journalistic autonomy and the three case studies show an unfortunate trend toward diminishing journalistic autonomy in both democratic and authoritarian contexts in the data age. Digital technology, the market and politics have played their respective parts in depleting rather than augmenting the level of autonomy that the news media enjoy.

END OF CHAPTER EXERCISE

By now, you have read about how journalistic autonomy has changed – more precisely been reduced – in different social contexts in the data age. What are your views on the ways that digital technologies have influenced journalistic autonomy? Are they liberating or limiting for journalism? Choose to focus on one country. Research the level of autonomy enjoyed by journalists in the country of your choice, and critically assess the respective roles of the state, the market and digital technologies in influencing journalistic autonomy.

FURTHER READING

Levi, Lili (2014). Journalism standards and 'the dark arts': the U.K.'s Leveson Inquiry and the U.S. media in the age of surveillance. *Georgia Law Review*, *48*(3), 907–948. This article offers a thorough discussion of the implications of the Leveson Inquiry for the UK and US news media.

Tandoc, Jr, Edson C. (2017). Follow the click? Journalistic autonomy and web analytics. In Bob Franklin and Scott Eldridge II (Eds.), *The Routledge Companion to Digital Journalism Studies* (pp. 293–301). London and New York: Routledge. This chapter discusses web analytics and their influence on the practices of journalists and their autonomy in reporting.

Tong, Jingrong (2017). The taming of critical journalism in China: a combination of political, economic and technological forces. *Journalism Studies*, *20*(1), 79–96. This article discusses how the joint forces of technology, the market and the state, have led to the taming of critical journalism in China. It analyses the changes in political cultures and media markets and explores how the capitalisation of digital platforms has damaged the material base for the practice of critical journalism. This article presents a good case study for us to consider in relation to the question: is digital technology a liberating force for journalism?

Note

1 There have been some debates about whether Donald Trump is a populist. This book follows Kellner's view that sees Donald Trump as an 'authoritarian populist' (Kellner, 2018).

TEN

JOURNALISTIC LEGITIMACY[1]

- What is journalistic legitimacy?
- What do news organisations and journalists need to gain and maintain journalistic legitimacy?
- What roles do digital technologies, politicians and the market play in influencing journalistic legitimacy?
- Is journalistic legitimacy weakened or strengthened in the data age? If so, to what extent and what has caused it?
- How do news organisations and journalists try to retain journalistic legitimacy in the data age?

━━━━━━━━ KEY CONCEPTS ━━━━━━━━

profession	credibility
journalistic legitimacy	immediacy
ethics	transparency
objectivity	boundary work

Legitimacy justifies the acts of social groups and organisations so that other members of society will accept these acts. All institutions or organisations thus need legitimacy. The concept of journalistic legitimacy provides an important perspective to understanding journalism and the changes in the contexts in which journalism operates. This chapter will discuss the challenges and opportunities faced by journalism today in the data age in relation to its legitimacy. It starts with a discussion of journalism as a 'profession', the concept of journalistic legitimacy and the three essentials required for news organisations and journalists to maintain journalistic legitimacy. The chapter then introduces two trends surrounding journalistic legitimacy. One indicates that journalistic legitimacy is in crisis, and the other suggests that legacy news organisations and journalists, joined by new digital news outlets, are trying to retain – or regain – journalistic legitimacy. They are adopting new technologies and practices in an attempt to rebrand and reinvigorate journalism, as well as to defend the professional boundaries of journalism.

Journalism as a 'Profession'

Journalism is not a classic profession. Conventionally, a profession is regarded as an occupation with particular traits that can distinguish it from other professions. These traits include professional autonomy, altruistic service, education or training, skills, organisation, ethical codes and licensing (for detailed discussions about the traits of a profession, see Dooley, 1997; Freidson, 1983; Johnson, 1972; Larson, 1977). These attributes justify regarding an occupation as a profession through establishing an easy differentiation between professions and non-professions. Classic professions, such as medicine and law, have such specialised and distinctive traits, which create clear boundaries for them to gain and maintain social legitimacy as well as market monopoly and privilege.

Judged from this perspective, journalism lacks sufficient and clear attributes to be a 'full' or 'true' profession and to be clearly distinguished from other professions. Journalistic legitimacy does not, therefore, come from its traits. Instead, the establishment of cultural authority in defining what counts as reality, and professional norms, such as objectivity and social responsibility, help journalists claim professional status and gain public recognition of their legitimacy and privilege.

━━━━━━━━━━━ **EXERCISE 10.1** ━━━━━━━━━━━

Think about what traits classic professions such as medicine and law have. Discuss if, and to what extent, the occupation of journalism has any of these traits.

Achieving and maintaining legitimacy

The legitimacy of journalism originates from public trust in its cultural authority in defining reality and the self-serving ideology of professionalism gained through establishing professional norms, such as objectivity and social responsibility. Instead of being a fixed, unchanging outcome, journalistic legitimacy is a dynamic process. It is intangible, symbolic, normative, discursive, changeable and fluid. Journalistic legitimacy, therefore, needs to be continuously maintained and sustained.

Achieving and maintaining journalistic legitimacy requires three essentials – cultural authority, market success and ethical practices. Journalists' cultural authority constructs and advances an image of themselves as exclusive, authoritative and reliable storytellers of reality. It is gained only if the public has faith in journalists' ability to decide what is the right information – the truth – and to collect, produce and distribute the right information.

Financial sustainability and stable success in commercial and job markets are essential for the maintenance of legitimacy. In spite of the ideal of journalism as serving the public interest and democracy, it is closely connected with money. It is expensive and may not survive without substantial financial support. For-profit, commercial news organisations will not give journalism the financial support it needs in the absence of success in the commercial market. Flourishing job markets are also important for journalists, for the maintenance of the professional prestige, boundaries and status of journalism, as individuals' career progression and pay can only be advanced if they are successful in the job market. Moreover, market success can help journalism resist state control and interference and maintain its independence.

Traditionally, journalism depends on news organisations to reconcile the conflicting needs to maximise profits and to serve the public interest. For most of the time, the relationship between journalism and news organisations is symbiotic – journalism needs the resources of news organisations to produce quality news, while news organisations need journalism for revenue. However, being more closely connected with money and materially focused than journalism, news organisations cater more to their commercial interests than to the public interest. With a paramount need to boost revenue, they may not treat serving the public interest as being as important as journalists would.

In addition, professions gain their professional status by demonstrating that they can be trusted (by the state) to control and regulate themselves. Journalism is no exception. Gaining and retaining journalistic legitimacy needs journalism to be ethical and trusted with the right to self-regulation and the ability to self-regulate by complying with high professional standards. The recent developments in media regulation and self-regulation in democratic contexts, such as Anglo-American societies (discussed in Chapter 9), have significant ramifications for the legitimacy of journalism.

Journalistic Legitimacy in Crisis

In the data age, journalistic legitimacy is in crisis in the wake of the changes in journalism and its environment discussed earlier in this book. The cultural authority to define reality, market success and ethical journalism – all of the three essential elements for maintaining journalistic legitimacy – are falling apart to various extents in the data age. Journalism's cultural authority is undermined in parallel with the popularity of the decentralisation of Internet-based communication that empowers ordinary users to write their versions of reality. Amateur reporters publish their stories on blogs, social media platforms, and even contribute materials to professional news articles. Journalists are no longer the only authoritative individuals who collect information about reality, inform the public and act as the watchdog of democracy. The augmented ability of amateurs to write about reality has changed who can, and should, produce news stories and define reality. The multiple versions of reality presented in user-generated content (UGC) may even differ from the 'truth' offered by journalists, and thus confront and challenge journalists' truth claims, which are at the heart of journalism's cultural authority.

In addition, the use of social media by journalists has changed their front-of-stage and backstage performances in the public sphere. In recent years, on the Internet, in particular on Twitter, journalists have increasingly revealed their performances that previously belonged to backstage areas. Journalistic processes that were hidden in the past are exposed in the pursuit of transparency in journalism. Although transparency is supposed to increase the credibility of journalism, the revelations regarding backstage performances may impair front-of-stage journalistic authority (Karlsson, 2011). The frequent social media presence of journalists and their online self-revelations of backstage performance de-mythologise the occupation and the work of journalism. These activities of journalists also narrow down the above-discussed information asymmetry between the performance of journalists and audiences' knowledge of journalistic performances. Audiences are, therefore, in a better position to evaluate journalists' performances and the credibility of their reports.

In addition, the pursuit of immediacy (see Box 10.1) turns online news reporting into a process where multiple versions of news stories about a news event may be published. These different versions may even contradict one another as an inevitable consequence of premature reporting of the event before it has fully unfolded. Such self-contradiction in different versions of news stories may harm the credibility of journalism.

BOX 10.1

Immediacy

The newly promoted journalistic principle of 'immediacy' has both positive and negative impacts on journalism. 'Immediacy' has been advanced in response to news media's need for instantaneous content publication and dissemination on the Internet. Promoting 'immediacy' shows that journalism embraces the instantaneity of online news dissemination (discussed in Chapter 4). However, instantaneous news production, distribution and consumption have turned journalistic reporting into an ongoing process. In this process, multiple, or even conflicting, versions of reality about the events may emerge, and errors may be made with the potential to damage journalistic legitimacy.

As discussed in Chapter 4, news organisations across the world have been trying to incorporate user-generated content (UGC) into news stories. However, the active incorporation in news articles of UGC – such as witness materials about emergencies or disasters – makes the credibility of news less controllable than in the past. Difficulties increase for journalists in checking the authenticity of UGC such as videos, and, therefore, news credibility is impaired. There have been some cases, where witnesses' claims or witness materials have later been found to be hoaxes. When a BA plane crashed in 2008, for example, Jason Johnson, who claimed to be on board, told Sky News: 'We came in very, very fast. It's something I've never been in before. Once it landed, it spun 90 degrees. I felt like I was in a washing machine.' This quote was widely cited by global media such as *The Guardian* (*The Guardian*, 2008) and CNN (CNN, 2008). However, it turned out to have been fabricated by Johnson, who was not on the plane at all (*The Sydney Morning Herald*, 2008).

In addition, it is extremely difficult for journalists to check the credibility of the websites to which their reports are linked, and to verify the accuracy of data analysed for news stories in data and computational journalism. When it comes to big data verification (the problems surrounding data verification have been discussed in Chapter 5), although news organisations have started to adopt high-level technologies, such as artificial intelligence, to curate data and to identify and remove fake news and misinformation, no perfect solutions have been achieved so far.

The emergence of online citizen news sites has a two-fold influence on journalistic legitimacy. First, they may complement the democratic role of professional journalism. Professional journalism is thus no longer the only fourth estate that is expected to shoulder democratic responsibilities. Second, they may offer different narratives of events to those constructed by the mainstream news media. For example, alternative accounts of reality provided by far-right online media have been found to challenge the journalistic authority of the legacy news media (Figenschou & Ihlebæk, 2019; Figenschou & Thorbjørnsrud, 2017).

Worsening the whole situation is the emerging practice of online native advertising (see Box 10.2) on news websites, which leads to doubts over their ethical practices, as demonstrated in the case of BuzzFeed. In 2016, BuzzFeed was found not to have clearly marked an article on '14 laundry fails' as an online advertorial paid for by a brand (Sweney, 2016). Another example is *The Atlantic* website. In 2013, *The Atlantic* published a sponsored article for the Church of Scientology; 11 hours later it removed it from its website and the next day published a statement apologising and admitting they had made a mistake because they failed to update their related native advertising policy. In the aftermath of this event, there were debates about whether or not the news site should carry native advertising, among and beyond *The Atlantic* staffers. In this case, native advertising triggered controversies and confusion even within the news organisations and among journalists.

================ **BOX 10.2** ================

Native advertising

Native advertising means the publication of a piece of paid-for content to make it look natural and 'native' to the media outlet that publishes it. Typical forms of native advertising include product placement, content marketing and sponsored content. These forms of advertising connect advertised brands with media content to various degrees. Product placement, for example, seeks to incorporate information about brands into programmes such as TV dramas, news articles and films published by news media outlets. Content marketing promotes the content that is produced and distributed by brands in media coverage, while sponsored content promotes brands by associating their name with the content produced and distributed by a publisher.

Native advertising existed prior to the arrival of digital technologies but has become much more prominent in the data age. The flourishing of different forms of native advertising on the Internet deepens the concern over the ubiquity of digital technologies that undermines journalistic legitimacy and authority.

On digital platforms, native advertising means an advertisement that bears the same features as the platform on which it appears. Digital media platforms have turned out to be an ideal platform for 'native' advertising. For example, a digital media outlet's native advertising content is designed to look like an article published on that platform, featuring multimedia content and being socially sharable. For news media to embrace the opportunities provided by digital technologies to increase revenue, they need to be adaptive to the new ways of advertising, and carrying native advertising could be a win-win situation for both advertisers and publishers. However, making advertising and news products look alike will impair the authenticity of news articles and damage public trust in journalism.

A growing danger associated with native advertising is sponsored native political advertisements. BuzzFeed piloted native political advertisements during the 2012 US Presidential election with the publication of a paid post entitled 'What Mitt Romney's "Binders Full of Women" Says About His Views'. It did label the item as a 'Paid Post' along with 'Obama for America, Brand Publisher' as a byline. Native political ads have since become increasingly popular. The danger of paid political advertisements is that they may catch audiences off guard with their promoted political ideology, and the impact of the labels on audiences remains unclear. What is worse than clearly labelled native political ads is unlabelled paid partisan news content appearing to be politically neutral. In 2020, *The New York Times* revealed that almost 1,300 local news websites and newspapers in the US, which claim to be objective, are actually secretly paid by Republicans to smear their opponents or to promote Republican candidates or companies. None of these ordered-up articles have been labelled as paid ads (Alba & Nicas, 2020). The decline of local newspapers has definitely left a void in which paid-for journalism can flourish. In a world that is politically turbulent and deeply polarised, however, such content not only damages journalistic legitimacy but also is potentially dangerous in its influence on voters who are unused to distinguishing authentic news and opinion from paid propaganda.

The challenges to the cultural authority of journalists may also come from a decrease in the occupational prestige of journalism as a consequence of the current financial plight of news organisations and the related unfavourable discourses about journalism in crisis. As discussed in previous chapters, journalists have encountered a hard time in job markets, let alone in terms of market success. It is a question of survival – rather than of thriving – in the face of financial turmoil. Naturally, journalists' feelings of precarity, or insecurity, may arise in tandem with media markets being transformed to the detriment of journalists and dramatic changes in journalistic practices prompted by the advent of new digital technologies. Such perceived precarity can be related to jobs, incomes or skills. This feeling may vary according to the actual situations of journalists – such as, for instance, whether they are 'freelance' or 'salaried' journalists. Overall, however, precarity in journalism may limit the ability of journalists to participate in civil life by producing quality journalism and thus cause a deterioration in their occupational prestige and professional identity.

Journalistic legitimacy is also in crisis because of the questionable ethical practices of some news organisations and their perceived inability to carry out effective self-regulation and to stick to ethical standards. In the Western context, in modern times, the most notorious journalistic scandal was the UK's phone-hacking scandal (discussed in Chapter 9), in which surveillance technologies were used to access private communications (Partridge, 2015). Newspapers have frequently become involved in phone-hacking scandals, but the 2011 scandal had the most severe consequences and led to the sudden closure of the *News of the World*. The phone-hacking scandals, of which the actions of the *News of the World* are the most well-known, arose from newspapers', especially tabloids', desire for scoops and profits. They of course have consequences, as shown in the demise of the *News of the World*. These scandals impaired the legitimacy of journalism in the Anglo-American news world, although major US and UK news organisations such as *The Guardian*, *The Times*, *The Telegraph*, the *Daily Mail*, *The New York Times* and *The Washington Post* tried to differentiate themselves from Murdoch's journalism, to reiterate journalistic norms and to maintain boundaries (see the discussions about the impact of these scandals on journalistic legitimacy in Carlson & Berkowitz, 2014; Eldridge, 2013; Moloney, Jackson, & McQueen, 2013).

Take the UK for example. In the UK, press ethics have been put under scrutiny since the phone-hacking scandals and the Leveson inquiry that followed in 2012 (see the discussion in the previous chapter). At the time, the call for regulatory reform was loud. The approval of IMPRESS by the Press Recognition Panel (PRP) in October 2016 is an example of this. Meanwhile, the press fought back hard to defend their right to self-regulation. In 2014, the press pushed to set up their own regulator, the Independent Press Standards Organisation (IPSO). However, newspapers such as *The Guardian* and the *Financial Times* still shun it, as its performance is not deemed to be satisfactory in terms of the speed or appropriateness of its judgements (Cathcart, 2021; Monbiot, 2019). Later, newspapers including both tabloids and broadsheets vocally advocated the scrapping of Leveson 2 and Section 40, which were cancelled in 2018.

Despite the cancellation of Leveson 2, the tightening of control over UK news media through regulations and laws is lurking. Examples of media abuse continue to emerge, acting as reminders of the importance of ethical practices and standards and, potentially, regulation. In 2021, it was disclosed by an inquiry that in the late 1980s, the *News of the World* and the Mirror Group illegally paid Southern Investigations, one of the founders of which, Daniel Morgan, was found brutally murdered, and police officers investigating the murder case for confidential information and stories (Sabbagh, 2021). In addition, in 2020, following the allegations of Earl Spencer about Martin Bashir's means of securing his famous interview with Princess Diana, the BBC commissioned an independent investigation led by Lord Dyson. In 2021, the Dyson report concluded that the BBC reporter set up the interview by using dishonest means and broke the ethical guidelines of the BBC (Lord Dyson, 2021). In the wake of this scandal the UK news media and politicians called on the BBC to act quickly to address its failure to meet the high standards expected of it and restore public trust in the public service broadcaster (Dowden, 2021). These instances were set against the backdrop of the UK government and politicians trying to limit press freedom (see a detailed discussion in Chapter 9) and thus have alarming implications for UK news media in terms of their regulatory system and legitimate status.

The status of journalistic legitimacy has also been exacerbated by top politicians' hostility towards the news media and journalism. In the Anglo-American contexts, this adverse situation is exemplified in Trump's clash with the news media and Boris Johnson's attempt to ban journalists from accessing officials and information (discussed in Chapter 9). In the 2010s, the relationships between politicians and journalists changed in liberal democracies. Politicians have delegitimised journalists by attacking their character and ethical standards, challenging the public-interest aspects and socially beneficial impact of their work, and linking them with illegitimate institutions (Van Dalen, 2019). They increasingly label journalism and news media as fake news makers. A similar situation can be found in authoritarian countries such as China (see the discussion in Chapter 9). Unethical journalistic practices and scandals have been used to de-legitimise journalism through tarnishing its public image.

Even traditional professional norms, like objectivity, may lead to the deterioration of journalistic legitimacy. While value divisions exist among the population and competing political actors and groups, and political hostility is shown towards journalism, the journalistic ideal of objectivity is thought by some observers (such as Carlson, 2018b) to be obsolete and to make journalists vulnerable to attacks from political actors. Journalists should reposition themselves, construct firm arguments in their writing and legitimise the strength of their judgements (Carlson, 2018b). That is to say, a strong, effective public articulation of the social values journalists support along with an attitude of self-reflection can help journalists defend themselves against criticisms made by political actors and groups. In addition, due to the problems surrounding data and data algorithms, objectivity is also considered to be inapplicable to the practice of data journalism, the values of which should be appreciated by its contribution to democracy (Tong & Zuo, 2021). Using objectivity as the main professional norm for data journalism, the credibility of which may be influenced by factors such as the problems in data that are beyond the control of journalists, may expose journalists to unfair criticism levelled at their work and practices. A reflection on, and revision of, journalism's professional norms would thus help revitalize journalistic legitimacy.

EXERCISE 10.2

Objectivity is one of the most important journalistic principles. However, in recent years, as discussed above in this section, scholars have started to argue that objectivity is no longer applicable. What are your views on this? Discuss whether, and to what extent, sticking to the journalistic principle of objectivity can still help journalists retain their legitimacy and authority in this current time of political and social turmoil, and in the data age. The aspects you can consider include, but are not limited to, the changes in journalistic practices, in the relationship between journalism and politicians, and in social dynamics, such as the resurgence of populism.

The Attempts of News Organisations and Journalists to Retain and Revive Journalistic Legitimacy

The previous section discussed the complicated circumstances under which public trust in journalism has been dramatically reduced and the legitimacy of journalism has been damaged. In the meantime, however, scholars (see, for example, Carlson, 2017; Solito & Sorrentino, 2020; Tong, 2018; Vos & Thomas, 2018) have also recognised the attempts of news organisations and journalists to restore journalistic legitimacy. The joint forces of digital technologies and contextual change also offer opportunities for them. Two principal tactics – defending the professional boundaries of journalism and rebranding journalism – are identifiable in the efforts of news outlets and journalists.

Defending the professional boundaries

With their professional status and cultural authority challenged, news media and journalists are endeavouring to construct and defend journalism's boundaries, which demarcate professional journalists from ordinary Internet users. Journalism practitioners question whether citizen journalism can be seen as journalism. Professional norms, such as telling the truth, fact-checking and accountability, are used as 'boundary markers' by journalists to differentiate themselves from ordinary Internet users in contexts such as the US, the UK, Finland, Sweden and China (see related studies in Andén-Papadopoulos & Pantti, 2013; Singer, 2015; Tong, 2015a).

In different social contexts, through boundary work, journalists continue to gatekeep and to refute the legitimacy of UGC producers. A study of the BBC, for example, found that despite the organisation's initiative to incorporate UGC into its traditional news production, journalists and editors still controlled the 'gate'. The inclusion of UGC did not contribute much to the diversity of news agendas in the BBC, and UGC was only used in reporting some disasters (Harrison, 2010). Journalists from the BBC and *The Guardian* tended to define UGC as 'non-journalism', in order to reduce the disruption to the journalistic field when incorporating it into their reports (Cooper, 2017). Reporting China's disasters, British and Chinese newspapers maintained their traditional journalistic practices and dissolved the content that was quoted from social media platforms as one type of news sources in their coverage (Tong, 2017b). Various studies (see, for example, Harrison, 2010; Singer, 2010; Williams, Wardle, & Wahl-Jorgensen, 2011) have found that UK journalists and reporters believe UGC damages journalistic values and norms, as well as editorial standards. Chinese journalists have also actively practised their boundary work and tried to restore journalistic legitimacy through criticising UGC producers for being irrational and not credible (Tong, 2015a, 2015b).

Journalists' professional norms and established standards for professional practice, particular news forms and collective narratives help them legitimate their work (Carlson, 2017). For example, journalists have been uniting online to form imagined or interpretive communities, stressing and reiterating their professional norms (Carlson, 2007). The members of these journalistic communities share and deliver collective interpretations of key events and form discourses about their profession, thus contributing to policing the boundaries of journalism. Political journalists, who produced narratives on stories about election campaigns on Twitter, for example, were seen to be able to reinforce their cultural authority on the social media platform (Mourão, 2015). Meanwhile, however, these activities may impair journalistic legitimacy by turning journalists' backstage performances into front-of-stage ones, as discussed above.

Rebranding journalism by using digital technologies

As legitimacy is discursive, the discourse and image of journalism is essential for maintaining or restoring legitimacy. As discussed earlier in this book, newsrooms and journalists across the world are actively adopting digital technologies in journalistic practices. The rise of new forms of journalism such as data journalism and their innovative techniques contribute to rebranding journalism as digital and tech- and data-savvy, which revises the narrative about what journalism is, should do, and can do. In an effort to adapt to the fast and continuously shifting digital media environment, big news organisations are trying to make the most of advanced digital technologies, ranging from developing new content apps for audiences to designing algorithms, to establishing databases for journalists and editors. The resultant changes in news production and journalistic practices redefine journalism as 24/7, multimedia journalism, celebrating the multimedia and data analytical skills of journalists and their ability to serve democracy.

Digital media innovations and the ubiquitous expansion of journalism to online, digital platforms demonstrate journalists' renewed ability to cover news with speed and immediacy, reiterating their legitimate right to report fast-changing reality. Immediacy has become a primary principle that online journalism should obey. A grasp of the relevant multimedia skills turns out to be vital for journalists in multimedia newsrooms, and more journalists are now able to edit, shoot and write for multiple media platforms. The availability of digital technologies, such as virtual reality (VR) devices and drones, further enhances the reporting ability of journalists. An image of journalists who are able to meet the requirements of the digital environment with their up-to-date skills is being presented to the public.

Against the backdrop of open data and big data, the emergence of data journalism advances the claims of journalists to having mastered advanced technology and to practising good journalism. The data skills of journalists and the data-dimension of journalism suggest the renewed potential of journalism to continue to fulfil its democratic role. Data-driven investigative reports published in recent years, such as the MPs' expenses scandal by The Guardian and The Daily Telegraph and the Panama Papers investigation (discussed in Chapter 5), have reimagined what journalists should do, and have declared that democracy still needs journalism. In the post-truth age, US journalists have been found to be renegotiating journalistic authority by shifting journalistic discourses back to stressing and embracing the democratic function of journalism (Vos & Thomas, 2018). Reiterating and re-stressing journalistic norms and principles reassures the public about the values and ethical codes of journalism and democracy's need for journalism.

The importance of the use of digital technologies by news organisations in rebranding journalism lies not only in the instrumental function of technology; it also lies in promoting a discourse of reinvented, tech-savvy, digital journalism. More important here is the symbolic meaning of using digital technologies in journalism: telling the world about what journalism is, and what journalists can and should do. Whenever they can, news organisations and journalists define what their journalism is, and what it should do, and they express their pride in their new abilities. An apt example of this occurred after the Brexit vote, on 29 June 2016, when Katharine Viner, editor-in-chief of Guardian News & Media, sent a statement to Guardian members through an email. In it, she said, 'The Guardian's role in producing fast, well-sourced, calm, accessible and intelligent journalism is more important than ever'. She then went on to say:

> I want to make sure that The Guardian's excellent journalists – from our political team and other reporters to Europe experts, opinion editors, commentators, leader writers, news editors, picture editors, subeditors, audience, video and visuals staff – along with our support and technology teams, continue to work 24 hours a day, seven days a week, across the world, to provide the answers that people desperately need at this time of anxiety and confusion.

This statement had a dual purpose: the first was to define and re-emphasise what Guardian journalism is, should do, and can do; the second was to mobilise Guardian readers to help fund the journalism practised in The Guardian. It aimed to polish up the image of The Guardian, to restore the legitimacy of its journalism, and to seek sustainability in the public interest.

New digital news outlets, alongside their counterparts in the traditional media, are making efforts to gain legitimacy in the journalistic field. A study found that in their manifestos, ten digital news start-ups tried to establish their legitimacy through critically reflecting on, but reinforcing, journalistic values, and through stressing their technology-facilitated innovations and the combination of journalism and technology (Carlson & Usher, 2016). Meanwhile, digital news organisations such as BuzzFeed and Vice are endeavouring to be recognised and accepted by their peers and the public. In their attempt to gain public recognition and journalistic legitimacy, BuzzFeed and Vice have hired young staff and invested in supporting the reporting of subject areas that are outside the traditional reporting focus but that interest their audiences (Stringer, 2018).

EXERCISE 10.3

Look for a statement made by a news outlet about their journalism and discuss what it says about their journalism. Think about the questions: By saying this in their statement, are they trying to defend their legitimacy and authority? If so, how?

Towards the rebuilding of journalistic legitimacy?

The image of journalism using digital technologies differs from that using pen and paper. The new image of journalism as digital and tech- and data-savvy tells the public about what journalism is, should do and can do. This image, thus, embodies and flags up the new type of journalism that is needed to produce and deliver the news to the public in the data age. In this sense, digital technologies have become a symbol of communication power, while possessing digital technologies is seen as having this power of communication. With the invention of new digital technologies, this may bring more opportunities for organisations and journalism to thrive. However, it is too early to conclude that journalism's legitimacy can be, or has been, rebuilt. Journalistic legitimacy will not be entirely rebuilt unless journalism can achieve success in media markets. Yet, how this can be accomplished is still an unsolved question. The future of journalism is, thus, promising but precarious.

Summary of this Chapter

The concept of journalistic legitimacy discussed in this chapter is closely associated with the cultural authority of journalism in defining reality. After comparing journalism with traditional professions, this chapter discusses factors that are crucial for journalism to gain and maintain its legitimacy: public trust in journalism's authority to define reality, journalism's market success, professional norms and an ethical image. The discussion in this chapter outlines two trends surrounding journalistic legitimacy identifiable in the data age. One suggests that journalistic legitimacy is in peril as a result of the changes in journalism and in the environment in which journalism operates. The other shows the efforts of legacy and new media news outlets and journalists to re-legitimate journalism through adopting digital technologies.

━━━━━━━━━ **END OF CHAPTER EXERCISE** ━━━━━━━━━

'Fake news' (see Box 9.5 in Chapter 9) can be a double-edged weapon for journalistic legitimacy. On the one hand, journalism may lose its legitimacy if it is closely associated with 'fake news' or journalists are labelled as 'fake news makers'. On the other hand, if 'fake news' is rampant on the Internet, and it is a big challenge for ordinary users to tell genuine from 'fake' news, then the news media are needed more than ever to fact-check and to produce reliable news. Think about the 'fake news' phenomenon. Discuss whether, and to what extent, the prevalence of 'fake news' on the Internet further damages journalistic legitimacy, or if it actually offers an opportunity to help journalists retain the legitimacy of their work.

━━━━━━━━━ **FURTHER READING** ━━━━━━━━━

Carlson, Matt (2017). *Journalistic Authority: Legitimating News in the Digital Era.* New York: Columbia University Press. Carlson's book discusses the way in which journalists achieve authority in the digital era. In particular, he explores three types of practices used by journalists to legitimate their work. He also scrutinises journalists' relationships with audiences, news sources and technologies in his discussion of journalistic authority.

Tong, Jingrong (2018). Journalistic legitimacy revisited: collapse or revival in the digital age? *Digital Journalism, 6*(2), 256–273. Tong's article outlines the de-legitimisation and re-legitimisation processes of journalism in Anglo-American contexts. She analyses how the contextual factors, such as the news media's financial difficulties, the challenges posed by decentralised online communication and the reformed relationship between politics and journalism, have influenced the two processes.

Note

1 This chapter is based on, and expands, the discussion in my published article: Journalistic legitimacy revisited: collapse or revival in the digital age? *Digital Journalism,* 6(2) (2018), 256–273.

ELEVEN
CONCLUSION

This concluding chapter summarises and highlights the state and status of journalism in the data age. As discussed in Chapter 2, the power of digital technologies is both disruptive and sustaining. Digital technologies have shown their 'disruptive' force in weakening the news media's gate-keeping authority, eroding their audience base, and toppling them from dominance in advertising markets.

The most significant disruption caused by digital technologies lies in transforming the communication environment in favour of the state and giant information companies. In both democratic and authoritarian contexts, the state has gained substantial technological and regulatory advantages to interfere with the work of journalism and control its performance. Should the news industry solve its decades-long, persistent financial problems, journalism will have more chance to win its tug-of-war with the state.

The news media do not have many advantages in their competition with tech giants over audiences and revenue. In many parts of the world, no matter whether they are broadsheets or tabloids, journalists in newsrooms rack their brains to engage – if not to entertain – audiences. The relationship between journalism and audiences has become so much more intricate than before, to the extent that audiences may be collaborators in, or even funders of, journalism. Big tech companies have overtaken the news media to become the leading advertising revenue generators and to channel the attention of users. The news media need to adapt further to this changing environment for their survival and then their success. Although big tech companies may not necessarily always be the rivals of news outlets, potential mutual-beneficial partnerships between them await to be explored.

The use of digital technologies in journalism has caused the quality of journalists' work to deteriorate, reduced autonomy in practice, threatened their jobs and triggered new ethical issues. While the news media's autonomy and reporting space is squeezed under the sway of political control, the autonomy of journalistic practice is reduced through the influence of using digital technologies, such as audience metrics, in journalism.

Journalism, thus, suffers triply – first, from the news media's financial losses, second, due to the increasing state interference and reduced media freedom, and, third, because of the collapse of legitimacy as the authoritative definer of reality. These substantial difficulties have led to a diminished social status for journalism, which has a weak financial foundation, less freedom, and lower levels of public trust. The present time is, thus, a tough time for journalism.

Journalism and news organisations – particularly those practising quality journalism – are endeavouring to boost the status of journalism, as a profession, in society. Overall, they are making a staunch effort to ensure that journalism thrives and serves its role in democracy. Making the most of digital technologies to rejuvenate journalism is part of this effort, as digital technologies also provide opportunities to help journalism and the news industry escape from their distressing situation. The advent and application of digital technologies contribute to reinvigorating journalism, defending its boundaries and reviving its legitimacy. Technologies such as algorithms are being used to boost income. The commercial interests of news organisations are strengthened – or even prioritised – with the assistance of algorithms. New funding opportunities are being actively explored in tandem with the vigorous establishment and management of new relationships with audiences. Where possible, in an attempt to defend journalistic autonomy and recover legitimacy, journalists and news outlets are pushing back against state interference, as well as aggressive attacks by politicians and measures to diminish media freedom.

In the data age, therefore, digital technologies can also help to revitalise journalism, as shown in the practice of these new forms of journalism. Being online, digital, multimedia, data-based and algorithm-powered, these key features portray a new face of smart, stylish journalism that keeps up with the latest developments and with the trends in digital technologies. A broad spectrum of digital technologies, ranging from everyday iPhones to more complicated automated algorithms, are at the disposal of journalists and help to improve their work. Skills that journalists need to grasp have expanded from journalism basics to include those in other disciplines, like data science and statistics. Tech-savvy and data-savvy journalists are hired to produce exciting, audience-engaging and (ideally) democracy-serving news stories that can be distributed instantly on the Internet to local, national and global audiences. The technological affordances of the Internet give rise to independent entrepreneurial journalism that seeks financial support from its audiences and private sponsors. Journalists may no longer be attached to news organisations, but they can practise journalism independently. Practising new forms of journalism facilitates the production of innovative types of news content and thus provides journalists with novel ways of fulfilling their role in democracy.

This is a time when the global arena has witnessed the rise of populist politicians, like Donald Trump, and authoritarian powers, like China. In this time, disinformation and fake news are increasing in tandem with information overload. Strikingly, the prevalence of disinformation and fake news further damages the health of democracy, while information overload will not help. This is thus a challenging time, in which we need quality journalism more than ever. This need is one of the primary reasons that journalism is obliged to survive and revive. This is also an exciting time for quality journalism to show its value for democracy and to make the most of digital technologies to serve this end.

Practising quality journalism, however, not only needs the updating of new skills and techniques but also requires an ability to think independently and critically, question and challenge what we are told, verify what is collected and provided and report events from diverse perspectives. In addition, when it comes to understanding the occupation of journalism and developing journalism as a career, journalists and future journalists should be well prepared with a self-reflexive, critical stance and mindset. For all these reasons, a thorough understanding of journalism in the data age is essential.

REFERENCES

Abdulla, R. (2013). *Mapping Digital Media: Egypt*. New York, NY: Open Society Foundations.

Abdulla, R. (2016). Navigating the boundaries between state television and public broadcasting in pre-and post-revolution Egypt. *International Journal of Communication, 10*, 4219–4238.

Abercrombie, N. & Longhurst, B. J. (1998). *Audiences: A Sociological Theory of Performance and Imagination*. London, Thousand Oaks, CA, and New Delhi: Sage.

Adams, C. (2018). Tinker, tailor, soldier, thief: an investigation into the role of drones in journalism. *Digital Journalism, 7*(5), 658–677, doi: 10.1080/21670811.2018.1533789.

Afful-Dadzie, E. & Afful-Dadzie, A. (2017) Liberation of public data: exploring central themes in open government data and freedom of information research. *International Journal of Information Management, 37*(6), 664–672.

Agence France-Presse (2019, 2 October 2019). 'Chilling': Singapore's 'fake news' law comes into effect. *The Guardian*. Retrieved from https://www.theguardian.com/world/2019/oct/02/chilling-singapores-fake-news-law-comes-into-effect

Åkesson, M., Sørensen, C., & Eriksson, C. I. (2018). Ambidexterity under digitalization: a tale of two decades of new media at a Swedish newspaper. *Scandinavian Journal of Management, 34*(3), 276–288.

Alba, D. & Nicas, J. (2020, 18 October, 2020). As local news dies, a pay-for-play network rises in its place. *The New York Times*. Retrieved from https://www.nytimes.com/2020/10/18/technology/timpone-local-news-metric-media.html

Albæk, E. (2011). The interaction between experts and journalists in news journalism. *Journalism, 12*(3), 335–348.

Albeanu, C. (2015, 2 September 2015). Contributoria closes, team still sees future for crowdfunding. *journalism.co.uk*. Retrieved from https://www.journalism.co.uk/news/contributoria-closes-but-its-team-still-sees-a-future-for-people-supported-journalism-/s2/a566305/

Albeanu, C. (2017, 22 June 2017). Advice for young journalists from Martin Baron, executive editor, The Washington Post. *journalism.co.uk*. Retrieved from https://www.journalism.co.uk/news/advice-for-young-journalists-from-martin-baron-executive-editor-the-washington-post/s2/a706092/

Aldhous, P. (2018, 25 October 2018). How Russia's online trolls engaged unsuspecting American voters – and sometimes duped the media. *BuzzFeed News*. Retrieved from https://www.buzzfeednews.com/article/peteraldhous/russia-online-trolls-viral-strategy

Aldridge, M. (1998). The tentative hell-raisers: identity and mythology in contemporary UK press journalism. *Media, Culture & Society, 20*(1), 109–127.

Ali, T. (2014, 7 August 2014). Local news outlets are joining the data journalism bandwagon. *Columbia Journalism Review*. Retrieved from https://archives.cjr.org/data_points/regional_data_journalism_becom.php

Allam, R. (2018). *Egypt – Media Landscape*. European Journalism Centre. Retrieved from https://medialandscapes.org/country/egypt

Amin, H. (2002). Freedom as a value in Arab media: perceptions and attitudes among journalists. *Political Communication, 19*(2), 125–135, doi: 10.1080/10584600252907407.

Andén-Papadopoulos, K. & Pantti, M. (2013). Re-imagining crisis reporting: professional ideology of journalists and citizen eyewitness images. *Journalism, 1-first*. doi: https://doi.org/10.1177/1464884913479055.

Anderson, B. & Borges-Rey, E. (2019). Encoding the UX: user interface as a site of encounter between data journalists and their constructed audiences. *Digital Journalism*, doi: 10.1080/21670811.2019.1607520.

Anderson, C. W. (2011). Between creative and quantified audiences: web metrics and changing patterns of newswork in local US newsrooms. *Journalism, 12*(5), 550–566.

Anderson, C. W. (2012). Towards a sociology of computational and algorithmic journalism. *New Media & Society, 15*(7), 1005–1021.

Andorfer, A. (2017). Spreading like wildfire: solutions for abating the fake news problem on social media via technology controls and government regulation. *Hastings Law Journal, 69*(5), 1409–1432.

Aneez, Z., Chattapadhyay, S., Parthasarathi, V., & Nielsen, R. K. (2016). *Indian Newspapers' Digital Transition: Dainik Jagran, Hindustan Times, and Malayala Manorama*. Oxford: Reuters Institute for the Study of Journalism, University of Oxford.

Aneez, Z., Neyazi, T. A., Kalogeropoulos, A., & Nielsen, R. K. (2019). *India Digital News Report*. Reuters Institute for the Study of Journalism, University of Oxford.

Ang, I. (1991). *Desperately Seeking the Audience*. London and New York: Routledge.

AP. (2016, 30 June 2016). AP expands Minor League Baseball coverage. *The Associated Press (AP)*. Retrieved from https://www.ap.org/press-releases/2016/ap-expands-minor-league-baseball-coverage

AP. (2018). Associated Press Data Team, in *Data Journalism – Data Exchange Network Data Journalism Awards*. Retrieved from https://datajournalismawards.org/projects/associated-press-data-team/ (accessed 2 September 2020)

Appelgren, E. (2016). Data journalists using Facebook. *Nordicom Review 37*(1), 156–169.

Appelgren, E. (2017). An illusion of interactivity: the paternalistic side of data journalism. *Journalism Practice, 12*(3), 1–18, doi: 10.1080/17512786.2017.1299032.

ARAB NEWS. (2020, 29 April 2020). Omnicom Mideast revenues plunge amid advertising dip. *ARAB NEWS*. Retrieved from https://www.arabnews.com/node/1666676/business-economy

Arrese, Á. (2016). From gratis to paywalls. *Journalism Studies, 17*(8), 1051–1067, doi: 10.1080/1461670X.2015.1027788.

Auletta, K. (2013, 30 September, 2013). Freedom of information. *The New Yorker*. Retrieved from https://www.newyorker.com/magazine/2013/10/07/freedom-of-information

Automated Insights. (No year). AP. Retrieved from https://automatedinsights.com/customer-stories/associated-press/

Azenha, G. S. (2006). The Internet and the decentralisation of the popular music industry: critical reflections on technology, concentration and diversification. *Radical Musicology* 1(1).

Bakker, P. (2011). *New Journalism 3.0 – Aggregation, Content Farms, and Huffinization: the Rise of Low-pay and No-pay Journalism*. Paper presented at the The Future of Journalism Conference, Cardiff.

Bakker, P. (2012). Aggregation, content farms and Huffinization: the rise of low-pay and no-pay journalism. *Journalism Practice*, 6(5–6), 627–637.

Balkin, J. M. (2014). Old-school/new-school speech regulation. *Harvard Law Review*, 127(8), 2296–2342.

Bandura, A., Ross, D., & Ross, S. A. (1963). Imitation of film-mediated aggressive models. *Journal of Abnormal and Social Psychology*, 66(1), 3–11.

Barnett, S. (2016, 22 January 2016). Why new regulator could be a game-changing moment for journalism. *The Conversation*. Retrieved from http://theconversation.com/why-new-regulator-could-be-a-game-changing-moment-for-journalism-53465

Barr, C. (2017, 28 November 2017). Child knife deaths in England and Wales set for nine-year peak. *The Guardian*. Retrieved from https://www.theguardian.com/membership/2017/nov/28/child-knife-deaths-in-england-and-wales-set-for-nine-year-peak

Barr, C., Chalabi, M., & Evershed, N. (2019 23 March 2019). A decade of the Datablog: 'There's a human story behind every data point'. *The Guardian*. Retrieved from https://www.theguardian.com/membership/datablog/2019/mar/23/a-decade-of-the-datablog-theres-a-human-story-behind-every-data-point

Barrett, D. (2021, 8 May 2021). Trump Justice Department secretly obtained Post reporters' phone records. *The Washington Post*. Retrieved from https://www.washingtonpost.com/national-security/trump-justice-dept-seized-post-reporters-phone-records/2021/05/07/933cdfc6-af5b-11eb-b476-c3b287e52a01_story.html

Barrowman, N. (2018). Why data is never raw. *The New Atlantis*, 56, 129–135.

Barstow, D., Craig, S., & Buettner, R. (2018). Trump engaged in suspect tax schemes as he reaped riches from his father. *The New York Times*. Retrieved from https://www.nytimes.com/interactive/2018/10/02/us/politics/donald-trump-tax-schemes-fred-trump.html

Beckers, K., Masini, A., Sevenans, J., van der Burg, M., De Smedt, J., Van den Bulck, H., & Walgrave, S. (2017). Are newspapers' news stories becoming more alike? Media content diversity in Belgium, 1983–2013. *Journalism*, doi: 10.1177/1464884917706860.

Bell, D. (1973). *The Coming of Post-industrial Society: A Venture in Social Forecasting*. New York: Basic Books.

Bell, D. (1976). The coming of the post-industrial society. *The Educational Forum*, 40(4), 574–579, doi: 10.1080/00131727609336501.

Bell, D. (1979). The social framework of the information society. In M. Dertouzos & J. Moses (Eds.), *The Computer Age: A Twenty-Year View*. Cambridge, MA: The MIT Press.

Bell, E. (2019, 2 February 2019). What 2,000 job cuts tell us: the free market kills digital journalism. *The Guardian*. Retrieved from https://www.theguardian.com/media/2019/feb/02/what-2000-job-cuts-tell-us-the-free-market-kills-digital-journalism

Benson, R. (2016). Institutional forms of media ownership and their modes of power. In M. Eide, L. O. Larsen, & H. Sjøvaag (Eds.), *Journalism Re-examined: Digital Challenges and Professional Reorientations* (pp. 27–48). Bristol: Intellect.

Benson, R. (2019). Paywalls and public knowledge: How can journalism provide quality news for everyone? *Journalism, 20*(1), 146–149.

Berg, H. & Hamed, I. (2017, 22 June 2017). No place for foreigners, *BR Data. SPIEGEL ONLINE*. Retrieved from https://www.hanna-und-ismail.de/english/index.html

Berte, K. & Bens, E. D. (2008). Newspapers go for advertising! *Journalism Studies, 9*(5), 692–703, doi: 10.1080/14616700802207623.

Bilton, R. (2016, 7 October 2016). ProPublica's Data Store, which has pulled in $200K, is now selling datasets for other news orgs. *NiemanLab*. Retrieved from http://www.niemanlab.org/2016/10/propublicas-data-store-which-has-pulled-in-200k-is-now-selling-datasets-for-other-news-orgs/ (accessed 28 March 2019).

Blankenship, J. C. (2016). Losing their 'mojo'?: Mobile journalism and the deprofessionalization of television news work. *Journalism Practice, 10*(8), 1055–1071, doi: 10.1080/17512786.2015.106308.

Blanquerna – Universitat Ramon Llull (Producer). (2014, 15 January 2014). The New York Times and their view on data journalism Part I by Aron Pilhofer. Retrieved 17 June 2021 from https://www.youtube.com/watch?v=OV18-RHKtSA

Boczkowski, P. J. (2005). *Digitizing the News: Innovation in Online Newspapers*. Cambridge, MA: The MIT Press.

Boczkowski, P. J. & de Santos, M. (2007). When more media equals less news: patterns of content homogenization in Argentina's leading print and online newspapers. *Political Communication, 24*(2), 167–180.

Bond, D. (2017). Guardian relies on readers' support to stave off crisis. *Financial Times*. Retrieved from https://www.ft.com/content/9044ff9a-358b-11e7-99bd-13beb0903fa3

Bor, S. E. (2014). Teaching social media journalism: challenges and opportunities for future curriculum design. *Journalism & Mass Communication Educator, 69*(3), 243–255.

Borger, J. (2013, 20 August 2013). NSA files: why the Guardian in London destroyed hard drives of leaked files. *The Guardian*. Retrieved from https://www.theguardian.com/world/2013/aug/20/nsa-snowden-files-drives-destroyed-london

Borges-Rey, E. (2016). Unravelling data journalism: a study of data journalism in British newsrooms. *Journalism Practice, 10*(7), 833–843, doi: 10.1080/17512786.2016.1159921.

Borges-Rey, E. (2017). Towards an epistemology of data journalism in the devolved nations of the United Kingdom: changes and continuities in materiality, performativity and reflexivity. *Journalism*, doi: 10.1177/1464884917693864.

Bouchart, M. (2017, 2 March 2017). How three women are influencing data journalism and what you can learn from them. *Data Journalism Awards*. Retrieved from https://medium.com/data-journalism-awards/how-three-women-are-influencing-data-journalism-and-what-you-can-learn-from-them-c3a9c32564ba

Boumans, J., Trilling, D., Vliegenthart, R., & Boomgaarden, H. (2018). The agency makes the (online) news world go round: the impact of news agency content on print and online news. *International Journal of Communication, 12*, 1768–1789.

Bourne, C. P. & Hahn, T. B. (2003). *A History of Online Information Services, 1963–1976*. Cambridge, MA and London: The MIT Press.

Boutyline, A. & Willer, R. (2017). The social structure of political echo chambers: variation in ideological homophily in online networks. *Political Psychology, 38*(3), 551–569.

Bowcott, O. (2014, 8 December 2014). Mass surveillance exposed by Snowden 'not justified by fight against terrorism'. *The Guardian*. Retrieved from https://www.theguardian.com/world/2014/dec/08/mass-surveillance-exposed-edward-snowden-not-justified-by-fight-against-terrorism

Bower, J. L. & Christensen, C. M. (1995). Disruptive technologies: catching the wave. *Harvard Business Review*, January–February.

Boyle, D. (2013, 12 November 2013). MP told by police that Met investigating Guardian over Snowden files. *PressGazette*. Retrieved from https://www.pressgazette.co.uk/metropolitan-police-confirm-investigation-guardian-over-snowden-leak-files-letter-tory-mp/

Boyles, J. L. & Meyer, E. (2016). Letting the data speak: role perceptions of data journalists in fostering democratic conversation. *Digital Journalism, 4*(7), 944–954, doi: 10.1080/21670811.2016.1166063.

Bozdag, E. (2013). Bias in algorithmic filtering and personalization. *Ethics and Information Technology, 15*(3), 209–227.

Bradshaw, P. (2014). Data journalism. In L. Zion & D. Craig (Eds.), *Ethics for Digital Journalists: Emerging Best Practices*. London and New York: Routledge.

Bradshaw, P. (2017). Chilling effect: regional journalists' source protection and information security practice in the wake of the Snowden and Regulation of Investigatory Powers Act (RIPA) revelations. *Digital Journalism, 5*(3), 334–352, doi: 10.1080/21670811.2016.1251329.

Bradshaw, P. & Rohumaa, L. (2011). *The Online Journalism Handbook*. Essex: Pearson.

Bradshaw, P. and Rohumaa, L. (2013). *The Online Journalism Handbook*. 2nd edn. Oxford and New York: Routledge.

Brake, D. (2017). The invisible hand of the unaccountable algorithm: how Google, Facebook and other tech companies are changing journalism. In J. Tong & S.-h. Lo (Eds.), *Digital Technology and Journalism: An International Comparative Perspective* (pp. 25–46). Cham: Palgrave Macmillan.

Brants, K. (1989). The social construction of the information revolution. *European Journal of Communication, 4*(1), 79–97.

Brevini, B. (2017). Metadata laws, journalism and resistance in Australia. *Media and Communication, 5*(1), 76–83.

Brevini, B., Hintz, A., & McCurdy, P. (Eds.) (2013). *Beyond WikiLeaks: Implications for the Future of Communications, Journalism and Society*. London: Palgrave Macmillan.

Brevini, B. & Murdock, G. (2013). Following the Monday: WikiLeaks and the political economy of disclosure. In B. Brevini, A. Hintz, & P. McCurdy (Eds.), *Beyond WikiLeaks:*

Implications for the Future of Communications, Journalism and Society (pp. 35–55). London: Palgrave Macmillan.

Briggs, M. (2012). *Entrepreneurial Journalism: How to Build What's Next for News*. Los Angeles, CA: Sage/CQ Press.

Brock, G. (2012). The Leveson Inquiry: There's a bargain to the struck over media freedom and regulation. *Journalism, 13*(4), 519–528

Brock, G. (2013). *Out of Print: Newspapers, Journalism and the Business of News in the Digital Age*. London, Philadelphia and New Delhi: KoganPage.

Brook, S. (2009, 13 January 2009). Telegraph Media Group tie-up firm charges just £45 to sub a page. *The Guardian*. Retrieved from https://www.theguardian.com/media/2009/jan/13/telegraph-media-group-sub-page

Brook, S. (2010, 5 January 2010). London Evening Standard to outsource some subbing to PA. *The Guardian*. Retrieved from https://www.theguardian.com/media/2010/jan/05/london-evening-standard-press-association

Brookes, S. (2018). The security reporter today – journalists and journalism in an age of surveillance. In J. Lidberg & D. Muller (Eds.), *In the Name of Security – Secrecy, Surveillance and Journalism* (pp. 209–230). London and New York: Anthem Press.

Brown, C. (1999). State of the American newspaper: fear.com. *American Journalism Review*, June.

Brüggemann, M., Humprecht, E., Nielsen, R. K., Karppinen, K., Cornia, A., & Esser, F. (2016). Framing the newspaper crisis: how debates on the state of the press are shaped in Finland, France, Germany, Italy, United Kingdom and United States. *Journalism Studies, 17*(5), 533–551, doi: 10.1080/1461670X.2015.1006871.

Bruno, N. & Nielsen, R. K. (2012). *Survival is Success: Journalistic Online Start-ups in Western Europe*. Oxford: Reuters Institute for the Study of Journalism, University of Oxford.

Bruns, A. (2008a). The active audience: transforming journalism from gatekeeping to gatewatching. In C. Paterson & D. Domingo (Eds.), *Making Online News: The Ethnography of New Media Production*. New York: Peter Lang Publishing, Inc.

Bruns, A. (2008b). *Blogs, Wikipedia, Second Life, and Beyond: From Production to Produsage*. New York: Peter Lang Publishing, Inc.

Bryant, A. (2016, 23 December 2016). Katherine Power of Clique Media: think like an entrepreneur. *The New York Times*. Retrieved from https://www.nytimes.com/2016/12/23/business/katherine-power-of-clique-media-think-like-an-entrepreneur.html

Bryant, J., Thompson, S., & Finklea, B. W. (2013). *Fundamentals of Media Effects*. Long Grove, IL: Waveland Press, Inc.

Bui, M. N. & Moran, R. E., (2019). Making the 21st century mobile journalist: examining definitions and conceptualizations of mobility and mobile journalism within journalism education. *Digital Journalism*, doi: 10.1080/21670811.2019.1664926.

Bunce, M. (2019). Management and resistance in the digital newsroom. *Journalism, 20*(7), 890–905.

Bureau Local. (No year). About Bureau Local. *The Bureau of Investigative Journalism Local*. Retrieved from https://www.thebureauinvestigates.com/explainers/about-the-project

Bureau of Justice Statistics. (2016). *Arrest-Related Deaths Program Redesign Study, 2015–16: Preliminary Findings*. U.S. Department of Justice, NCJ 250112.

Büren, K. (2011). *Mobile Media Services at Sub-Saharan African Newspapers: A Guide to Implementing Mobile News and Mobile Business*. Paris: The World Association of Newspapers (WAN-IFRA) and the African Media Initiative (AMI).

Buschow, C. (2020). Why do digital native news media fail? An investigation of failure in the early start-up phase. *Media and Communication, 8*(2), 51–61.

Carlson, M. (2007). Making memories matter: journalistic authority and the memorializing discourse around Mary McGrory and David Brinkley. *Journalism, 8*(2), 165–183.

Carlson, M. (2017). *Journalistic Authority: Legitimating News in the Digital Era*. New York: Columbia University Press.

Carlson, M. (2018a). Automating judgment? Algorithmic judgment, news knowledge, and journalistic professionalism. *New Media & Society, 20*(5), 1755–1772.

Carlson, M. (2018b). The information politics of journalism in a post-truth age. *Journalism Studies, 19*(13), 1879–1888, doi: 10.1080/1461670X.2018.1494513.

Carlson, M. & Berkowitz, D. (2014). 'The emperor lost his clothes': Rupert Murdoch, *News of the World* and journalistic boundary work in the UK and USA. *Journalism, 15*(4), 389–406.

Carlson, M. & Usher, N. (2016). News startups as agents of innovation. *Digital Journalism, 4*(5), 563–581, doi: 10.1080/21670811.2015.107634.

Carson, A. (2015). Behind the newspaper paywall – lessons in charging for online content: a comparative analysis of why Australian newspapers are stuck in the purgatorial space between digital and print. *Media, Culture & Society, 37*(7), 1022–1041. doi: https://doi.org/10.1177/0163443715591669.

Casero-Ripollés, A. & Izquierdo-Castillo, J. (2013). Between decline and a new online business model: the case of the Spanish newspaper industry. *Journal of Media Business Studies, 10*(1), 63–78, doi: 10.1080/16522354.2013.11073560.

Casero-Ripollés, A., Izquierdo-Castillo, J., & Doménech-Fabregat, H. (2016). The journalists of the future meet entrepreneurial journalism. *Journalism Practice, 10*(2), 286–303, doi: 10.1080/17512786.2015.1123108.

Castells, M. (1996). *The Rise of The Network Society: The Information Age: Economy, Society and Culture*, Vol. 1. Cambridge, MA and Oxford, UK: Blackwell Publishers.

Castells, M. (2001). *The Internet Galaxy: Reflections on the Internet, Business and Society*. London: Oxford University Press.

Cathcart, B. (2021). *The Guardian* and press reform: a wheel come full circle. *The Political Quarterly, 92*(1), 48–56.

Cellan-Jones, R. (2020, 25 June 2020). Google to pay for 'high quality' news in three countries. *The BBC*. Retrieved from https://www.bbc.co.uk/news/technology-53176945

Centre for Community Journalism. (2017). *A Contestable Funding Scheme for Hyperlocal News in Wales*. Briefing Note, Cardiff University: Centre for Community Journalism.

Chadha, K. & Koliska, M. (2016). Re-legitimizing the institution of journalism: the Indian news media's response to the 'Radia Tapes' scandal. *Journalism Studies, 17*(2), 199–215.

Channel 4. (2020, 24 December 2020). Deepfake Queen to deliver Channel 4's alternative Christmas message. *Channel 4*. Retrieved from https://www.channel4.com/press/news/deepfake-queen-deliver-channel-4s-alternative-christmas-message

Chen, S. (2020, 26 January 2020). Where have those over 5 million people who left Wuhan gone? Big data tells you (*likai wuhan de wubai duowan ren qule nali dashuju gaosu ni*). *First Financial News (Yicai)*. Retrieved from https://www.yicai.com/news/100481655.html

Cheruiyot, D., Baack, S., & Ferrer-Conill, R. (2019). Data journalism beyond legacy media: the case of African and European civic technology organizations. *Digital Journalism*, doi: 10.1080/21670811.2019.1591166.

China Daily. (No year). About China Daily Group. *China Daily*. Retrieved from http://www.chinadaily.com.cn/e/static_e/about

Christensen, C. M., Skok, D., & Allworth, J. (2012, 15 September 2012). Breaking news: Mastering the art of disruptive innovation in journalism. *Nieman Reports, 66*(3), 6–20.

Chyi, H. I. (2012). Paying for what? How much? And why (not)? Predictors of paying intent for multiplatform newspapers. *International Journal on Media Management, 14*(3), 227–250, doi: 10.1080/14241277.2012.657284.

Chyi, H. I. & Lee, A. M. (2013). Online news consumption: a structural model linking preference, use, and paying intent. *Digital Journalism, 1*(2), 194–211.

CNN. (2008, January 17, 2008). Crash passenger: We just dropped. *CNN*. Retrieved from http://edition.cnn.com/2008/WORLD/europe/01/17/heathrow.witnesses/index.html

Coates Nee, R. (2014). Social responsibility theory and the digital nonprofits: should the government aid online news startups? *Journalism, 15*(3), 326–343.

Coddington, M. (2015). Clarifying journalism's quantitative turn. *Digital Journalism, 3*(3), 331–348.

Cohen, N. S. (2015). Entrepreneurial journalism and the precarious state of media work. *South Atlantic Quarterly, 114*(3), 513–533.

Committee to Protect Journalists. (2018, 29 March 2018). New US Espionage Act prosecution has troubling implications for press freedom. Retrieved from https://cpj.org/2018/03/new-us-espionage-act-prosecution-has-troubling-imp/

Constantaras, E. (2018). Data journalism by, about and for marginalised communities. In J. Gray & L. Bounegru (Eds.), *The Data Journalism Handbook 2*. European Journalism Centre and Google News Initiative.

Cook, C. (2012, 5 August 2012). London state schools best in England. *Financial Times*. Retrieved from https://www.ft.com/content/2c0866fe-dbca-11e1-aba3-00144feab49a#axzz22l672AfD

Cook, C. & Sirkkunen, E. (2013). What's in a niche? Exploring the Business Model of Online Journalism. *Journal of Media Business Studies, 10*(4), 63–82, doi: 10.1080/16522354.2013.11073576.

Cook, L. R. (2019, 12 June 2019). How we helped our reporters learn to love spreadsheets. *The New York Times*. Retrieved from https://open.nytimes.com/how-we-helped-our-reporters-learn-to-love-spreadsheets-adc43a93b919

Cooper, G. (2017). UGC creators and use of their content by mainstream media. In J. Tong & S.-h. Lo (Eds.), *Digital Technology and Journalism: An International Comparative Perspective* (pp. 71–90). Cham: Palgrave Macmillan.

Cottle, S. & Ashton, M. (1999). From BBC newsroom to BBC newscentre: on changing technology and journalist practices. *Convergence: The International Journal of Research into New Media Technologies, 5*(3), 22–43.

Cox, M. (2000). *The Development of Computer-Assisted Reporting*. Paper presented at the Newspaper Division, Association for Education in Journalism and Mass Communication,

Southeast Colloquium, University of North Carolina, Chapel Hill. http://citeseerx.ist.psu.edu/viewdoc/download?doi=10.1.1.631.6220&rep=rep1&type=pdf

Curran, J. (2010). The future of journalism. *Journalism Studies*, 11(4), 1–13, doi: https://doi.org/10.1080/14616701003722444.

Curran, J. & Park, M.-J. (Eds.). (2000). *De-Westernizing Media Studies*. London: Routledge.

Dans, E. (2019, 6 February 2019). Meet Bertie, Heliograf and Cyborg, the new journalists on the block. *Forbes*. Retrieved from https://www.forbes.com/sites/enriquedans/2019/02/06/meet-bertie-heliograf-and-cyborg-the-new-journalists-on-the-block/#256ba74138d1

Darcy, O. & Kludt, T. (2019, 24 January 2019). Media industry loses about 1,000 jobs as layoffs hit news organizations. *CNN Business*. Retrieved from https://edition.cnn.com/2019/01/24/media/media-layoffs-buzzfeed-huffpost-gannett/index.html

data.europa.eu. (2017). New Open Data Act in Germany. Retrieved from https://data.europa.eu/en/news/new-open-data-act-germany (accessed 17 June 2021)

Davies, N. & Leigh, D. (2010, 25 July 2010). Afghanistan war logs: massive leak of secret files exposes truth of occupation. *The Guardian*. Retrieved from https://www.theguardian.com/world/2010/jul/25/afghanistan-war-logs-military-leaks

de Burgh, H. (Ed.). (2008). *Investigative Journalism* (2nd edn). London: Routledge.

De Maeyer, J. (2012). The journalistic hyperlink. *Journalism Practice*, 6(5–6), 692–701.

Dedman, B. (1988). *The Color of Money: Home Mortgage Lending Practices Discriminate against Blacks*. The Atlanta Journal and The Atlanta Constitution. Retrieved from http://powerreporting.com/color/ (accessed 04 June 2019)

DeFleur, M. H. (2013). *Computer-Assisted Investigative Reporting: Development and Methodology*. London: Routledge.

Dencik, L. & Cable, J. (2017). The advent of surveillance realism: public opinion and activist responses to the Snowden leaks. *International Journal of Communication*, 11, 763–781.

Dennis, E. E., Martin, J. D., Lance, E. A., & Hassan, F. (2019). *Media Use in the Middle East: A Five-Year Retrospection*. Northwestern University in Qatar.

Deuze, M. (2006). Participation, remediation, bricolage: considering principal components of a digital culture. *The Information Society*, 22(2), 63–75, doi: 10.1080/01972240600567170.

Deuze, M. (2008). The changing context of news work: liquid journalism and monitorial citizenship. *International Journal of Communication*, 2, 848–865.

Devi, S. (2019). Making sense of 'views' culture in television news media in India. *Journalism Practice*, 13(9), 1075–1090, doi: 10.1080/17512786.2019.1635041.

Dewey, C. (2016, 17 November 2016). Facebook fake-news writer: 'I think Donald Trump is in the White House because of me'. *The Washington Post*. Retrieved from https://www.washingtonpost.com/news/the-intersect/wp/2016/11/17/facebook-fake-news-writer-i-think-donald-trump-is-in-the-white-house-because-of-me/

Diakopoulos, N. (2010). A functional roadmap for innovation in computational journalism. Retrieved from: http://www.nickdiakopoulos.com/2011/04/22/a-functional-roadmap-for-innovation-in-computational-journalism/ (accessed 15 May 2019)

Diakopoulos, N. (2014). *Algorithmic Accountability Reporting: On the Investigation of Black Boxes*. PhD, Columbia University, Columbia. Retrieved from https://academiccommons.columbia.edu/doi/10.7916/D8ZK5TW2

Díaz-Struck, E. & Carvajal, R. (2018, 19 December 2018). Algorithms, analysis and adverse events: how ICIJ used machine learning to help find medical device issues. *The*

International Consortium of Investigative Journalists (ICIJ). Retrieved from https://www.icij.org/investigations/implant-files/algorithms-analysis-and-adverse-events-how-icij-used-machine-learning-to-help-find-medical-device-issues/ (accessed 5 June 2020)

Dick, M. (2012). The re-birth of the 'beat': a hyperlocal online newsgathering model. *Journalism Practice*, 6(5–6), 754–765.

Dimitrova, D. V., Connolly-Ahern, C., Williams, A. P., Kaid, L. L., & Reid, A. (2003). Hyperlinking as gatekeeping: online newspaper coverage of the execution of an American terrorist. *Journalism Studies*, 4(3), 401–414.

Domínguez, E. (2017). Going beyond the classic news narrative convention: the background to and challenges of immersion in journalism. *Frontiers in Digital Humanities*, 17 May, doi: https://doi.org/10.3389/fdigh.2017.00010.

Donsbach, W. (2004). Psychology of news decisions: factors behind journalists' professional behavior. *Journalism*, 5(2), 131–157.

Dooley, P. L. (1997). *Taking Their Political Place: Journalists and the Making of an Occupation*. Westport, CT and London: Greenwood Press.

Doudaki, V. & Spyridou, L.-P. (2015). News content online: patterns and norms under convergence dynamics. *Journalism*, 16(2), 257–277.

Douglas, G. (Producer). (2018, 29 August 2018). Data visualisation, from 1987 to today. *The Economist*. Retrieved from https://medium.economist.com/data-visualisation-from-1987-to-today-65d0609c6017

Dowden, O. (2021, 24 May 2021). Bashir scandal: BBC needs to shine a light on its failings. *The Times*. Retrieved from https://www.thetimes.co.uk/article/bashir-scandal-bbc-needs-to-shine-a-light-on-its-failings-j5vvhkf67

Downie, L. Jr & Rafsky, S. (2013). *The Obama Administration and the Press: Leak Investigations and Surveillance in post-9/11 America. Committee to Protect Journalists*. Retrieved from https://cpj.org/reports/2013/10/obama-and-the-press-us-leaks-surveillance-post-911.php (accessed 19 September 2019)

Dubois, E. & Blank, G. (2018). The echo chamber is overstated: the moderating effect of political interest and diverse media. *Information, Communication & Society*, 21(5), 729–745, doi: 10.1080/1369118X.2018.1428656.

Dunn, H. S. (2013). 'Something old, something new …': WikiLeaks and the collaborating newspapers – exploring the limits of conjoint approaches to political exposure. In B. Brevini, A. Hintz, & P. McCurdy (Eds.), *Beyond WikiLeaks: Implications for the Future of Communications, Journalism and Society* (pp. 85–100). London: Palgrave Macmillan Limited.

Edmonds, R. (2021, 15 March 2021). Meet Tortoise, the British digital startup hoping to pioneer 'slow news'. *Poynter*. Retrieved from https://www.poynter.org/business-work/2021/meet-tortoise-the-british-digital-startup-hoping-to-pioneer-slow-news/ (accessed 7 June 2021)

Ekdale, B., Tully, M., Harmsen, S., & Singer, J. B. (2015). Newswork within a culture of job insecurity. *Journalism Practice*, 9(3), 383–398, doi: 10.1080/17512786.2014.9633.

Eldridge II, S. A. (2013). Boundary maintenance and interloper media reaction: differentiating between journalism's discursive enforcement processes. *Journalism Studies*, 15(1), 1–16.

Elgot, J. & Allegretti, A. (2021, 7 June 2021). Tory rebels await Speaker's decision on bid to restore aid pledge. *The Guardian*. Retrieved from https://www.theguardian.com/global-development/2021/jun/07/tory-rebels-thwarted-in-bid-to-force-vote-on-uk-foreign-aid-cut

El Issawi, F. (2016). A comparative analysis of traditional media industry transitions in Tunisia, Libya, and Egypt. In M. Zayani & S. Mirgani (Eds.), *Bullets and Bulletins: Media and Politics in the Wake of the Arab Uprisings*. New York: Oxford University Press.

El Issawi, F. & Cammaerts, B. (2016). Shifting journalistic roles in democratic transitions: lessons from Egypt. *Journalism*, *17*(5), 549–566, doi: 10.1177/1464884915576732.

Elmer, C. (2018). Algorithms in the spotlight: collaborative investigations at Spiegel Online. In J. Gray & L. Bounegru (Eds.), *The Data Journalism Handbook 2*. Retrieved from https://datajournalismhandbook.org/handbook/two/investigating-data-platforms-and-algorithms/algorithms-in-the-spotlight-collaborative-investigations-at-spiegel-online-christina-elmer-spiegel-online (accessed 8 April 2019)

Erdal, I. J. (2009). Cross-media (re)production cultures. *Convergence: The International Journal of Research into New Media Technologies*, *15*(2), 215–231.

European Data News Hub (EDNH) (No year). We are journalists, designers, developers, planners. Retrieved from https://www.ednh.news/about/

European Data Portal. (2018). *Open Data Maturity in Europe*. Retrieved from https://www.europeandataportal.eu/sites/default/files/edp_landscaping_insight_report_n4_2018.pdf (accessed 17 June 2021)

Evershed, N. (2019, 1 February 2019). Why I created a robot to write news stories. *The Guardian*. Retrieved from https://www.theguardian.com/commentisfree/2019/feb/01/why-i-created-a-robot-to-write-news-stories

Farmanfarmaian, R. (2017). Media and the politics of the sacral: freedom of expression in Tunisia after the Arab Uprisings. *Media, Culture & Society*, *39*(7), 1043–1062.

Farrer, M. (2018, 23 December 2018). Sunda Strait tsunami is latest in a series of Indonesian disasters in 2018. *The Guardian*. Retrieved from https://www.theguardian.com/world/2018/dec/23/sunda-strait-tsunami-is-latest-in-a-series-of-indonesian-disasters-in-2018

Fengler, S. (2012). From media self-regulation to 'crowd-criticism': media accountability in the digital age. *Central European Journal of Communication*, *5*(9), 175–189.

Fenton, N. (Ed.). (2010). *New Media, Old News: Journalism and Democracy in the Digital Age*. London: Sage.

Fielden, L. (2016). UK press regulation: taking account of media convergence. *Convergence*, *22*(5), 472–477.

Figenschou, T. U. & Ihlebæk, K. A. (2019). Challenging journalistic authority: media criticism in far-right alternative media. *Journalism Studies*, *20*(9), 1221–1237, doi: 10.1080/1461670X.2018.150086.

Figenschou, T. U. & Thorbjørnsrud, K. (2017). Disruptive media events: managing mediated dissent in the aftermath of terror. *Jouranalism Practice*, *11*(8), 942–959.

Figl, B. (2017). *Bigger Is Not Always Better: What We Can Learn about Data Journalism from Small Newsrooms*. Reuters Fellowship Paper. Oxford: University of Oxford.

Findley, A. (2013, 20 May 2013). A rare peek into a Justice Department leak probe. *The Washington Post.* Retrieved from http://www.washingtonpost.com/local/a-rare-peek-into-a-justice-department-leak-probe/2013/05/19/0bc473de-be5e-11e2-97d4-a479289a31f9_story.html

Finer, J. (2017, 20 February 2017). A dangerous time for the press and the Presidency. *The Atlantic.* Retrieved from https://www.theatlantic.com/politics/archive/2017/02/a-dangerous-time-for-the-press-and-the-presidency/517260/

Fink, K. & Anderson, C. W. (2015). Data journalism in the United States: beyond the 'usual suspects'. *Journalism Studies, 16*(4), 467–481.

Flamingo and the Reuters Institute for the Study of Journalism, University of Oxford. (2019). *How Young People Consume News and the Implications for Mainstream Media.* Report.

Fletcher, J., Kirby, D. G., & Cunningham, S. (2006). Tapeless and paperless: automating the workflow in TV studio production. Retrieved from http://downloads.bbc.co.uk/rd/pubs/whp/whp-pdf-files/WHP141.pdf (accessed 28 May 2020)

Ford, H. & Hutchinson, J. (2019). Newsbots that mediate journalist and audience relationships. *Digital Journalism, 7*(8), 1013–1031, doi: 10.1080/21670811.2019.1626752.

Forester, T. (Ed.). (1986). *The Information Technology Revolution.* Cambridge, MA: The MIT Press.

Forester, T. (1990). *High-tech Society: The Story of the Information Technology Revolution.* Cambridge, MA: The MIT Press.

Franklin, B. (2012). The future of journalism. *Journalism Studies, 13*(5–6), 663–681.

Franklin, B. (2014). The future of journalism: in an age of digital media and economic uncertainty. *Digital Journalism, 2*(3), 254–272.

Freedman, D. (2012). The phone hacking scandal: implications for regulation. *Television & New Media, 13*(1), 17–20, doi: 10.1177/1527476411425253 (accessed 30 April 2019)

Freedom House. (2018). *Freedom on the Net 2018.* Retrieved from https://freedomhouse.org/sites/default/files/FOTN_2018_Final.pdf (accessed 19 May 2020)

Freedom House. (2019). *Freedom in the World 2019.* Retrieved from https://freedomhouse.org/sites/default/files/Feb2019_FH_FITW_2019_Report_ForWeb-compressed.pdf

Freidson, E. (1983). The theory of professions: the state of the art. In R. Dingwall and P. Lewis (Eds.), *The Sociology of the Professions.* London: Macmillan.

Froomkin, D. (2014, 28 July 2014). Top journalists and lawyers: NSA surveillance threatens press freedom and right to counsel. *The Intercept.* Retrieved from https://theintercept.com/2014/07/28/nsa-surveillance-threatens-press-freedom-right-counsel-survey-finds/

Gade, P. J. & Lowrey, W. (2011). Reshaping the journalistic culture. In W. Lowrey & P. J. Gade (Eds.), *Changing the News: The Forces Shaping Journalism in Uncertain Times* (pp. 22–42). New York and London: Routledge.

Gallagher, R. (2013, 10 October 2013). Government surveillance is crippling press freedoms, report shows. *Slate.* Retrieved from https://slate.com/technology/2013/10/committee-to-protect-journalists-report-shows-government-surveillance-hurting-press-freedom.html

Gallagher, R. (2015, 24 July 2015). U.K. police confirm ongoing criminal probe of Snowden leak journalists. *The Intercept.* Retrieved from https://theintercept.com/2015/07/24/uk-met-police-snowden-investigation-journalists/

Gans, H. J. (1979) *Deciding What's News: A Study of CBS Evening News, NBC Nightly News, Newsweek, and Time*. London: Constable.

García Avilés, J., Meier, K., Kaltenbrunner, A., Carvajal, M., & Kraus, D. (2009). Newsroom integration in Austria, Spain and Germany: models of media convergence. *Journalism Practice, 3*(3), 285–303.

García Avilés, J. A., León, B., Sanders, K., & Harrison, J. (2006). Journalists at digital television newsrooms in Britain and Spain: workflow and multi-skilling in a competitive environment. *Journalism Studies, 5*(1), 87–100.

Garrett, R. K. (2009). Politically motivated reinforcement seeking: reframing the selective exposure debate. *Journal of Communication, 59*(4), 676–699.

Gentzkow, M. & Shapiro, J. M. (2010). *Ideological Segregation Online and Offline*. NBER Working Paper Series (15916, NBER).

Geradin, D. & Katsifis, D. (2020, 3 June 2020). Competition in ad tech: a response to Google. Submission before the Australian Competition and Consumer Commission (ACCC). Retrieved from https://www.accc.gov.au/system/files/Damien%20Geradin%20and%20Dimitrios%20Katsifis%20%283%20June%202020%29.pdf (accessed 5 January 2022)

Giddens, A. (1990). *The Consequences of Modernity*. Cambridge: Polity Press.

Gilbert, C. & Bower, J. L. (2002). Disruptive change: when trying harder is part of the problem. *Harvard Business Review, 80*(5), 94–101.

Gilbert, C. G. (2005). Unbundling the structure of inertia: resource versus routine rigidity. *The Academy of Management Journal, 48*(5), 741–763.

Gillespie, T. (2010). The politics of 'platforms'. *New Media & Society, 12*(3), 347–364.

Gillmor, D. (2006). We the media: grassroots journalism by the people, for the people. Sebastopol, CA: O'Reilly Media, Inc.

Glahn, H. R. (1970). Computer-produced worded forecasts. *Bulletin of the American Meteorological Society, 51*(12), 1126–1132.

Glasser, T. & Ettema, J. (1989). Investigative journalism and the moral order. *Critical Studies in Mass Communication, 6*(1), 1–20.

Glendinning, L., Swaine, J., Laughland, O., Lartey, J., & Popovich, N. (2016, 11 April 2016). How we record every police killing in the United States [video]. *The Guardian*. Retrieved from https://www.theguardian.com/us-news/video/2016/apr/11/the-counted-police-killings-guardian-us-video

GNM press office. (2020, 15 July 2020). Guardian Media Group plc (GMG) publishes 2019/20 statutory financial results and announces proposals to position the business for future growth and reduce costs. *The Guardian*. Retrieved from https://www.theguardian.com/gnm-press-office/2020/jul/15/guardian-media-group-plc-gmg-publishes-201920-statutory-financial-results-and-announces-proposals-to-position-the-business-for-future-growth-and-reduce-costs

Goggin, G. (2011). Ubiquitous apps: politics of openness in global mobile cultures. *Digital Creativit [Creativity], 22*(3), 148–159.

Gold, H. (2016, 26 February 2016). Donald Trump: We're going to 'open up' libel laws. *Politico*. Retrieved from https://www.politico.com/blogs/on-media/2016/02/donald-trump-libel-laws-219866

Graefe, A. (2016). Guide to automated journalism. *Tow Center for Digital Journalism.*

Graefe, A., Haim, M., Haarmann, B., & Brosius, H.-B. (2018). Readers' perception of computer-generated news: credibility, expertise, and readability. *Journalism, 19*(5), 595–610.

Granados, S., Murphy, Z., & Schaul, K. (2016, 17 October 2016). A new age of walls, episode 3: Concrete divisions. *The Washington Post.* Retrieved from https://www.washingtonpost.com/graphics/world/border-barriers/us-mexico-border-crossing/

Grant, A. M. (2019). Bringing *The Daily Mail* to Africa: entertainment websites and the creation of a digital youth public in post-genocide Rwanda. *Journal of Eastern African Studies, 13*(1), 106–123.

Greenslade, R. (2008, 3 July 2008). Outsourced subbing is on the way. *The Guardian.* Retrieved from https://www.theguardian.com/media/greenslade/2008/jul/03/outsourcedsubbingisonthew#comment-3043807

Greenslade, R. (2020, 15 March 2020). It's time to break the silence about Mirror phone hacking. *The Guardian.* Retrieved from https://www.theguardian.com/business/commentisfree/2020/mar/15/its-time-to-break-the-silence-about-mirror-phone-hacking

Grice, A. (2017). Fake news handed Brexiteers the referendum – and now they have no idea what they're doing. *The Independent.* Retrieved from https://www.independent.co.uk/voices/michael-gove-boris-johnson-brexit-eurosceptic-press-theresa-may-a7533806.html

Grieco, E. (2018). Newsroom employment dropped nearly a quarter in less than 10 years, with greatest decline at newspapers. *Pew Research Center.* Retrieved from https://www.pewresearch.org/fact-tank/2021/07/13/u-s-newsroom-employment-has-fallen-26-since-2008/

Grosser, K. M., Hase, V., & Wintterlin, F. (2019). Trustworthy or shady?: Exploring the influence of verifying and visualizing user-generated content (UGC) on online journalism's trustworthiness. *Journalism Studies, 20*(4), 500–522, doi: 10.1080/1461670X.2017.1392255.

Grynbaum, M. M. (2017, 26 January 2017). Trump strategist Stephen Bannon says media should 'keep its mouth shut'. *The New York Times.* Retrieved from https://www.nytimes.com/2017/01/26/business/media/stephen-bannon-trump-news-media.html

Gu, J. (2018, 15 March 2018). Women lose out to men even before they graduate from college. *Bloomberg.* Retrieved from https://www.bloomberg.com/graphics/2018-women-professional-inequality-college/

Guaaybess, T. (2019). *The Media in Arab Countries: From Development Theories to Cooperation Policies.* Hoboken, NJ and London: John Wiley & Sons.

Guardian staff. (2013, 19 August 2013). Glenn Greenwald's partner detained at Heathrow airport for nine hours. *The Guardian.* Retrieved from https://www.theguardian.com/world/2013/aug/18/glenn-greenwald-guardian-partner-detained-heathrow

Halal, W. (1993). The information technology revolution: computer hardware, software, and services into the 21st century. *Technological Forecasting and Social Change, 44*(1), 69–86.

Hall, S. (1980). Encoding/decoding. In S. Hall, D. Hobson, A. Lowe, & P. Willis (Eds.), *Culture, Media, Language* (pp. 128–138). London: Routledge.

Halliday, J. (2013, 21 January 2013). Financial Times editor announces digital-first strategy. *The Guardian.* Retrieved from https://www.theguardian.com/media/2013/jan/21/financial-times-digital-first

Hallin, D. C. & Mancini, P. (2004). *Comparing Media Systems: Three Models of Media and Politics.* New York: Cambridge University Press.

Hamilton, J. T. & Turner, F. (2009). *Accountability Through Algorithm: Developing the Field of Computational Journalism*. Center for Advanced Study in the Behavioral Sciences, Summer Workshop, Stanford University.

Hammond, P. (2017). From computer-assisted to data-driven: journalism and big data. *Journalism, 18*(4), 408–424, doi: 10.1177/1464884915620205.

Hanusch, F. (2017). Web analytics and the functional differentiation of journalism cultures: individual, organizational and platform-specific influences on newswork. *Information, Communication & Society, 20*(10), 1571–1586.

Hanusch, F. & Tandoc, E. C. (2019). Comments, analytics, and social media: the impact of audience feedback on journalists' market orientation. *Journalism, 20*(6), 695–713.

Harlow, S. & Chadha, M. (2019). Indian entrepreneurial journalism : building a typology of how founders' social identity shapes innovation and sustainability. *Journalism Studies, 20*(6), 891–910, doi: 10.1080/1461670X.2018.146317.

Harrison, J. (2010). User-generated content and gatekeeping at the BBC hub. *Journalism Studies, 11*(2), 243–256.

Harvey, D. (1990). *The Condition of Postmodernity: An Enquiry into the Origins of Cultural Change*. Oxford: Blackwell.

Hassard, J. (2002). Essai: Organizational time: modern, symbolic and postmodern reflections. *Organization Studies, 23*(6), 885–892.

Heft, A. & Dogruel, L. (2019). Searching for autonomy in digital news entrepreneurism projects. *Digital Journalism, 7*(5), 678–697, doi: 10.1080/21670811.2019.1581070.

Hemmingway, E. (2008). *Into the Newsroom: Exploring the Digital Production of Regional Television News*. London and New York: Routledge.

Heravi, B. R. (2019). 3Ws of data journalism education: what, where and who?. *Journalism Practice, 13*(3), 349–366, doi: 10.1080/17512786.2018.1463167.

Herbert, J. (2000). *Journalism in the Digital Age: Theory and Practice for Broadcast, Print and On-line Media*. Oxford: Focal Press.

Hermida, A. (2010). Twittering the news: the emergence of ambient journalism. *Journalism Practice, 4*(3), 297–308.

Hermida, A., Fletcher, F., Korell, D., & Logan, D. (2012). Share, like, recommend: decoding the social media news consumer. *Journalism Studies, 13*(5–6), 815–824, doi: 10.1080/1461670X.2012.664430.

Hermida, A. & Young, M. L. (2019). *Data Journalism and the Regeneration of News*. London and New York: Routledge.

Hern, A. (2021, 17 February 2021). News Corp agrees deal with Google over payments for journalism. *The Guardian*. Retrieved from https://www.theguardian.com/media/2021/feb/17/news-corp-agrees-deal-with-google-over-payments-for-journalism

Hill, S. & Lashmar, P. (2014). *Online Journalism: The Essential Guide*. London: Sage.

Hinchcliffe, K. & Dukes, T. (2018, 23 May). School arrest disparity methodology. *WRAL*. Retrieved from https://wral.com/school-arrest-disparity-methodology/17575769/

Hodge, B. & Coronado, G. (2005). Speculations on a Marxist theory of the virtual revolution. *The Fibreculture Journal, 5*, 1449–1443.

Hoogvelt, A. (1997) *Globalisation and the Postcolonial World: The New Political Economy of Development*. Basingstoke and London: Macmillan Press Ltd.

Howard, P. N. & Hussain, M. M. (2011). The upheavals in Egypt and Tunisia: the role of digital media. *Journal of Democracy, 22*(3), 35–48.

Howatt, G. & Webster, M. (2019, 23 March 2019). With fewer kids vaccinated, more Minnesota schools are vulnerable to measles and chickenpox. *Star Tribune*. Retrieved from https://www.startribune.com/with-fewer-kids-vaccinated-more-minnesota-schools-are-vulnerable-to-measles-and-chickenpox/507568022/

Hoyer, M., Minkoff, M., & Thibodeaux, T. (2016, 24 May 2016). Branching out in data journalism. *The Associated Press (AP) Insights*.

Human Rights Watch. (2014). *With Liberty to Monitor All: How Large-Scale US Surveillance Is Harming Journalism, Law and American Democracy*. New York: HRW.

Humprecht, E. & Esser, F. (2018). Diversity in online news: on the importance of ownership types and media system types. *Journalism Studies*, *19*(2), 1825–1847.

Hunter, A. (2015). Crowdfunding independent and freelance journalism: negotiating journalistic norms of autonomy and objectivity. *New Media & Society*, *17*(2), 272–288.

Hunter, A. (2016). 'It's like having a second full-time job': Crowdfunding, journalism and labour. *Journalism Practice*, *10*(2), 217–232, doi: 10.1080/17512786.2015.11231.

Hyvarinen, J. (2018). SLAPP: shadowy legal actions are being used to silence the media. Retrieved from https://www.indexoncensorship.org/2018/01/shadowy-legal-actions-are-silencing-the-media/

ICNN. (2021). Connect with hyperlocals around the world. Retrieved from https://www.communityjournalism.co.uk/ (accessed 28 May 2020)

Iglesias, C. (2013). *European Public Sector Information Platform Topic Report No. 2013/12: A Year of Open Data in the EMEA Region*. EPSIplatform. Retrieved from https://data.europa.eu/sites/default/files report/2013_a_year_of_open_data_in_the_emea_region.pdf (accessed 25 November 2019)

Ingold, D. & Soper, S. (2016, 21 April 2016). Amazon doesn't consider the race of its customers. Should it? *Bloomberg*. Retrieved from https://www.bloomberg.com/graphics/2016-amazon-same-day/

Ingram, M. (2018, 16 May 2018). The platform patrons: how Facebook and Google became two of the biggest funders of journalism in the world. *Colulmbia Journalism Review*. Retrieved from https://www.cjr.org/special_report/google-facebook-journalism.php (accessed 19 February 2019)

Ipsos. (2018, 3 April 2018). *AIB*. Retrieved from https://aib.org.uk/rt-weekly-tv-audience-grows-by-more-than-a-third-now-100-mln-ipsos/

IRE. (No year). *Investigative Reporters & Editors (IRE)*. Retrieved from https://www.ire.org/resource-center/listservs

Irion, K. & Valcke, P. (2015). Cultural diversity in the digital age: EU competences, policies and regulations for diverse audiovisual and online content. In E. Psychogiopoulou (Ed.), *Cultural Governance and the European Union* (pp. 75–90). London: Palgrave Macmillan.

Islam, A. (2018, 1 December 2018). Making sense of data journalism from Bangladesh perspective. *Global Media Journal*, *16*(31).

Jamil, S. (2021). Increasing accountability using data journalism: challenges for the Pakistani journalists. *Journalism Practice*, *15*(1), 19–40, doi: 10.1080/17512786.2019.1697956.

Jarvis, J. (2006, 5 July 2006). Networked journalism. Retrieved 23 August 2013 from http://buzzmachine.com/2006/07/05/networked-journalism/

Jin, X., Wah, B. W., Cheng, X., & Wang, Y. (2015). Significance and challenges of big data research. *Big Data Research*, *2*(2), 59–64.

Joffé, G. (2014). Government–media relations in Tunisia: a paradigm shift in the culture of governance? *The Journal of North African Studies*, *19*(5), 615–638, doi: 10.1080/13629387.2014.975664.

Johnson, T. J. (1972). *Professions and Power*. Houndmills, UK: Macmillan.

Johnston, C. (2014, 14 November 2014). Trinity Mirror to close seven local newspapers with the loss of 50 jobs. *The Guardian*. Retrieved from https://www.theguardian.com/media/2014/nov/14/trinity-mirror-close-local-newspapers-job-losees

Johnston, L. (2016). Social news = journalism evolution? *Digital Journalism*, *4*(7), 899–909, doi: 10.1080/21670811.2016.1168709.

Jones, B. & Jones, R. (2019). Public service chatbots: automating conversation with BBC News. *Digital Journalism*, *7*(8), 1032–1053.

Jones, R. A. & West, S. R. (2017). The fragility of the free American press. Northwestern University Law Review, *112*(3), 567–596.

Jung, J., Song, H., Kim, Y., Im, H., & Oh, S. (2017). Intrusion of software robots into journalism: the public's and journalists' perceptions of news written by algorithms and human journalists. *Computers in Human Behavior*, *71*, 291–298.

Kakade, S. (2017, 9 June 2017). How the Hindustan Times is introducing Indian readers to interactive stories. Retrieved from http://www.storybench.org/hindustan-times-introducing-indian-readers-interactive-stories/

Kakar, A. (2018, 17 January 2018). European Commission pressured by MEPs to protect media from 'abusive' high-cost lawsuits. *PressGazette*. Retrieved from https://www.pressgazette.co.uk/european-commission-pressured-by-meps-to-protect-media-from-abusive-high-cost-lawsuits/

Kalyani, C. (2017). The Indian news media industry: structural trends and journalistic implications. *Global Media and Communication*, *13*(2), 139–156.

Kang, C., McCabe, D., & Wakabayashi, D. (2020, 20 October 2020). U.S. accuses Google of illegally protecting monopoly. *The New York Times*. Retrieved from https://www.nytimes.com/2020/10/20/technology/google-antitrust.html

Kaplan, R. L. (2002). *Politics and the American Press: The Rise of Objectivity, 1865–1920*. Cambridge: Cambridge University Press.

Karlsson, M. (2011) The immediacy of online news, the visibility of journalistic processes and a restructuring of journalistic authority. *Journalism 12*(3), 279–295.

Katz, E., Blumler, J. G., & Gurevitch, M. (1973). Uses and gratifications research. *Public Opinion Quarterly*, *37*(4), 509–523.

Kellam, M. & Stein, E. (2017). Trump's war on the news media is serious. Just look at Latin America. *The Washington Post*. Retrieved from https://www.washingtonpost.com/news/monkey-cage/wp/2017/02/16/trumps-war-on-the-news-media-is-serious-just-look-at-latin-america/

Kellner, D. (2018). Donald Trump as authoritarian populist: a Frommian analysis. In J. Morelock (Ed.), *Critical Theory and Authoritarian Populism* (pp. 71–82). London: University of Westminster Press.

Kelly, K. J. (2016). Bloomberg turning to robots to deliver the news. Retrieved from https://nypost.com/2016/04/27/bloomberg-turning-to-robots-to-deliver-the-news/

Kennedy, P. M. (1993). *Preparing for the Twenty-First Century*. London: Random House.

Kenny, P. D. (2020). 'The enemy of the people': populists and press freedom. *Political Research Quarterly, 73*(2), 261–275.

Kiel, P. & Waldman, A. (2015, 8 October 2015). The color of debt: how collection suits squeeze black neighborhoods. *ProPublica.* Retrieved from https://propublica.org/article/debt-collection-lawsuits-squeeze-black-neighborhoods

Kim, D. & Kim, S. (2017). Newspaper companies' determinants in adopting robot journalism. *Technological Forecasting & Social Change, 117,* 184–195.

Kirk, A. (2015, 17 January 2015). Nurses at breaking point as number off work with stress soars. *The Guardian.* Retrieved from https://www.theguardian.com/society/2015/jan/17/nurses-nhs-stress-leave-staff-breaking-point

Kiss, J. (2008, 11 July 2008). Rafat Ali: from blogs to riches. *The Guardian.* Retrieved from https://www.theguardian.com/media/pda/2008/jul/11/rafatalifromblogstoriches

Klein, S. (2016, 16 March). Infographics in the time of cholera. *ProPublica.* Retrieved from https://www.propublica.org/nerds/infographics-in-the-time-of-cholera

Kolodzy, J. (2012). *Practicing Convergence Journalism: An Introduction to Cross-Media Storytelling.* Lanham, MD: Rowman & Littlefield.

Kopf, E. W. (1916). Florence Nightingale as statistician. *Publications of the American Statistical Association, 15*(116), 388–404.

Kormelink, T. G. & Meijer, I. C. (2018). What clicks actually mean: exploring digital news user practices. *Journalism, 19*(5), 668–683.

Kumar, A. & Haneef, M. S. M. (2018). Is *Mojo* (en)de-skilling? Unfolding the practices of mobile journalism in an Indian newsroom. *Journalism Practice, 12*(10), 1292–1310.

Larrondo, A., Domingo, D., Erdal, I. J., Masip, P., & Van den Bulck, H. (2016). Opportunities and limitations of newsroom convergence: a comparative study on European public service broadcasting organisations. *Journalism Studies, 17*(3), 277–300.

Larson, M. S. (1977). *The Rise of Professionalism: A Sociological Analysis.* Berkeley: University of California Press.

Lashmar, P. (2017). No more sources? : The impact of Snowden's revelations on journalists and their confidential sources. *Journalism Practice, 11*(6), 665–688, doi: 10.1080/17512786.2016.1179587.

Latar, N. L. (2015). The robot journalist in the age of social physics: the end of human journalism? In G. Einav (Ed.), *The New World of Transitioned Media: Digital Realignment and Industry Transformation* (pp. 65–80). Cham: Springer.

Latar, N. L. (2018). Robot journalism. In L. N. Lemelshtrich (Ed.), *Robot Journalism: Can Human Journalism Survive?* (pp. 29–40). Singapore: World Scientific Publishing.

Laughey, D. (2010). User authority through mediated interaction: a case of eBay-in-use. *Journal of Consumer Culture, 10*(1), 105–128.

Lauk, E., Uskali, T., Kuutti, H., & Hirvinen, H. (2016). Drone journalism: the newest global test of press freedom. In U. Carlsson (Ed.), *Freedom of Expression and Media in Transition: Studies and Reflections in the Digital Age* (pp. 117–125). Gothenburg: Nordicom.

Laville, S. & Taylor, M. (2019, 17 November 2019). Scientists and climate advisors condemn Tory environmental record *The Guardian.* Retrieved from https://www.

theguardian.com/environment/2019/nov/17/scientists-and-climate-advisers-condemn-tory-environmental-record

Lee, A. M., Lewis, S. C., & Powers, M. (2014). Audience clicks and news placement: a study of time-lagged influence in online journalism. *Communication Research, 41*(4), 505–530.

Lee, C.-C. (2001). Rethinking political economy: implications for media and democracy in Greater China. *Javnost – The Public, 8*(4), 81–102.

Lee, C.-C., He, Z., & Huang, Y. (2006). 'Chinese Party Publicity Inc.' conglomerated: the case of the Shenzhen Press Group. *Media, Culture & Society, 28*(4), 581–602.

Lee, E. (2020, 5 November 2020). New York Times hits 7 million subscribers as digital revenue rises. *The New York Times.* Retrieved from https://www.nytimes.com/2020/11/05/business/media/new-york-times-q3-2020-earnings-nyt.html

Lehtisaari, K. (2015). *Market and Political Factors and the Russian Media.* Working Paper. Oxford: Reuters Institute for the Study of Journalism, University of Oxford.

Leigh, D. (2019). *Investigative Journalism: A Survival Guide.* London and New York: Springer International Publishing.

Leonhardt, D. (No year). Navigating the news with the Upshot. *The New York Times.* Retrieved from https://www.facebook.com/notes/the-new-york-times-the-upshot/navigating-the-news-with-the-upshot/1453536644883143?smid=tw-upshotnyt

Levi, L. (2014). Journalism standards and 'the dark arts': The U.K.'s Leveson Inquiry and the U.S. media in the age of surveillance. *Georgia Law Review, 48*(3), 907–948.

Levi, L. (2015). Taming the 'feral beast': cautionary lessons from British press reform. *Santa Clara Law Review, 55*(2), 323–401.

Levi, L. (2017). The weaponised lawsuit against the media: litigation funding as a new threat to journalism. *American University Law Review, 66*(3), 761–828.

Lewis, N. P. & Al Nashmi, E. (2019). Data journalism in the Arab region: role conflict exposed. *Digital Journalism, 7*(9), 1200–1214.

Lewis, N. P. & Waters, S. (2018). Data journalism and the challenge of shoe-leather epistemologies. *Digital Journalism, 6*(6), 719–736, doi: 10.1080/21670811.2017.1377093.

Lewis, P., Barr, C., Clarke, S., Voce, A., Levett, C., & Gutiérrez, P. (2019). Revealed: the rise and rise of populist rhetoric. *The Guardian.* Retrieved from https://www.theguardian.com/world/ng-interactive/2019/mar/06/revealed-the-rise-and-rise-of-populist-rhetoric

Lewis, P., Clarke, S., & Barr, C. (2019, 6 March 2019). How we combed leaders' speeches to gauge populist rise. *The Guardian.* Retrieved from https://www.theguardian.com/world/2019/mar/06/how-we-combed-leaders-speeches-to-gauge-populist-rise

Lewis, P. H. (1996, 22 January 1996). The New York Times introduces a web site. *The New York Times.* Retrieved from https://www.nytimes.com/1996/01/22/business/the-new-york-times-introduces-a-web-site.html

Lewis, S. C., Sanders, A. K., & Carmody, C. (2019). Libel by algorithm? Automated journalism and the threat of legal liability. *Journalism & Mass Communication Quarterly, 96*(1), 60–81, doi: 10.1177/1077699018755983.

Lewis, S. C. & Usher, N. (2014). Code, collaboration, and the future of journalism: a case study of Hacks/Hackers global network *Digital Journalism, 2*(3), 383–393, doi: 10.1080/21670811.2014.895504.

Lewis, S. C. & Westlund, O. (2015). Big data and journalism: epistemology, expertise, economics, and ethics. *Digital Journalism, 3*(3), 447–466.

Lievrouw, L. & Livingstone, S. (2002). The social shaping and consequences of ICTs. In L. Lievrouw & S. Livingstone (Eds.), *The Handbook of New Media* (pp. 1–21). London: Sage.

Linden, C.-G. (2018). Algorithms are a reporter's new best friend: news automation and the case for augmented journalism. In S. Eldridge II & B. Franklin (Eds.), *The Routledge Handbook of Developments in Digital Journalism Studies* (pp. 237–250). London and New York: Routledge.

Lischka, J. A. (2019). A badge of honor?: How The New York Times discredits President Trump's fake news accusations *Journalism Studies, 20*(2), 287–304, doi: 10.1080/1461670X.2017.1375385.

Liu, C. & Bruns, A. (2007). *Cell Phone SMS News in Chinese Newspaper Groups: A Case Study of Yunnan Daily Press Group.* Paper presented at the Mobile Media Conference, Sydney.

Liu, H.-C., Chang, C.-C., Liang, C.-T., Yin, C. I., & Liang, C. (2019). Kindling social entrepreneurial journalism. *Journalism Practice, 13*(7), 873–885.

Livingstone, S. (2005). On the relation between audiences and publics. In S. Livingstone (Ed.), *Audiences and Publics: When Cultural Engagement Matters for the Public Sphere* (pp. 17–41). Bristol: Intellect Books.

Livingstone, S. & Das, R. (2013). The end of audiences? Theoretical echoes of reception amid the uncertainties of use. In J. Hartley, J. Burgess, & A. Bruns (Eds.), *A Companion to New Media Dynamics* (pp. 104–121). Oxford: Wiley-Blackwell.

Lo, S.-h (2020, 14 October, 2020). Personal Communication.

Lohner, J., Banjac, S., & Neverla, I. (2016). *Mapping Structural Conditions of Journalism in Egypt, Kenya, Serbia and South Africa.* Working Paper, MeCoDEM. Retrieved from http://eprints.whiterose.ac.uk/117303/

Lord Dyson. (2021). *Report of the Dyson Investigation.* Retrieved from http://downloads.bbc.co.uk/aboutthebbc/reports/reports/dyson-report-20-may-21.pdf (accessed 3 June 2021)

Lowenstein, R. L. & Merrill, J. C. (1990). *Macromedia: Mission, Message and Morality.* New York: Longman.

Maheshwari, S. & Sparks, C. (2018). Political elites and journalistic practices in India: A case of institutionalized heteronomy. *Journalism*, doi: 10.1177/1464884918761630.

Mancini, P. (2018). 'Assassination campaigns': corruption scandals and news media instrumentalization. *International Journal of Communication, 12*, 3067–3086.

Manfredi, J. L. & Artero, J. P. (2014). New business models for the media: the Spanish case. In E. Psychogiopoulou (Ed.), *Media Policies Revisited*: The Challenge for Media Freedom and Independence (pp. 160–174). Houndmills, UK: Palgrave Macmillan.

Manovich, L. (2005, 16 November 2005). Remix and remixability. Retrieved from https://www.nettime.org/Lists-Archives/nettime-l-0511/msg00060.html

Mason, R. & Sparrow, A. (2020, 3 February 2020). Political journalists boycott No 10 briefing after reporter ban. *The Guardian.* Retrieved from https://www.theguardian.com/politics/2020/feb/03/political-journalists-boycott-no-10-briefing-after-reporter-ban

Mayer-Schönberger, V. & Cukier, K. (2013). *Big Data: A Revolution That Will Transform How We Live, Work and Think.* London: John Murray.

Mayhew, F. (2017, 26 October 2017). Guardian says money from readers has overtaken advertising as it boasts 500,000 paying supporters. *PressGazette*. Retrieved from https://www.pressgazette.co.uk/guardian-says-money-from-readers-has-overtaken-advertising-as-it-boasts-500000-paying-supporters-and-subscribers/

Mayhew, F. (2018, 16 October 2018). James Harding's Tortoise Media launches campaign to raise £75,000 as it promises a 'different kind of newsroom'. *PressGazette*. Retrieved from https://www.pressgazette.co.uk/james-hardings-tortoise-media-launches-campaign-to-raise-75000-as-it-promises-a-different-kind-of-newsroom/

Mayhew, F. (2019a, 14 October 2019). Independent rebrands content behind paywall as 'premium'. *PressGazette*. Retrieved from https://pressgazette.co.uk/independent-premium-content-rebrand-paywall/

Mayhew, F. (2019b, 15 October). Some 20 national newspaper staff face redundancy as Reach restructure continues. *PressGazette*. Retrieved from https://pressgazette.co.uk/some-20-national-newspaper-staff-face-redundancy-as-reach-restructure-continues/

Mayhew, F. (2020, 13 January 2020). Every national editor signs letter to Boris Johnson urging Lobby changes rethink. *PressGazette*. Retrieved from https://www.pressgazette.co.uk/every-national-uk-editor-signs-letter-to-boris-johnson-urging-lobby-changes-rethink/.

Meyer, P. (1973/1991) *Precision Journalism: A Reporter's Introduction to Social Science Methods*. Lanham, MD: Rowman & Littlefield

McIntyre, N. & Pegg, D. (2018, 16 September 2018). Councils use 377,000 people's data in efforts to predict child abuse. *The Guardian*. Retrieved from https://www.theguardian.com/society/2018/sep/16/councils-use-377000-peoples-data-in-efforts-to-predict-child-abuse

McLuhan, M. (1964). *Understanding Media: The Extensions of Man*. New York: McGraw-Hill.

McQuail, D. (1997). *Audience Analysis*. London: Sage.

Mediapart. (2017). *News Starts Here*. Retrieved from https://static.mediapart.fr/files/2017/04/06/mediapart-2008-2017-english.pdf (accessed 28 May 2021)

Mehendale, S. G. (2019). Immersion is 'hear': a practitioners' perspective on immersive podcasts. *Journal of Content, Community & Communication*, 9(5), 68–74.

Menke, M., Kinnebrock, S., Kretzschmar, S., Aichberger, I., Broersma, M., Hummel, R., Kirchhoff, S., Prandner, D., Ribeiro, N., & Salaverría, R. (2018). Convergence culture in European newsrooms : comparing editorial strategies for cross-media news production. *Journalism Studies*, 19(6), 881–904, doi: 10.1080/1461670X.2016.1232175.

Mihailidis, P. & Viotty, S. (2017). Spreadable spectacle in digital culture: civic expression, fake news, and the role of media literacies in 'post-fact' society. *American Behavioral Scientist*, 61(4), 441–454.

Milakovich, M. E. & Gordon, G. J. (2009). *Public Administration in America* (10th edn). Boston, MA: Wadsworth Cengage Learning.

Miller, C., & Fitzgerald T. (2017, 19 January 2017) Find out how your child's school performed at GCSEs using our gadget. *Manchester Evening News*. Retrieved from https://manchestereveningnews.co.uk/news/greater-manchester-news/find-out-how-your-childs-12475621.

Mills, C., Pidd, M., & Ward, E. (2012). *Data Journalism in Sweden – Opportunities and Challenges*. Paper presented at the Proceedings of the Digital Humanities Congress, Sheffield.

Mitchell, A. & Rosenstiel, T. (2011). Navigating news online: where people go, how they get there and what lures them away. *Pew Research Centre Journalism & Media*. Retrieved from https://www.journalism.org/2011/05/09/navigating-news-online/

Moloney, K., Jackson, D., & McQueen, D. (2013). News journalism and public relations: a dangerous relationship. In K. Fowler-Watt & S. Allan (Eds.), *Journalism: New Challenges* (pp. 259–281). Bournemouth: Centre for Journalism & Communication Research, Bournemouth University.

Monbiot, G. (2019, 10 December 2019). Why do I have to break an embargo in order to expose press lies about Labour? *The Guardian*. Retrieved from https://www.theguardian.com/commentisfree/2019/dec/10/break-embargo-expose-press-lies-labour

Montal, T. & Reich, Z. (2017). I, robot. You, journalist. Who is the author? Authorship, bylines and full disclosure in automated journalism. *Digital Journalism, 5*(7), 829–849, doi: 10.1080/21670811.2016.1209083.

Moreira, S. V. & Oller Alonso, M. O. (2018). Journalists in newsrooms: professional roles, influences, and changes to journalism. *Brazilian Journalism Research, 14*(2), 304–317.

Morris, F. (2018). Can a new business model save small-town papers? *NPR*. Retrieved from https://www.npr.org/2018/05/08/609304180/can-a-new-business-model-save-small-town-papers?t=1550587264904

Mosalski, R. (2017, 3 April 2017). The parts of Cardiff where most (and least) crimes are committed. WalesOnline. Retrieved from https://walesonline.co.uk/news/local-news/parts-cardiff-most-and-least-12836137

Mourão, R. R. (2015). The boys on the timeline: political journalists' use of Twitter for building interpretive communities. *Journalism, 16*(8), 1107–1123.

Mullin, B. (2016, 27 April 2016). Bloomberg EIC: automation is 'crucial to the future of journalism'. *Poynter*. Retrieved from https://www.poynter.org/tech-tools/2016/bloomberg-eic-automation-is-crucial-to-the-future-of-journalism/

Musariri, D. (2018, 26 September 2018). Independent puts up partical paywall offering readers exclusive content from £55 per year. *PressGazette*. Retrieved from https://www.pressgazette.co.uk/independent-launches-new-subscription-offer-to-readers-from-55-per-year-but-editor-says-this-is-not-simply-a-case-of-creating-a-paywall/

Mutiara, F. & Priyonggo, A. (2020). Analysis of sustainability business media from hyperlocal and entrepreneurial journalism perspectives: a case study of DI's Way Daily. *Journal of Entrepreneurship & Business, 1*(2), 102–113.

Mutsvairo, B., Bebawi, S., & Borges-Rey, E. (Eds.). (2020). *Data Journalism in the Global South*. London: Palgrave Macmillan.

Na, J.-H. (2011). *Introducing the Digital News System into a TV Newsroom: A Case of SBS, South Korea*. PhD, University of Sheffield, Sheffield.

Nechepurenko, I. (2016, 24 June 2016). Russia moves to tighten counterterror law; rights activists see threat to freedoms. *The New York Times*. Retrieved from https://www.nytimes.com/2016/06/25/world/europe/russia-counterterrorism-yarovaya-law.html?module=inline

Newman, N., Fletcher, R., Kalogeropoulos, A., Levy, D. A. L., & Nielsen, R. K. (2017). *Reuters Institute Digital News Report 2017*. Oxford: Reuters Institute for the Study of Journalism, University of Oxford.

Newman, N., Fletcher, R., Kalogeropoulos, A., Levy, D. A. L., & Nielsen, R. K. (2018). *Reuters Institute Digital News Report 2018*. Oxford: Reuters Institute for the Study of Journalism, University of Oxford.

Newman, N., Fletcher, R., Kalogeropoulos, A., & Nielsen, R. K. (2019). *Reuters Institute Digital News Report 2019*. Oxford: Reuters Institute for the Study of Journalism, University of Oxford.

News & Tech Staff Report. (2021). Wave of newspapers outsourcing printing. *News & Tech*.

Nikunen, K. (2014). Losing my profession: age, experience and expertise in the changing newsrooms. *Journalism, 15*(7), 868–888.

Nocetti, J. (2015). Russia's 'dictatorship-of-the-law' approach to internet policy. *Internet Policy Review, 4*(4), doi: 10.14763/2015.4.380.

Nygren, G. (2012). Autonomy: a crucial element of professionalization. In G. Nygren (Ed.), *Journalism in Russia, Poland and Sweden: Traditions, Cultures and Research*. Södertørn: Södertörns Högskola.

Obermaier, F. & Obermayer, B. (2017). *The Panama Papers: Breaking the Story of How the Rich and Powerful Hide Their Money*. London: Oneworld.

O'Neill, S. (2013, 12 November 2013). Police to investigate Guardian's role in Snowden affair. *The Times*. Retrieved from https://www.thetimes.co.uk/article/police-to-investigate-guardians-role-in-snowden-affair-sp0fk89wghd

O'Neill, S. (2020, 24 October 2020). New laws will protect journalists as threats on social media increase. *The Times*. Retrieved from https://www.thetimes.co.uk/article/new-laws-will-protect-journalists-as-threats-on-social-media-increase-j9wdkhp5q

Oborne, P. (2015, 17 February). Why I have resigned from the Telegraph. Retrieved from https://www.opendemocracy.net/en/opendemocracyuk/why-i-have-resigned-from-telegraph/

Odriozola-Chéné, J. & Llorca-Abad, G. (2014). The homogeneity process in the online media agenda: a comparative analysis of Spanish and Foreign online media. *Communication & Society, XXVII* (3), 19–41.

Ofcom. (2021). *Online Nation 2021 Report*. Retrieved from https://www.ofcom.org.uk/__data/assets/pdf_file/0013/220414/online-nation-2021-report.pdf (accessed 17 June 2021)

Ombelet, P.-J., Kuczerawy, A., & Valcke, P. (2016a). *Employing Robot Journalists: Legal Implications, Considerations and Recommendations*. Paper presented at the 25th International Conference Companion on World Wide Web.

Ombelet, P.-J., Kuczerawy, A., & Valcke, P. (2016b). Supervising automated journalists in the newsroom: liability for algorithmically produced news stories. KU Leuven Centre for IT & IP Law. Working Paper 25/2016.

Ottewell, D. (2018). Highlights from the Trinity Mirror Data Unit this week. Retrieved from https://towardsdatascience.com/highlights-from-the-trinity-mirror-data-unit-this-week-e9e811cf62d9

Owen, P. & Kiss, J. (2013). NSA files – live coverage of all developments and reaction. *The Guardian*. Retrieved from https://www.theguardian.com/world/2013/oct/14/

nsa-files-live-coverage-of-all-developments-and-reaction#block-525ff1d3e4b0010b6627a956

Oxford Business Group. (No year). Social media and digital content transform Saudi Arabia's media sector. Retrieved from https://oxfordbusinessgroup.com/overview/shifting-tide-social-media-and-digital-content-are-transforming-sector (accessed 17 June 2021)

Parasie, S. (2015). Data-driven revelation? Epistemological tensions in investigative journalism in the age of 'big data'. *Digital Journalism, 3*(3), 364–380.

Parasie, S. & Dagiral, E. (2012). Data-driven journalism and the public good: 'computer-assisted-reporters' and 'programmer-journalists' in Chicago. *New Media & Society, 15*(6), 853–871.

Parkinson, H. J. (2016, 14 November 2020). Click and elect: how fake news helped Donald Trump win a real election. *The Guardian*. Retrieved from https://www.theguardian.com/commentisfree/2016/nov/14/fake-news-donald-trump-election-alt-right-social-media-tech-companies

Partridge, T. (2015). *To What Extent Has Human Thought and Personality Become Encapsulated by Technology-Related Activity?* Paper presented at the IEEE International Symposium on Technology and Society (ISTAS).

Paulussen, S. (2012). Technology and the transformation of news work: are labor conditions in (online) journalism changing? In E. Siapera & A. Veglis (Eds.), *The Handbook of Global Online Journalism* (pp. 192–208). West Sussex: Wiley-Blackwell.

Peiser, J. (2019a, 6 February 2019). The New York Times Co. reports $709 million in digital revenue for 2018. *The New York Times*. Retrieved from https://www.nytimes.com/2019/02/06/business/media/new-york-times-earnings-digital-subscriptions.html

Peiser, J. (2019b, 5 February 2019). The rise of the robot reporter. *The New York Times*. Retrieved from https://www.nytimes.com/2019/02/05/business/media/artificial-intelligence-journalism-robots.html

Perez, S. & Cremedas, M. (2014). The multimedia journalist in large-market television newsrooms: Can old dogs learn new tricks? Do they want to? *Electronic News, 8*(3), 159–176.

Perreault, G. & Stanfield, K. (2019). Mobile journalism as lifestyle journalism? *Journalism Practice, 13*(3), 331–348, doi: 10.1080/17512786.2018.1424021.

Pew Research Center. (2018). Newspapers Fact Sheet.

Phillips, A. (2010). Old sources, new bottles. In N. Fenton (Ed.), *New Media, Old News : Journalism and Democracy on the Digital Age* (pp. 87–101). London: Sage.

Picard, R. G. (1989). *Media Economics: Concepts and Issues*. London: Sage.

Picard, R. G. (2006). *Journalism, Value Creation and the Future of News Organizations*. Working Paper Series, the Joan Shorenstein Center on the Press, Politics and Public Policy (Vol. R-27).

Pickard, V. (2011). Can government support the press? Historicizing and internationalizing a policy approach to the journalism crisis. *The Communication Review, 14*(2), 73–95.

Pickard, V. & Williams, A. T. (2014). Salvation or folly? The promises and perils of digital paywalls. *Digital Journalism, 2*(2), 195–213.

Ponsford, D. (2014, 28 March 2014). Rusbridger on how no journalist's sources are safe, joining ipso and why he would have kept News of the World open. *PressGazette*.

Retrievedfromhttp://www.pressgazette.co.uk/rusbridger-how-no-journalists-sources-are-now-safe-joining-ipso-and-why-he-would-have-kept-news/

Ponsford, D. (2015, 7 September 2015). IPSO's first year report card: it has been a tougher complaints handler than the PCC, but is failing as a regulator. *PressGazette*. Retrieved from https://www.pressgazette.co.uk/ipsos-first-year-report-card-it-has-been-a-tougher-complaints-handler-than-the-pcc-but-is-failing-as-a-regulator/

Ponsford, D. (2017, 15 December 2017). Telegraph to recruit 39 more journalists in 2018 as it plans to reach 10m registered readers. *PressGazette*. Retrieved from https://www.pressgazette.co.uk/telegraph-to-recruit-39-more-journalists-in-2018-as-it-plans-to-reach-10m-registered-readers/

Porlezza, C. & Splendore, S. (2016). Accountability and transparency of entrepreneurial journalism: unresolved ethical issues in crowdfunded journalism projects. *Journalism Practice*, *10*(2), 196–216, doi: 10.1080/17512786.2015.1124731.

Prasad, R. (2019). Digital disruption? Journalism startups in India. *Journalism*, doi: 10.1177/1464884919852446.

Price, J. (2017). Can The Ferret be a watchdog? : Understanding the launch, growth and prospects of a digital, investigative journalism start-up *Digital Journalism*, *5*(10), 1336–1350.

ProPublica. (2017, 24 April 2017). ProPublica is hiring a data editor. *ProPublica*. Retrieved from https://www.propublica.org/atpropublica/propublica-is-hiring-a-data-editor

Pulitzer. (2019, 5 December 2019). Pulitzer Prize Board announces new Audio Reporting category. Retrieved from https://pulitzer.org/news/pulitzer-prize-board-announces-new-audio-reporting-category

Qiang, X. (2019). The road to digital unfreedom: President Xi's surveillance state. *Journal of Democracy*, *30*(1), 53–67.

Quinn, S. (2005). Convergence's fundamental question. *Journalism Studies*, *6*(1), 29–38. doi: 10.1080/1461670052000328186.

Raseef22. (2017, 11 July 2017). 'The Arab World can no longer ignore data journalism': ADP and Raseef22. *Raeseef22*. Retrieved from https://raseef22.com/article/1069587-arab-world-can-no-longer-ignore-data-journalism-adp-raseef22Reece, D. (2006, 5 September 2006). Telegraph raises its game at news hub. *The Telegraph*. Retrieved from http://www.telegraph.co.uk/finance/2946710/Telegraph-raises-its-game-at-news-hub.html

Reid, A. (2014, 2 May 2014). 5 lessons in start-up journalism from De Correspondent. journalism.co.uk. Retrieved from https://www.journalism.co.uk/news/5-lessons-for-start-ups-from-de-correspondent/s2/a556629/

Reinardy, S. (2011). Newspaper journalism in crisis: burnout on the rise, eroding young journalists' career commitment. *Journalism*, *12*(1), 33–50.

Reißmann, O. (2019). The rise of vertical storytelling. *NiemanLab*. Retrieved 5 March 2019 http://www.niemanlab.org/2019/01/the-rise-of-vertical-storytelling/

Remnick, D. (2018, 15 August 2018). Trump and the enemies of the people. *The New Yorker*. Retrieved from https://www.newyorker.com/news/daily-comment/trump-and-the-enemies-of-the-people

ReporterMate. (2019, 31 January 2019). Political donations plunge to $16.7m – down from average $25m a year. *The Guardian*. Retrieved from https://www.theguardian.

com/australia-news/2019/feb/01/political-donations-plunge-to-167m-down-from-average-25m-a-year

Reporters Without Borders. (2020, 3 February 2020). UK: banning of journalists from Downing Street press briefing latest worrying move by Boris Johnson's new government. Retrieved from https://prod.rsf.mis.ovh/en/news/uk-banning-journalists downing downing-street-press-briefing-latest-worrying-move-boris-johnsons-new

Reporters Without Borders. (2021). *2021 World Press Freedom Index*. Retrieved from https://rsf.org/en/ranking/2021

Reuters. (2018a). Producing data stories and visualisations the Reuters way – Data Journalism Awards. Retrieved from https://datajournalismawards.org/2018/06/14/producing-data-stories-and-visualisations-the-reuters-way/ (accessed 2 September 2020)

Reuters. (2018b). United States added to list of most dangerous countries for journalists for first time. *NBCNews*. Retrieved from https://www.nbcnews.com/news/world/united-states-added-list-most-dangerous-countries-journalists-first-time-n949676?fbc lid=IwAR1S8SHpe3pvDVm6RKlxcMr0ECJT-ZIN00clwVlsMVlQiSQ0BTEjjH0n4iw

Reuters. (2020, 26 November 2020). Drone footage shows expanded burial grounds for COVID-19 victims in Jakarta. *Reuters*. Retrieved from https://reuters.screenocean.com/record/1588445

Risen, J. (2016, 30 December 2016). If Donald Trump targets journalists, thank Obama. *The New York Times*. Retrieved from https://www.nytimes.com/2016/12/30/opinion/sunday/if-donald-trump-targets-journalists-thank-obama.html

Rodrigues, U. M. (2017, 28 January 2017). Indian print media defying the odds? *East Asia Forum*. Retrieved from https://www.eastasiaforum.org/2017/01/28/indian-print-media-defying-the-odds/

Rogers, S. (2009, 18 June 2009). How to crowdsource MPs' expenses. *The Guardian*. Retrieved from https://www.theguardian.com/news/datablog/2009/jun/18/mps-expenses-houseofcommons

Rogers, S. (2010, 13 August 2010). Florence Nightingale, datajournalist: information has always been beautiful. *The Guardian*. Retrieved from https://www.theguardian.com/news/datablog/2010/aug/13/florence-nightingale-graphics

Rogers, S. (2012). Behind the scenes at the Guardian Datablog. In J. Gray, L. Chambers, & L. Bounegru (Eds.), *The Data Journalism Handbook: How Journalists Can Use Data to Improve the News* (pp. 34–36). Sebastopol, CA: O'Reilly. Media, Inc.

Rogers, S. (2013a). *Facts are Sacred: The Power of Data*. London: Faber and Faber.

Rogers, S. (2013b, 15 March 2013). John Snow's data journalism: the cholera map that changed the world. *The Guardian*. Retrieved from https://www.theguardian.com/news/datablog/2013/mar/15/john-snow-cholera-map

Rogers, S. (2014, 25 May 2014). Introduction to data journalism. Retrieved from https://simonrogers.net/2014/05/25/introduction-to-data-journalism/ (accessed 19 May 2021)

Rogers, S., Schwabish, J., & Bowers, D. (2017). *Data Journalism in 2017: The Current State and Challenges Facing the Field Today*. Retrieved from https://newslab.withgoogle.com/assets/docs/data-journalism-in-2017.pdf (accessed 21 March 2019)

Ronning, H. (2005). African journalism and democratic media. In H. de Burgh (Ed.), *Making Journalists: Diverse Models, Global Issues* (pp. 157–180). London: Routledge.

Rosenstiel, T. & Mitchell, A. (2012). *The Future of Mobile News*. Pew Research Center. Retrieved from https://pewresearch.org/journalism/2012/10/01/future-mobile-news/

Roston, E. & Migliozzi, B. (2017, 19 April 2017). How a melting Arctic changes everything. *Bloomberg*. Retrieved from https://www.bloomberg.com/graphics/2017-arctic/

Rottwilm. P. (2014) *The Future of Journalistic Work: Its Changing Nature and Implications*. Oxford: The Reuters Institute for the Study of Journalism. Retrieved from https://reutersinstitute.politics.ox.ac.uk/our-research/future-journalistic-work

Ruotsalainen, J. & Villi, M. (2018). Hybrid engagement: discourses and scenarios of entrepreneurial journalism. *Media and Communication, 6*(4), 79–90, doi: https://doi.org/10.17645/mac.v6i4.1465.

Rusbridger, A. (2011, 28 January 2011). WikiLeaks: The Guardian's role in the biggest leak in the history of the world. *The Guardian*. Retrieved from https://www.theguardian.com/media/2011/jan/28/wikileaks-julian-assange-alan-rusbridger

Rusbridger, A. (2013, 19 August 2013). David Miranda, schedule 7 and the danger that all reporters now face. *The Guardian*. Retrieved from https://www.theguardian.com/commentisfree/2013/aug/19/david-miranda-schedule7-danger-reporters

Ryabinska, N. (2011). The media market and media ownership in post-Communist Ukraine: impact on media independence and pluralism. *Problems of Post-Communism, 58*(6), 3–20, doi: 10.2753/PPC1075-8216580601.

Ryley, S., Singer-Vine, J., & Campbell, S. (2019, 24 January 2019). Shoot someone in a major US city, and odds are you'll get away with it. *BuzzFeed News*. Retrieved from https://www.buzzfeednews.com/article/sarahryley/police-unsolved-shootings

Sabbagh, D. (2021, 15 June 2021). Daniel Morgan inquiry highlights murky links between police and media. *The Guardian*. Retrieved from https://www.theguardian.com/uk-news/2021/jun/15/daniel-morgan-inquiry-highlights-murky-links-between-police-and-media

Sala, I. M. (2015, 20 May 2015). Hong Kong to get new crowdfunded independent newspaper. *The Guardian*. Retrieved from https://www.theguardian.com/world/2015/may/20/hong-kong-to-get-new-crowdfunded-independent-newspaper

Saltzis, K. V. (2006). *Media Convergence in News Organisations: How Digital Technologies Affect Journalists and the Management of News Production*. PhD, University of Leicester, Leicester.

Satija, N., Collier, K., Shaw, A., & Larson, J. (Producers). (2016, 3 March 2016). Hell and high water. Retrieved from https://projects.propublica.org/houston/

Savage, C. & Benner, K. (2021, 2 June 2021). Trump administration secretly seized phone records of Times reporters. *The New York Times*. Retrieved from https://www.nytimes.com/2021/06/02/us/trump-administration-phone-records-times-reporters.html

Schmidt, C. (2019, 14 February 2019). Inside Inside's new local newsletters and its plans to keep scaling (with 750,000 active subscribers on board). *NiemanLab*. Retrieved from https://www.niemanlab.org/2019/02/inside-insides-new-local-newsletters-and-its-plans-to-keep-scaling-with-750000-active-subscribers-on-board/ (accessed 04 June 2019)

Scott, C. (2018, 29 May 2018). BBC mobile journalism pilot scheme sees 15 experienced camera operators shoot with iPhones over three months. *journalism.co.uk*. Retrieved from https://www.journalism.co.uk/news/-mixed-economy-is-king-bbc-mobile-journalism-pilot-scheme-sees-15-experienced-camera-operators-shoot-with-iphones/s2/a722552/

Seyser, D. & Zeiller, M. (2018). *Scrollytelling – An Analysis of Visual Storytelling in Online Journalism*. Paper presented at the 2018 22nd International Conference Information Visualisation (IV). https://ieeexplore.ieee.org/stamp/stamp.jsp?arnumber=8564193

Shane, S. & Mazzetti, M. (2018, 20 September 2020). The plot to subvert an election: unraveling the Russia story so far. *The New York Times*. Retrieved from https://www.nytimes.com/interactive/2018/09/20/us/politics/russia-interference-election-trump-clinton.html?module=inline&mtrref=www.nytimes.com&gwh=D841C79D2DF28615C242A8C946D66543&gwt=pay&assetType=PAYWALL

Shao, C., Ciampaglia, G. L., Varol, O., Flammini, A., & Menczer., F. (2017). The spread of fake news by social bots. *arXiv preprint 707.07592*, 96–104.

Shaw, D. (Producer). (2019). This is quoted from a post by Dougal Shaw of BBC News, on the Facebook group: "#mojofest community Where the global Mojo Community meet and share". Retrieved from https://en-gb.facebook.com/groups/mojofest/ (accessed 17 June 2021)

Shawli, N. K. (2021). *The Challenges of a Changing Communication Landscape: An Examination of Saudi Arabian Media*. PhD, Université d'Ottawa/University of Ottawa. Retrieved from https://ruor.uottawa.ca/bitstream/10393/41662/3/Shawli_Nidaa_Khalid_2021_thesis.pdf (accessed 15 February 2021)

Shields, R. (2003). *The Virtual*. London and New York: Routledge.

Shin, A. (2018, 11 January. 2018). Twenty years ago, the Drudge Report broke the Clinton-Lewinsky scandal. *The Washington Post*. Retrieved from https://www.washingtonpost.com/lifestyle/magazine/twenty-years-ago-the-drudge-report-broke-the-clinton-lewinsky-scandal/2018/01/09/3df90b7a-e0ec-11e7-89e8-edec16379010_story.html

Siapera, E. & Papadopoulou, L. (2016). Entrepreneurialism or cooperativism?: An exploration of cooperative journalistic enterprises *Journalism Practice*, *10*(2), 178–195.

Siebert, F. S., Peterson, T., & Schramm, W. (1956). *Four Theories of the Press: The Authoritarian, Libertarian, Social Responsibility, and Soviet Communist Concepts of What the Press Should Be and Do*. Urbana: University of Illinois Press.

Silow-Carroll, A. (2019, 5 February 2019). News-writing robots may be the future of Jewish news, according to a news-writing robot. *Jewish Telegraphic Agency*. Retrieved from https://www.jta.org/2019/02/05/opinion/news-writing-robots-may-be-the-future-of-jewish-news-according-to-a-news-writing-robot

Silverman, C. (2016, 16 November 2016). This analysis shows how viral fake election news stories outperformed real news on Facebook. *BuzzFeedNews*. Retrieved from https://www.buzzfeednews.com/article/craigsilverman/viral-fake-election-news-outperformed-real-news-on-facebook

Silverman, C., Rajagopalan, M., Pham, S., & Yang, W. (2018, 19 December 2018). Please welcome China's WeChat to the #Resistance. *BuzzFeed News*. Retrieved from https://www.buzzfeednews.com/article/craigsilverman/china-censor-trump-content-wechat

Simon, J. (2017, 25 February 2017). Trump is damaging press freedom in the US and abroad. *The New York Times*. Retrieved from https://www.nytimes.com/2017/02/25/opinion/trump-is-damaging-press-freedom-in-the-us-and-abroad.html

Simons, M. (Ed.). (2013). *What's Next in Journalism?*: New-Media Entrepreneurs Tell Their Stores Brunswick: Scribe.

Singer, J. B. (2006). Partnerships and public service: normative issues for journalists in converged news-rooms. *Journal of Mass Media Ethics, 21*(1), 30–53.

Singer, J. B. (2007). Contested autonomy: professional and popular claims on journalistic norms. *Journalism Studies, 8*(1), 79–95.

Singer, J. B. (2010). Quality control: perceived effects of user-generated content on newsroom norms, values and routines. *Journalism Practice, 4*(2), 127–142.

Singer, J. B. (2015). Out of bounds: professional norms as boundary markers. In M. Carlson & S. C. Lewis (Eds.), *Boundaries of Journalism: Professionalism, Practices and Participation* (pp. 21–36). Oxford: Routledge.

Singer, J. B. (2018). Entrepreneurial journalism. In T. P. Vos (Ed.), *Journalism* (pp. 355–372). Berlin: De Gruyter Mouton.

Sjøvaag, H. (2016). Introducing the paywall : a case study of content changes in three online newspapers. *Journalism Practice, 10*(3), 304–322.

Smith, D. (2020, 8 June 2020). 'Denigrated and discredited': how American journalists became targets during protests. *The Guardian.* Retrieved from https://www.theguardian.com/media/2020/jun/08/us-journalists-media-protests-donald-trump?CMP=Share_AndroidApp_Gmail

Smythe, D. (1977). Communications: blindspot of western Marxism. *Canadian Journal of Political and Social Theory, 1*(3), 1–27.

Solito, L. & Sorrentino, C. (2020). New forms of journalistic legitimization in the digital world. In J. Vázquez-Herrero, S. Direito-Rebollal, A. Silva-Rodríguez, & X. López-García (Eds.), *Journalistic Metamorphosis: Media Transformation in the Digital Age* (pp. 185–197). Cham: Springer.

Solomon, G. & Schrum, L. (2007). *Web 2.0: New Tools, New Schools.* Eugene, Oregon and Washington, DC: International Society for Technology in Education.

Son, J. (2016, 15 May 2016). Will robot reporters replace humans? *The Korea Observer.*

Sørensen, J. K. & Hutchinson, J. (2018). Algorithms and public service media. In G. F. Lowe, H. Van den Bulck, & K. Donders (Eds.), *Public Service Media in the Networked Society* (pp. 91–106). Gothenburg: Nordicom.

Southern, L. (Producer). (2019, 26 February 2019). Inside Bloomberg's 30-person international data journalism team. *Digiday.* Retrieved from https://digiday.com/media/inside-bloombergs-30-person-international-data-journalism-team/

Sparkes, M. (2014, 4 March 2014). Twitter users believe news should be fact-checked. *The Telegraph.* Retrieved from https://www.telegraph.co.uk/technology/twitter/10675634/Twitter-users-believe-news-should-be-fact-checked.html

Splendore, S. (2016). Quantitatively oriented forms of journalism and their epistemology. *Sociology Compass, 10*(5), 343–352.

Spyridou, L.-P., Matsiola, M., Veglis, A., Kalliris, G., & Dimoulas, C. (2013). Journalism in a state of flux: journalists as agents of technology innovation and emerging news practices. *International Communication Gazette, 75*(1), 76–98.

Spyridou, L.-P. & Veglis, A. (2016). Convergence and the changing labor of journalism: towards the 'super journalist' paradigm. In A. Lugmayr & Dal Zotto, C. (Eds.), *Media*

Convergence Handbook, Vol. 1: Journalism, Broadcasting, and Social Media Aspects of Convergence. Berlin and Heidelberg: Springer-Verlag.

Stalph, F. (2020). Evolving data teams: tensions between organisational structure and professional subculture. *Big Data & Society, 7*(1), doi: 10.1177/2053951720919964.

Stark, J. & Diakopoulos, N. (2016, 10 March 2016). Uber seems to offer better service in areas with more white people. That raises some tough questions. *The Washington Post.* Retrieved from https://www.washingtonpost.com/news/wonk/wp/2016/03/10/uber-seems-to-offer-better-service-in-areas-with-more-white-people-that-raises-some-tough-questions/?utm_term=.5b1eac9e6ced

Stavelin, E. (2013). *Computational Journalism: When Journalism Meets Programming.* PhD, The University of Bergen.

Steensen, S. (2018). What is the matter with newsroom culture? A sociomaterial analysis of professional knowledge creation in the newsroom. *Journalism, 19*(4), 464–480.

Stetka, V. & Örnebring, H. (2013). Investigative journalism in Central and Eastern Europe: autonomy, business models and democratic roles. *The International Journal of Press/Politics, 18*(4), 413–435.

Stoneman, J. (2015). *Does Open Data Need Journalism?* Working Paper, Reuters Institute for the Study of Journalism, University of Oxford. Retrieved from https://reutersinstitute.politics.ox.ac.uk/our-research/does-open-data-need-journalism

Stotz, P. (2019, 23 February 2019). Tempolimit könnte bis zu 140 Todesfälle im Jahr verhindern. *Der Spiegel.* Retrieved from https://www.spiegel.de/auto/aktuell/tempolimit-koennte-jaehrlich-bis-zu-140-todesfaelle-verhindern-a-1254504.html

Stringer, P. (2018) Finding a place in the journalistic field. *Journalism Studies, 19*(13), 1991–2000.

Stuart-Turner, R. (2017, 5 September). Trinity Mirror announces more local newspaper closures. *Printweek.* Retrieved from https://www.printweek.com/print-week/news/1162143/trinity-mirror-announces-more-local-newspaper-closures (accessed 19 February 2019)

Sunne, S. (2016, 9 March 2016). How data journalism is different from what we've always done. Retrieved from https://www.americanpressinstitute.org/publications/reports/strategy-studies/how-data-journalism-is-different/

Sunstein, C. R. (2007). *Republic.com 2.0. Revenge of the Blogs.* Princeton, NJ: Princeton University Press.

svt NYHETER. (2017) The Swedes in Paradise Papers. *svt NYHETER.* Retrieved from https://www.svt.se/special/the-swedes-in-paradise-papers/

Swaine, J. & McCarthy, C. (2016, 15 December 2016). Killings by US police logged at twice the previous rate under new federal program. *The Guardian.* Retrieved from https://www.theguardian.com/us-news/2016/dec/15/us-police-killings-department-of-justice-program

Sweney, M. (2016, 13 January 2016). BuzzFeed breaks UK ad rules over misleading advertorial. *The Guardian.* Retrieved from https://www.theguardian.com/media/2016/jan/13/buzzfeed-breaks-uk-ad-rules-over-misleading-advertorial

Sweney, M. (2018a, 1 March 2018). Leveson 2 explained: what was it meant to achieve? *The Guardian.* Retrieved from https://www.theguardian.com/media/2018/mar/01/leveson-2-explained-what-was-it-meant-to-achieve

Sweney, M. (2018b, 4 July 2018). Telegraph Media Group profits fall 50% after sales and ad slide. *The Guardian*. Retrieved from https://www.theguardian.com/media/2018/jul/04/telegraph-media-group-profits-fall-50-per-cent-amid-sales-and-ad-slide

Swindells, K. (2021, 15 February 2021). Revealed: the army of Big Tech lobbyists targeting Capitol Hill. *The New Statesman*. Retrieved from https://www.newstatesman.com/business/companies/2021/02/revealed-army-big-tech-lobbyists-targeting-capitol-hill?_gl=1*saqo2p*_ga*MTY1ODc4MjU4NC4xNjIzMzQwMDA4*_ga_4GW6S7C2VR*MTYyMzM0MDAwOC4xLjAuMTYyMzM0MDAwOC42MA

Tameling, K. & Broersma, M. (2013). De-converging the newsroom: strategies for newsroom change and their influence on journalism practice. *International Communication Gazette, 75*(1), 19–34, doi: 10.1177/1748048512461760.

Tan, Y., Zhang, W., & Chen, Y. (2017). Big data news: experiments and practice (*dashuju xinwen de tansuo yu shijian*). In Z. Zhao & J. Zhao (Eds.), *New Media and News*. Beijing: China Communication University Press (*zhongguo chuanmei daxue chubanshe*).

Tandoc, Jr, E. C. (2014). Journalism is twerking? How web analytics is changing the process of gatekeeping. *New Media & Society, 16*(4), 559–575.

Tandoc, Jr, E. C. (2015). Why web analytics click: factors affecting the ways journalists use audience metrics. *Journalism Studies, 16*(6), 782–799.

Tandoc, Jr, E. C. (2017). Follow the click? Journalistic autonomy and web analytics. In B. Franklin & S. Eldridge II (Eds.), *The Routledge Companion to Digital Journalism Studies* (pp. 293–301). London and New York: Routledge.

Tandoc, Jr, E. C., Lim, Z. W., & Ling, R. (2018). Defining 'fake news'. *Digital Journalism, 6*(2), 137–153, doi: 10.1080/21670811.2017.1360143.

Tandoc, Jr, E. C. & Oh, S.-K. (2017). Small departures, big continuities? : Norms, values, and routines in The Guardian's big data journalism. *Journalism Studies, 18*(8), 997–1015, doi: 10.1080/1461670X.2015.1104260.

Tandoc, Jr, E. C. & Thomas, R. J. (2015). The ethics of web analytics : implications of using audience metrics in news construction. *Digital Journalism, 3*(2), 243–258, doi: 10.1080/21670811.2014.909122.

Tang, L. & Yang, P. (2011). Symbolic power and the internet: the power of a 'horse'. *Media, Culture & Society, 33*(5), 675–691.

Tedeschi, J. T. & Quigley, B. M. (1996). Limitations of laboratory paradigms for studying aggression. *Aggression and Violent Behavior, 1*(2), 163–177.

Tencent News. (2015). Interactive map of Tianjin Explosion. *Tencent News*. Retrieved from https://news.qq.com/a/20150813/011368.htm (accessed 18 June 2021)

The Associated Press. (2013, 13 May 2013). Gov't obtains wide AP phone records in probe. *The Associated Press*. Retrieved from https://www.ap.org/ap-in-the-news/2013/govt-obtains-wide-ap-phone-records-in-probe

The BBC. (2013, 9 September 2013). China issues new internet rules that include jail time. *The BBC*. Retrieved from https://www.bbc.co.uk/news/world-asia-china-23990674

The BBC. (2014, 18 March 2014). Robot writes LA Times earthquake breaking news article. *The BBC*. Retrieved from https://www.bbc.co.uk/news/technology-26614051

The BBC. (2015, 17 February 2015). Daily Telegraph's Peter Oborne resigns over HSBC coverage. *The BBC*. Retrieved from https://www.bbc.co.uk/news/uk-31510152

The BBC. (2016, 13 April 2016). Press regulation: what you need to know. *The BBC.* Retrieved from https://www.bbc.co.uk/news/uk-politics-36034956

The BBC. (2019a, 18 June 2019). BBC international audience soars to record high of 426m. *The BBC.* Retrieved from https://www.bbc.co.uk/mediacentre/latestnews/2019/bbc-international-audience-record-high

The BBC. (2019b, 17 October 2019). Google and BBC scrap VR projects. *The BBC.* Retrieved from https://www.bbc.co.uk/news/technology-50080594

The BBC. (2019c, 19 August 2019). Hong Kong protests: huge crowds rally peacefully. *The BBC.* Retrieved from https://www.bbc.co.uk/news/world-asia-china-49386298

The BBC. (2020, 21 May 2020). ABC figures: newspapers will no longer have to publish sales. *The BBC.* Retrieved from https://www.bbc.co.uk/news/entertainment-arts-52754762

The BBC. (2021, 18 February 2021). Facebook blocks Australian users from viewing or sharing news. *The BBC.* Retrieved from https://www.bbc.co.uk/news/world-australia-56099523

The Cabinet Office. (2021, 9 Feb 2021). Response to points raised in openDemocracy article, 08/02/21. Retrieved from https://www.gov.uk/government/news/response-to-points-raised-in-opendemocracy-article-080221 (accessed 8 June 2021)

The Canadian Press. (2018, 14 June 2018). Rogers Media cuts 75 jobs in digital content and publishing. *The Star.* Retrieved from https://www.thestar.com/business/2018/06/14/rogers-media-cuts-75-jobs-in-digital-content-and-publishing.html

The Correspondent. (2021). About The Correspondent. Retrieved from https://thecorrespondent.com/834/the-correspondent-will-stop-publishing-on-1-january-2021-wed-like-to-thank-our-members-for-their-support/12825252-8c4236ca (accessed 19 June 2021)

The Detroit Urban League. (1967). The People beyond 12th Street: A Survey of Attitudes of Detroit Negroes after the Riot of 1967. The Detroit Urban League and *The Detroit Free Press.* Retrieved from https://s3.amazonaws.com/s3.documentcloud.org/documents/2070181/detroit1967.pdf (accessed 30 April 2019)

The Economist. (2018, 22 October 2018). Turning a page: The Economist's data journalism gets its own place in print. *The Economist.* Retrieved from https://medium.economist.com/turning-a-page-the-economists-data-journalism-gets-its-own-place-in-print-664c2e5bdfe9

The Economist. (2019, 14 February 2019). The Economist collaborates with ABC to release new certificates for greater transparency on audited circulation figures. *The Economist.* Retrieved from https://press.economist.com/story/9946/the-economist-collaborates-with-abc-to-release-new-certificates-for-greater-transparency-on-audited-circulation-figures

The Guardian. (2008, 18 January 2008). 'We came in fast. I felt like I was in a washing machine'. *The Guardian.* Retrieved from https://www.theguardian.com/uk/2008/jan/18/world.theairlineindustry

The Guardian. (2011–2012) *Reading the riots series. The Guardian.* Retrieved from https://www.theguardian.com/uk/series/reading-the-riots

The Guardian. (2015, 12 September 2015). Tianjin explosion: China sets final death toll at 173, ending search for survivors. *The Guardian*. Retrieved from https://www.theguardian.com/world/2015/sep/12/tianjin-explosion-china-sets-final-death-toll-at-173-ending-search-for-survivors

The Guardian. (2019, 2 May 2019). Julian Assange and the story of WikiLeaks. *The Guardian* [podcast]. Retrieved from https://www.theguardian.com/media/audio/2019/may/02/julian-assange-and-the-story-of-wikileaks-podcast

The Guardian. (No year-a). The new populism series. *The Guardian*. Retrieved from https://www.theguardian.com/world/series/the-new-populism?page=5

The Guardian. (No year-b). The NSA files. *The Guardian*. Retrieved from https://www.theguardian.com/us-news/the-nsa-files

The Independent. (2010, 11 March 2010). Social networks a challenge to cable news: CNN US president. *The Independent*. Retrieved from https://www.independent.co.uk/incoming/social-networks-a-challenge-to-cable-news-cnn-us-president-5527636.html

The Justice Department of the United States. (2020). The Justice Department of the United States' complaint in a lawsuit against Google, submitted to The United States District Court for The District of Columbia.

The New York Times. (2017). *Journalism That Stands Apart*. *The New York Times*. Retrieved from https://www.nytimes.com/projects/2020-report/index.html

The Nielsen Company. (2014, 24 February 2014). How smartphones are changing consumers' daily routines around the globe. *Nielsen*. Retrieved from https://www.nielsen.com/us/en/insights/article/2014/how-smartphones-are-changing-consumers-daily-routines-around-the-globe/

The Oxford Dictionary. (No year). Algorithm. *The Oxford Dictionary*. Retrieved from: https://www.oxfordlearnersdictionaries.com/definition/american_english/algorithm (accessed 19 June 2021)

The Pew Research Center's Project for Excellence in Journalism. (2013). *The State of the News Media 2013: An Annual Report on American Journalism*. Washington: Pew Research Center.

The Shift Team (2017). Henley and Partners threatens legal action against *The Shift*. Retrieved from https://theshiftnews.com/2017/12/24/henley-and-partners-threatens-legal-action-against-the-shift/

The Southern Metropolitan Daily. (2015, 13 August 2015). 20 hours after the Tianjin explosion in graphs. *The Southern Metropolitan Daily (nanfang dushibao)*. Retrieved from http://news.sina.com.cn/c/2015-08-13/221232201817.shtml

The Sydney Morning Herald. (2008, 18 January 2008). Aussie 'hoaxer' version. *The Sydney Morning Herald*. Retrieved from http://www.smh.com.au/news/travel/aussie-hoaxer-version/2008/01/18/1200590657902.html

The Telegraph. (No year). MPs expenses scandal website. *The Telegraph*. Retrieved from https://www.telegraph.co.uk/news/mps-expenses-scandal/

Thienthaworn, E. (2018). *Data Journalism: Principle Development and Knowledge Adaptation in Thailand*. PhD, National Institute of Development Administration, Bangkok. Retrieved from https://repository.nida.ac.th/bitstream/handle/662723737/4366/b204596.pdf?sequence=1

Thurman, N. (2011). Making 'The Daily Me': technology, economics and habit in the mainstream assimilation of personalized news. *Journalism*, *12*(4), 395–415.

Thurman, N., Dörr, K., & Kunert, J. (2017). When reporters get hands-on with robo-writing: professionals consider automated journalism's capabilities and consequences. *Digital Journalism*, *5*(10), 1240–1259, doi: 10.1080/21670811.2017.1289819.

Thurman, N. & Lupton, B. (2008). Convergence calls: multimedia storytelling at British news websites. *Convergence: The International Journal of Research into New Media Technologies*, *14*(4), 439–455, doi: 10.1177/1354856508094662.

Thurman, N. & Schifferes, S. (2012). The future of personalization at news websites: lessons from a longitudinal study. *Journalism Studies*, *13*(5–6), 775–790.

Thurman, N. & Walters, A. (2013). Live blogging – digital journalism's pivotal platform? A case study of the production, consumption, and form of live blogs at Guardian. co.uk. *Digital Journalism*, *1*(1), 82–101.

Thussu, D. (2005). Adapting to globalisation: the changing contours of journalism in India. In H. de Burgh (Ed.), *Making Journalists: Diverse Models, Global Issues* (pp. 127–141). London: Routledge.

Tobitt, C. (2018, 11 May 2018). Reach data unit boss says it should be 'more the merrier' as huge amount of local data 'still not interrogated properly by journalists'. *PressGazette*. Retrieved from https://www.pressgazette.co.uk/trinity-mirror-data-unit-boss-says-it-should-be-the-more-the-merrier-as-huge-amount-of-local-data-still-not-interrogated-properly-by-journalists/

Tobitt, C. (2020, 11 February 2020). Reach creates five new journalist jobs as it expands Cornwall and Devon news websites. *PressGazette*. Retrieved from https://www.pressgazette.co.uk/reach-creates-five-new-journalist-jobs-as-it-expands-cornwall-and-devon-news-websites/

Toffler, A. (1980). *The Third Wave*. New York, NY: William Morrow.

Tong, J. (2015a). Chinese journalists' views of UGC producers and journalism: a case study of the boundary work of journalism. *Asian Journal of Communication*, online first. doi: 10.1080/01292986.2015.1019526.

Tong, J. (2015b). The defence of journalistic legitimacy in media discourse in China: an analysis of the case of Deng Yujiao. *Journalism*, *16*(3), 429–446.

Tong, J. (2017a). The taming of critical journalism in China: a combination of political, economic and technological forces. *Journalism Studies*, *20*(1), 79–96.

Tong, J. (2017b). Technology and journalism: 'dissolving' social media content into disaster reporting on three Chinese disasters. *International Communication Gazette*, *79*(4), 400–418.

Tong, J. (2018). Journalistic legitimacy revisited: collapse or revival in the digital age? *Digital Journalism*, *6*(2), 256–273.

Tong, J. (2020). Paradigm reinforcing: the assimilation of data journalism in the UK. *Journal of Applied Journalism and Media Studies*. doi: doi.org/10.1386/ajms_00043_1

Tong, J. & Lo, S.-h. (2017). Uncertainty, tabloidisation, and the loss of prestige: new media innovations and journalism cultures in two newspapers in mainland China and Taiwan. In J. Tong & S.-h. Lo (Eds.), *Digital Technology and Journalism: An International Comparative Perspective*. Cham: Palgrave Macmillan.

Tong, J. & Sparks, C. (2009). Investigative journalism in China today. *Journalism Studies*, *10*(3), 337–352.

Tong, J. & Zuo, L. (2021). The inapplicability of objectivity: understanding the work of data journalism. *Journalism Practice*, *15*(2), 153–169.

Touri, M., Kostarella, I., & Theodosiadou, S. (2017). Journalism culture and professional identity in transit: technology, crisis and opportunity in the Greek media. In J. Tong & S.-h. Luo (Eds.), *Digital Technology and Journalism: An International Comparative Perspective* (pp. 115–139). Cham: Palgrave Macmillan.

Townend, J. (2009, 29 October 2009). Jeff Jarvis: 'The future is entrepreneurial not institutional'. *journalism.co.uk*. Retrieved from https://www.journalism.co.uk/news/jeff-jarvis–the-future-is-entrepreneurial-not-institutional-/s2/a536283/

Tufekci, Z. (2017). *Twitter and Tear Gas: The Power and Fragility of Networked Protest*. New Haven, CT: Yale University Press.

Turow, J. & Draper, N. (2014). Industry conceptions of audience in the digital space. *Cultural Studies*, *28*(4), 643–656, doi: 10.1080/09502386.2014.88892.

Udupa, S. & Chakravartty, P. P. (2012). Changing with *The Times of India* (Bangalore): remaking a post-political media field. *South Asian History and Culture*, *3*(4), 491–510.Undurraga, T. (2017). Making news, making the economy: technological changes and financial pressures in Brazil. *Cultural Sociology*, *11*(1), 77–96.

Uricchio, W. (2017). Data, culture and the ambivalence of algorithms. In M. T. Schäfer & K. van Es (Eds.), *The Datafied Society: Studying Culture through Data* (pp. 139–146). Amsterdam: Amsterdam University Press.

Usher, N. (2013). Al Jazeera English Online: understanding Web metrics and news production when a quantified audience is not a commodified audience. *Digital Journalism*, *1*(3), 335–351, doi: 10.1080/21670811.2013.80169.

Van Dalen, A. (2012). The algorithms behind the headlines: how machine-written news redefines the core skills of human journalists. *Journalism Practice*, *6*(5–6), 648–658, doi: http://dx.doi.org/10.1080/17512786.2012.667268.

Van Dalen, A. (2019). Rethinking journalist–politician relations in the age of populism: how outsider politicians delegitimize mainstream journalists, *Journalism*. doi: 10.1177/1464884919887822.

Van Damme, K., All, A., De Marez, L., & Van Leuven, S. (2019). 360° video journalism: experimental study on the effect of immersion on news experience and distant suffering. *Journalism Studies*, *20*(14), 2053–2076, doi: 10.1080/1461670X.2018.1561208.

Van der Kaa, H. & Krahmer, E. (2014). *Journalist Versus News Consumer: The Perceived Credibility of Machine Written News*. Paper presented at the Proceedings of the Computation+ Journalism Conference, New York.

van Dijk, J. A. G. M. (2006). *The Network Society: Social Aspects of New Media*. London: Sage.

Viner, K. (2018, 12 November 2018). Katharine Viner: 'The Guardian's reader funding model is working. It's inspiring'. *The Guardian*. Retrieved from https://www.theguardian.com/membership/2018/nov/12/katharine-viner-guardian-million-reader-funding

Vos, T. P. & Singer, J. B. (2016). Media discourse about entrepreneurial journalism: implications for journalistic capital. *Journalism Practice*, *10*(2), 143–159, doi: 10.1080/17512786.2015.11247.

Vos, T. P. & Thomas, R. J. (2018). The discursive construction of journalistic authority in a post-truth age. *Journalism Studies, 19*(13), 2001–2010, doi: 10.1080/1461670X.2018.1492879.

Vu, H. T. (2014). The online audience as gatekeeper: the influence of reader metrics on news editorial selection. *Journalism, 15*(8), 1094–1110.

Vujnovic, M., Singer, J. B., Paulussen, S., Heinonen, A., Reich, Z., Quandt, T., Hermida, A., & Domingo, D. (2010). Exploring the political-economic factors of participatory journalism. *Journalism Practice, 4*(3), 285–296, doi: 10.1080/17512781003640588.

Waddell, T. (2018). A robot wrote this?: How perceived machine authorship affects news credibility. *Digital Journalism, 6*(2), 236–255, doi: 10.1080/21670811.2017.1384319.

Wagemans, A., Witschge, T., & Deuze, M. (2016). Ideology as resource in entrepreneurial journalism: the French online news startup Mediapart. *Journalism Practice, 10*(2), 160–177, doi: 10.1080/17512786.2015.11247.

Wahl-Jorgensen, K., Williams, A., & Wardle, C. (2010). Audience views on user-generated content: exploring the value of news from the bottom up. *Northern Lights: Film & Media Studies Yearbook, 8*(1), 177–194.

Wakabayashi, D. & Hsu, T. (2021, 17 January 2020). Behind a secret deal between Google and Facebook. *The New York Times*. Retrieved from https://www.nytimes.com/2021/01/17/technology/google-facebook-ad-deal-antitrust.html

Wang, H. & Sparks, C. (2018). Marketing credibility : Chinese newspapers' responses to revenue losses from falling circulation and advertising decline. *Journalism Studies*, doi: 10.1080/1461670X.2018.1513815.

Wang, S. (2018, 2 July 2018). As The New York Times extends its reach across countries (and languages and cultures), it looks to locals for guidance. *NiemanLab*. Retrieved from https://www.niemanlab.org/2018/07/as-the-new-york-times-extends-its-reach-across-countries-and-languages-and-cultures-it-looks-to-locals-for-guidance/ (accessed 19 June 2021)

WashPostPR. (2017, 1 September 2017). The Washington Post leverages automated storytelling to cover high school football. *The Washington Post*. Retrieved from https://www.washingtonpost.com/pr/wp/2017/09/01/the-washington-post-leverages-heliograf-to-cover-high-school-football/

Waterson, J. (2018a, 24 July 2018). Guardian Media Group digital revenues outstrip print for first time. *The Guardian*. Retrieved from https://www.theguardian.com/media/2018/jul/24/guardian-media-group-digital-revenues-outstrip-print-for-first-time

Waterson, J. (2018b, 5 November 2018). More than a million readers contribute financially to the Guardian. *The Guardian*. Retrieved from https://www.theguardian.com/media/2018/nov/05/guardian-passes-1m-mark-in-reader-donations-katharine-viner

Waterson, J. (2019a, 11 February 2019). 'It's really missed': the death of the Harlow Star newspaper. *The Guardian*. Retrieved from https://www.theguardian.com/media/2019/feb/11/its-really-missed-the-death-of-the-harlow-star-newspaper

Waterson, J. (2019b, 1 May 2019). Guardian breaks even helped by success of supporter strategy. *The Guardian*. Retrieved from https://www.theguardian.com/media/2019/may/01/guardian-breaks-even-helped-by-success-of-supporter-strategy?CMP=share_btn_tw

Webb, A. (2016). Journalism as a service. *NiemanLab*. Retrieved from https://www.niemanlab.org/2016/12/journalism-as-a-service/ (accessed 04 June 2020)

Weber, P. (2016, August 31, 2016). Megyn Kelly wonders if she can sue over fake Facebook Trending article. *The Week*. Retrieved from https://theweek.com/speedreads/646052/megyn-kelly-wonders-sue-over-fake-facebook-trending-article

Webster, F. (1997). Is this the information age? : Towards a critique of Manuel Castells. *City*, 2(8), 71–84, doi: 10.1080/13604819708713517.

Webster, F. (2006). *Theories of the Information Society* (3rd edn). London and New York: Routledge.

Webster, J., Phalen, P., & Lichty, L. (2014). *Ratings Analysis: Audience Measurement and Analytics* (4th edn). New York and London: Routledge.

Webster, J. G. & Ksiazek, T. B. (2012). The dynamics of audience fragmentation: public attention in an age of digital media. *Journal of Communication*, 62(1), 39–56, doi: https://doi.org/10.1111/j.1460-2466.2011.01616.x.

Webster, M. (2016, 19 September 2016). What is a 'data state of mind'? : And how you can develop it. *DataJournalism.com*. Retrieved from https://datajournalism.com/read/longreads/what-is-a-data-state-of-mind-and-how-you-can-develop-it

Welbers, K., van Atteveldt, W., Kleinnijenhuis, J., Ruigrok, N., & Schaper, J. (2016). News selection criteria in the digital age: professional norms versus online audience metrics. *Journalism*, 17(8), 1037–1053.

Wenger, D. H. & Owens, L. C. (2012). Help wanted 2010: an examination of new media skills required by top U.S. news companies. *Journalism & Mass Communication Educator*, 67(1), 9–25.

Wenger, D. H., Owens, L. C., & Cain, J. (2018). Help wanted: realigning journalism education to meet the needs of top U.S. news companies. *Journalism & Mass Communication Educator*, 73(1), 18–36.

Westlund, O. (2013). Mobile news: a review and model of journalism in an age of mobile media. *Digital Journalism*, 1(1), 6–26, doi: 10.1080/21670811.2012.740273.

Williams, A., Wardle, C., & Wahl-Jorgensen, L. (2011). The limits of audience participation: UGC @ the BBC. In B. Franklin & M. Carlson (Eds.), *Journalists, Sources, and Credibility: New Perspectives*. London and New York: Routledge.

Wölker, A. & Powell, T. E. (2018). Algorithms in the newsroom? News readers' perceived credibility and selection of automated journalism. *Journalism*, doi: 10.1177/1464884918757072.

Wong, J. C. & Solon, O. (2018, 24 April 2018). Facebook releases content moderation guidelines – rules long kept secret. *The Guardian*. Retrieved from https://www.theguardian.com/technPonsfordology/2018/apr/24/facebook-releases-content-moderation-guidelines-secret-rules

Woodhouse, J. (2018). Press regulation after Leveson. Research Briefing Paper Number 07576, House of Commons Library.

Wrenn, N. & Cox-Brooker, S. (2018, 19 November 2018). Facebook launches UK Community News Project. *Facebook Journalism Project*. Retrieved from https:/www.facebook.com/journalismproject/facebook-uk-community-news-project-launch.

Wright, S. & Doyle, K. (2018). The evolution of data journalism: a case study of Australia. *Journalism Studies*, 20(13), 1811–1827.

Xin, X. (2010). The impact of 'citizen journalism' on Chinese media and society. *Journalism Practice, 4*(3), 333–344.

Yang, N. (2012, 4 December 2012). Building the wall: Will digital subscriptions save the newspaper industry? *Editor & Publisher* Retrieved from https://www.editorandpublisher.com/stories/building-the-wall-will-digital-subscriptions-save-the-newspaper-industry,67739?.

Young, M. L. & Hermida, A. (2015). From Mr. and Mrs. Outlier to central tendencies. *Digital Journalism, 3*(3), 381–397, doi: 10.1080/21670811.2014.976409.

Young, M. L., Hermida, A., & Fulda, J. (2018). What makes for great data journalism? A content analysis of data journalism awards finalists 2012–2015. *Journalism Practice, 12*(1), 115–135.

Younge, G. (2017, 28 March 2017). Beyond the blade: the truth about knife crime in Britain. *The Guardian*. Retrieved from https://www.theguardian.com/uk-news/2017/mar/28/beyond-the-blade-the-truth-about-knife-in-britain

Yu, H. (2006). From active audience to media citizenship: the case of post-Mao China. *Social Semiotics, 16*(2), 303–326.

Zamith, R. (2019). Transparency, interactivity, diversity, and information provenance in everyday data journalism. *Digital Journalism*, doi: 10.1080/21670811.2018.1554409.

Zaripova, A. (2017). 'My boss is 18,000 people': journalism practices in crowdfunded media organizations. *MedieKultur: Journal of Media and Communication Research, 33*(62), doi: 10.7146/mediekultur.v33i62.24767.

Zhang, S. I. (2009). Newsroom convergence models of China's *Beijing Youth Daily* and Denmark's *Nordjyske*. *Chinese Journal of Communication, 2*(3), 330–347.

Zhang, S. I. (2012). The newsroom of the future : newsroom convergence models in China. *Journalism Practice, 6*(5–6), 776–787, doi: 10.1080/17512786.2012.667281.

Zheng, Y., Zhong, B., & Yang, F. (2018). When algorithms meet journalism: the user perception to automated news in a cross-cultural context. *Computers in Human Behaviour, 86*, 266–275.

INDEX